POP MUSIC LEGENDS

"Hank Moore has a wealth of knowledge. Not only is he fascinating to talk with, he's a fabulous writer as well. I'm so glad that he put all of his extensive knowledge of pop culture and business history down in books for generations to come. Now we can all have access to the amazing stories behind many of the histories, corporations and who's who. Thanks, Hank for sharing these wonderful stories. You Rock."

—**Kathryn C. Wheat Wiggins**, author of *Networking: Naked and Unafraid*

"Hank Moore is a prolific writer with an amazing knowledge of his subject. Everyone will love *Pop Music Legends*."

—**Douglas B. Gehrman**

POP MUSIC LEGENDS

Compendium Of Recorded Music

ULTIMATE MUSIC RESOURCE BOOK.

HANK MOORE

NEW YORK

LONDON • NASHVILLE • MELBOURNE • VANCOUVER

POP MUSIC LEGENDS
Compendium Of Recorded Music
ULTIMATE MUSIC RESOURCE BOOK.

Published in New York, New York, by Morgan James Publishing. Morgan James is a trademark of Morgan James, LLC. www.MorganJamesPublishing.com

Proudly distributed by Ingram Publisher Services.

Morgan James
BOGO™

A **FREE** ebook edition is available for you or a friend with the purchase of this print book.

CLEARLY SIGN YOUR NAME ABOVE

Instructions to claim your free ebook edition:
1. Visit MorganJamesBOGO.com
2. Sign your name CLEARLY in the space above
3. Complete the form and submit a photo of this entire page
4. You or your friend can download the ebook to your preferred device

ISBN 9781631959653 paperback
ISBN 9781631959677 hardcover
ISBN 9781631959660 ebook
Library of Congress Control Number:
2022938550

Cover Design by:
Rachel Lopez
www.r2cdesign.com

Interior Design by:
Bonnie Bushman

Cover Photos:
"Lady Gaga at the 2018 Toronto International Film Festival" by John Bauld
"The Beatles, The Ed Sullivan Show" by Bernard Gotfryd
"Harry Belafonte and Nat King Cole in 1957" by Gerald Smith
"Mariah" by Raph_PH
"Madonna MDNA Concert Live" by Youngrobv
"Frank Sinatra with a Paper Coffee Cup" by Ken Veeder
"David Matthews Performing…Outside Lands 2009" by Moses Namkung
"Elvis Presley Meeting Richard Nixon" by Ollie Atkins
"Beyoncé Knowles with Necklaces" by Tony Duran
"Alica Keys at the 2009 American Music Awards Red Carpet" by burningkarma

Morgan James is a proud partner of Habitat for Humanity Peninsula and Greater Williamsburg. Partners in building since 2006.

Get involved today! Visit MorganJamesPublishing.com/giving-back

Dedicated to Joan Moore.

CONTENTS

ACKNOWLEDGMENTS

Remembrances to some of the legends whom I met and interviewed: Roy Acuff, Herb Alpert, Patty Andrews, Stan Applebaum, Eddy Arnold, Frankie Avalon, Burt Bacharach, Count Basie, The Beach Boys, The Beatles, Tony Bennett, Leonard Bernstein, Chuck Berry, Beyoncé, Perry Botkin Jr., James Brown, Glen Campbell, Diahann Carroll, Johnny Cash, David Cassidy, Chubby Checker, Chicago, Dick Clark, Crosby Stills Nash & Young, Kathryn Crosby, Vic Dana, Danny & the Juniors, Sammy Davis Jr., Doris Day, Al DeLory, Walt Disney, Placido Domingo, Fats Domino, Duke Ellington, Shelley Fabares, The Fifth Dimension, Ella Fitzgerald, Pete Fountain, Peter Frampton, Aretha Franklin, Benny Goodman, Robert Goulet, Merle Haggard, Roy Head, Florence Henderson, Woody Herman, Harry James, Sonny James, Billy Joel, Lady Bird Johnson, Lyndon B. Johnson, George Jones, Shirley Jones, Janis Joplin, Stan Kenton, Carole King, The Kingston Trio, Kris Kristofferson, Frankie Laine, Brenda Lee, Little Richard, Kenny Loggins, Dean Martin, Richard Marx, Johnny Mathis, Rod McKuen, Liza Minnelli, Jim Nabors, Ozzie Nelson, Rick Nelson, Helen O'Connell, Roy Orbison, Buck Owens, Patti Page, Luciano Pavarotti, Peter Paul & Mary, The Platters, Elvis Presley, Andre Previn, Ray Price, Cactus Pryor, Della Reese, Nelson Riddle, Kenny Rogers, The Rolling Stones, Linda Ronstadt, Diana Ross & the Supremes, Billy Joe Royal, Neil Sedaka, Bobby Sherman, Dinah Shore, Beverly Sills, Simon & Garfunkel, Frank Sinatra, Sonny & Cher, Rick Springfield, Barbra Streisand, Ed Sullivan, B.J.

xi

Thomas, Kenneth Threadgill, Mel Torme, Conway Twitty, Dionne Warwick, Barry White, Don Williams, Hank Williams Jr., Wolfman Jack, ZZ Top.

Also, acknowledgments to Imad Abdullah, Sharon Connally Ammann, Judy Blake, Tom Britton, Dr. Lee P. Brown, Tony Castiglie, Glenn Chisman, Donna Clairfield, Sandra Collins, George Connelly, Rob Cook, Hector & Arleigh De Leon, R.J. Diamond, Sue Ditsch, Deborah Duncan, Tom & Anna Dutta, Alan & Gay Erwin, Dr. Ron Evans, Felix Fraga, Martin Gaston, Douglas & Christine Gehrman, Andrea Gold, Diane Payton Gomez, Sonia Guimbellot, Phillip Hatfield, Bubba & Glenna Hawkins, Royce Heslep, Michael Hick, Mary Higginbotham, Bruce Hillegeist, Larry Holgerson, Derrill Holly, Kathy Fulbright Hradecky, Richard Huebner, Susan & Robert Hutsko, Hiett Ives, Chris Kelso, Dana Kervin, Soulat Khan, Jon King, Kirby Lammers, Nancy Lauterbach, Torre Lee, Steve & Barbara Levine, Mike Linares, Jayce Love, Anya Albert Lucas, Jackie Lyles, Kate Lyon, Tammy Collins Markee RCC, Bertrand McHenry, Kathleen McKeague, Bruce Merrin, Amber Mesorana, Julie Moore, Larry Moore, Phil Morabito, Jesse Mueller, Larry Mueller, Lizz Mueller, Bill Nash, Howard Partridge, Dan Parsons, Dru & Anne Pencak, Monte & Linda Pendleton, Tom Perrone, Sue Pistone, Anthony Pizzitola, Travis Posey, Doug Quinn, Sally Mathis Ramsay, Roy & Gail Randolph, Ronney Reynolds, Tamra Battle Rogers, Mike Rosen, Melissa Rotholz, Monica Ryan, Rita Santamaria, Rick Schissler, Jack Shabot, Bill Spitz, Gail Stolzenburg, Bill & Cindy Taylor, Deborah Taylor, Jon & Paige Taylor, Jane Moore Taylor, Charlie & Laura Thorp, Rich Tiller, James & Carolyn Todd, Linda Toyota, Mary & Paul Vandenberg, David Wadler, Kathryn C. Wheat, Chris Wiggins, Robert Willeby, Melissa Williams, Ronald Earl Wilsher, Beth Wolff, Dr. Martha Wong.

INTRODUCTION

This book evolved over sixty-five years. I started my career as a ten-year-old radio DJ. I played the hits of the day. I had to learn about what we were playing as golden oldies, records from the 1930s and 1940s.

I pioneered radio oldies shows in several genres: pop, rock, big-band, country, soul and show music, from 1959–1982. I wrote magazine articles and appeared on talk shows, discussing music and business topics. I emceed concerts with major stars and proudly watched nostalgia waves.

I progressed to being a business guru, which is why several of my previous books are about business, leadership and strategy. I often believed and said that the entertainment industry is more flexible and adaptive than other business sectors.

I wrote the first prospectus for this book in 1984. I was too young to write history books and continued to amass research, as music styles changed and evolved. Chapter 2 of this book was written in 1998 as a stand-alone monograph. My first entertainment book was "The Classic TV Reference," written in 2005 and including articles that I had written for TV Guide and other publications.

In 2014, I started the Legends series. One was "Pop Icons and Business Legends," written in the style that evolved into this book. The next book followed the same concept and focused on my other favorite topic, "Non-Profit Legends."

Then came "The Big Picture of Business, Books 1-2-3-4," written and published as I was preparing this book.

This is my legacy book. I wrote chapters about 100 years of the recording industry, covering the decades and music trends. This is the book that I could not have written decades ago. In addition to the historical chapters, I wrote chapters on music genres, most of which are not in other niche books or on fan websites on the internet.

My business books all had entertainment chapters. "Big Picture of Business, Book 3" had a study of how the automobile affected society and business. "Book 4" had a chapter on development of the internet. "Book 1" had fun facts about the number seven, anniversaries and branding. "Book 2" covered cultural trends and reframing the future through nostalgic studies of the past. In "Non-Profit Legends," I wrote the first-ever nostalgic review of public television and radio. "Power Stars to Light the Flame" was chocked full of celebrity and music quotes.

This book is about widening the scope much further. Whenever we review what made the business successful, we see that pop culture thinking took part in past times. Chapters are written in such a way as to be interpreted on several levels. Part common sense and part deep wisdom, they are intended to widen your focus and inspire the music vision that exists within you the reader.

Concluding with statements from some of my friends in the music world:

Beyoncé: "I get nervous when I don't get nervous. If I'm nervous I know I'm going to have a good show."

Elvis Presley: "Truth is like the sun. You can shut it out for a time, but it isn't going away. Some people tap their feet, some people snap their fingers, and some people sway back and forth. I just do them all together. I learned very early in life that without a song, the day would never end. So, I keep singing a song."

Paul McCartney: "Nothing pleases me more than to go into a room and come out with a piece of music. You can tell your guitar things that you can't tell people. And it will answer you with things people can't tell you."

Benny Goodman: "It takes the black keys and white keys both to make perfect harmony. After you've done all the work and prepared as much as you can, what the hell, you might as well go out and have a good time."

Frank Sinatra: "Nobody is Number 1 forever. Life goes in cycles. I'm for anything that gets you through the night. Cock your hat because angles are attitudes. I would like to be remembered as a man who had a wonderful time living life, a man who had good friends, fine family and couldn't ask for anything more than that."

Doris Day: "When I was a little girl, I was in dancing school, and I sang. We had to put a dance to a song, so I went to the 10-cent store one day and looked at all the sheet music. It was all laid out, and I picked Life Is Just a Bowl of Cherries."

Mick Jagger: "The only performance that makes it, that makes it all the way is the one that achieves madness. I don't think people care about the mechanics of songwriting. Songs are very much of a moment, that you just encapsulate. They come to you, you write them, and you feel good that day or bad that day."

Tony Bennett: "I'm still learning about music. The best way to learn is to listen to the audience. When you listen to the audience, they will tell you what they like. I wish these big corporations, instead of telling the audience what they should have, would listen."

Cher: "All of us invent ourselves. Some of us just have more imagination than others. I am the girl who everyone said was never going anywhere. I guess I shocked a few people. If you can't go straight ahead, you go around the corner."

One never forgets being in the presence of greatness and their shared wisdom.

Chapter 1
MUSIC FOR GENERATIONS

Music affects every person. It is the soundtrack of our happiness, zest for achievement and relationships to others. Music brings great ideas and feelings. It soothes the soul. It creates and sustains memories.

This book is written for young people. Yes, it is a nostalgic journey through 100 years of music history. It is intended to show what has transpired in the perspective of today.

We all still hear many of the golden oldies on TV commercials, on the radio, in concerts, on sound systems and via the internet. We acclimate to many musical styles and share the music with younger generations. I wrote this book from the perspective of a young person who learned what came before me, with the quest to pass it on.

The growth and expanse of pop music in the last 125 years parallels the growth of generations. The GI or Greatest includes persons born through 1926. The front half of the generation became music fans in the 1920s. The second half became the standard bearers of the Big Band Era.

The Silent Generation, born 1927–1945, grew in the 1950s, the Happy Days. Their growth years brought 45RPM and 33-1/3RPM records, television and modern radio as a pipeline to the latest music. They were the first fans of rock and roll, giving it a face and attitude.

Baby Boomers, born 1946–1964, were teens in the 1960s and came of age in the 1970s. They embraced teen pop, Motown, the British Invasion, singer-songwriters, disco and much more. They took rock and roll to the mainstream of culture, thus influencing next generations.

Generation X, born 1965–1983, has 1980s music as the gold standard. Their era brought us video tape, cassette tape, 8-tracks, CDs and DVDs, the media that further transported music and culture. In their growth, music videos came of age, along with cable TV.

Generation Y, aka Millennials, born 1984–2002, championed dance music of the 1990s and 2000s. They brought music access into the digital age, including internet, streaming tunes, downloads, cell phones and websites.

Generation Z, born 2003–2021, reaped the benefit of these evolutions from previous generations. They embrace it all and are poised to share with the next generation.

I grew up listening to the music of the early 1950s on radio and on TV variety shows. I became a huge fan of music by watching "Your Hit Parade" on NBC-TV, where top songs of the week were staged live. I saw the presentation of music evolve into music videos, MTV, YouTube and other media. I started working in radio as a DJ when I was ten years old. Rock and roll had just hit, and I got to play the latest hit records by the top stars of the day, including Elvis Presley, Buddy Holly, Chuck Berry, Little Richard, Fats Domino and The Everly Brothers.

The first star that I ever met was Elvis Presley, the King of Rock and Roll. I met Elvis in 1958. He came to visit me at KTBC Radio in Austin, TX, when he was a private in the US Army. The next time was in 1962 at the Seattle World's Fair, where he was making a movie. The last time was backstage at his 1975 concert in Houston, TX.

The first question that I asked Elvis Presley was his favorite food. Answer: burnt bacon, because that's what they served to him in Army basic training at Fort Hood. He kept the affinity for burnt bacon the rest of his life. The second question was about the staying power of rock n' roll, then known as kids' music. His answer: "They won't always be kids."

While Elvis was in the Army, music transitioned from that 1950s format. Other trends came and went. The music industry remained nimble and willing to change and update. I observed and chronicled every style, genre and heyday of music and share via this book.

Dick Clark was known as "America's oldest teenager," a seminal influence on music for 50 years. He started hosting "American Bandstand" in 1956, and every performer of the late 1950s, 1960s, 1970s, 1980s and beyond held him in high esteem.

I met Dick Clark in 1971, appeared on an "American Bandstand" special and spoke at his final tribute dinner in 2011 in Los Angeles, CA. I sat at the head table between Frankie Avalon and Burt Bacharach. After speaking about his influence on the music industry, I introduced Beyoncé to give her tribute to Dick Clark. At the time of his death on April 18, 2012, Clark was worth $200 million. In 1972, he introduced "New Year's Rockin' Eve," in 1973 went into game shows with "$10,000 Pyramid" and created American Music Awards. Dick Clark said: "Rock had a huge impact. Anything that the older generation hates is usually loved by kids. Nothing changes, and that still continues today."

I hosted and innovated radio oldies shows. They covered such formats as Top 40, big band, rock and roll, easy listening, soul and country. I produced 150 radio documentaries on the music and its stars. I wrote about music in newspapers and magazines. I taught music appreciation classes.

I introduced in performance such stars as Frank Sinatra, The Beach Boys, Kenny Rogers, Duke Ellington, Ella Fitzgerald, Roy Orbison, George Jones, Don Williams, Chuck Berry, Little Richard, Dionne Warwick, Count Basie, Chicago, Johnny Dee & the Rocket 88s, Simon & Garfunkel, Nelson Riddle, Danny & the Juniors, Ray Price, The Beatles, Janis Joplin, Rick Nelson, Conway Twitty, Chubby Checker, Benny Goodman, Kay Starr, Crosby, Stills, Nash & Young, Della Reese, Billy Joe Royal, Sonny & Cher and others.

Since the beginning of recorded time, music has been with us. The ancient Greeks strummed instruments such as kithara and aulos players at festivals with instrumentals and vocals.

By the fifth century, music became prominent in church services. Roman chants and liturgies embodied community and aesthetic values of the time. The years of

1000–1200 saw an increase in trading and commerce throughout the world. Songs traveled from town to town, with additional verses added to the vocals.

The concept of raising notes and pitches for dramatic effect surfaced in 14th Century French and Italian music. Dancing and festivals created opportunity for happy, perky tunes. Humanism was characteristic of the Renaissance era, with music theory and practice expanded to widening popular cultures.

The sixteenth century witnessed the rise of native musical idioms. Categories of instrumental music included dance crazes, improvisatory pieces, contrapuntal genres, sonatas and variations. Church music expanded and adapted to reformation and baroque periods. The sixteenth century brought Christmas classics still being sung: "God Rest Ye Merry Gentlemen," "O Christmas Tree" and "Twelve Days of Christmas." Carols and symphony suites in the 19th century, including "O Holy Night," "O Little Town of Bethlehem" and "Silent Night."

Opera came in the seventeenth century, as did vocal chamber music. Instrumentals utilized organs and harpsichords. The eighteenth century saw classical music by such esteemed composers as Johann Sebastian Bach, Antonio Vivaldi, Franz Joseph Haydn, Wolfgang Amadeus Mozart, George Fredric Handel and Jean-Philippe Rameau. Nineteenth-century romanticism classical music came from Ludwig Van Beethoven, Franz Schubert, Felix Mendelssohn, Robert Schumann, Frederyk Chopin, Franz Liszt, Johannes Brahms, Richards Wagner and Antonio Dvorak. There were symphonies, chamber music and vocal music.

In the pop music in the twentieth century, the classics were often updated as instrumentals for big bands, jazz groups and rock ensembles. Often, pop lyrics were added to create memorable songs that charted well and enjoyed longevity in the public psyche. Most of the classics were in the public domain, and their familiarity with the public assured that pop tunesmiths would go back to the well of classical music regularly.

Great composers such as Beethoven, Rachmaninoff, Bach, Chopin, Schubert, Liszt, Brahms, Wagner, Mahler, Verdi, Debussy, Tchaikovsky, Strauss, Rimsky-Korsakov, Ravel and others provided great melodies for pop standards. The popular operas influenced stage musicals, which influenced pop vocals in grandiose ballads.

This brings music history up to where this book begins. It was at this dawn that the recording industry was established. The twentieth century saw an exponential rise in pop music and industries that supported it. The next thirty-six chapters describe and pay homage to it.

Hank Moore with Dick Clark

Hank Moore with Sonny & Cher

Chapter 2

QUESTIONS IN LIFE, ASKED THROUGH MUSIC

S ome people ask too many questions. Most don't ask enough of the right ones. Some seek true answers. Some try to glean keen insights between the lines of the answers. For an "outside-the-box" reflection through everyone's memory base (the entertainment genre), here are some of life's most probing questions, taken from the lexicons of pop music.

Are

- "Are the stars out tonight? I don't know if it's cloudy or bright. I only have eyes for you, dear." Harry Warren & Al Dubin (1933)
- "Are you sincere when you say you'll be true? Do you mean every word that my ears have heard? Are really mine every day, all the time? I'd like to know which way to go." Andy Williams (1958)
- "Are you lonesome tonight? Are you sorry we drifted apart? Does your memory stray to a bright summer day? Shall I come back again?" 1920s song by Ray Turk & Lou Handman (later revived by Elvis Presley)

- "I hear the music coming out of your radio. Are you there with another girl?" Burt Bacharach & Hal David (1965)
- "Are you ready to sit by the throne? Are you ready not to be alone? Somebody's coming to take you home." Pacific Gas & Electric (1970)
- "Aren't you glad you're you?" Bing Crosby (1946)

Can

- "I swear the day is going to come so soon. The truth is going to burst a lot of balloons. Mister, can't you see?" Buffy Sainte-Marie (1972)
- "Can you find it in your heart? Can't we make another start? I'm repenting, Think it over." Tony Bennett (composed by Stillman & Allen)
- "Can't you see that she's mine? Don't you know I love her so? I don't care what the people say. I'm going to keep on holding her hand." Dave Clark Five (1964)

Did

- "Did you ever see a dream walking? Well, I did." Song hit of 1933
- "Did you ever have to make up your mind? Say yes to one and let the other one ride? So many changes and tears you must hide." John Sebastian & the Lovin' Spoonful (1965)
- "Didn't I blow your mind this time?" The Delfonics (1968)

Do

- "Do you want to dance and hold my hand? Tell me that I'm your man? Squeeze me all through the night." Bobby Freeman (1958)
- "Do you love me, now that I can dance?" The Contours (1962)
- "Do you know the way to San Jose? In a week or two, they'll make you a star. And all the stars that ever were are parking cars and pumping gas." Burt Bacharach & Hal David (1968)
- "Do you believe in magic in a young girl's heart? If you believe like I believe." John Sebastian/Lovin' Spoonful (1965)
- "Do you want to know a secret? Let me whisper in your ear. I'm in love with you." The Beatles (1964)
- "Do you love as good as you look?" The Bellamy Brothers (1981)

- "Do you know what it means to miss New Orleans? I know I'm not wrong. The feelings get stronger, the longer I'm away." Louis Armstrong (1956)
- "Do you really want to hurt me? Do you really want to make me cry? That's a step a step too far. Give me time to realize my crime." Culture Club (1983)
- "Do you see what I see? A song high above the tree with a voice as big as the sea. Do you know what I know? Let us bring him silver and gold." Christmas song

Does

- "Does anybody really know what time it is? Does anybody really care? If so, I can't imagine why." Chicago (1970)
- "Does your chewing gum lose its flavor on the bedpost overnight? If only I could know the answer to my question, is it yes or no." 1924 song, revived by Lonnie Donegan (1961)
- "Does my ring hurt your finger?" Charley Pride (1967)

Don't

- "Don't it make you want to go home? Now the grass won't grow, and the river doesn't flow like it did in my childhood days." Joe South (1970)
- "Don't you want me baby? You'd better change it back or we will both be sorry." The Human League (1982)

Have

- "Have you ever been lonely? Have you ever been blue?" Ted Lewis (1933)
- "Have you ever seen the rain coming down on a sunny day?" Creedence Clearwater Revival (1970)
- "Have I told you lately that I love you? Well darling, I'm telling you now." Gene Autry (1946)
- "Have you heard who's kissing her now? Do you think she's blue? Did she say we're through? Does she say who's to blame?" hit for Joni James & The Duprees

How

- "How can I be sure, in a world that's constantly changing?" The Rascals (1967)
- "How am I supposed to live without you? Now that I've been loving you for so long." Michael Bolton, 1982
- "How can people be so heartless? How can people be so cruel? Easy to be hard, easy to be cold." from 1968 Broadway musical *Hair*
- "How much do I love you? I'll tell you no lie. How deep is the ocean? How high is the sky?" song by Irving Berlin
- "How will I know if he really loves me? Tell me, is it real love." Whitney Houston (1986)
- "How'd we ever get this way? I wonder how it all began." Andy Kim (1968)
- "How many times must a man turn his head and pretend he just doesn't see? The answer, my friend, is blowing in the wind." Bob Dylan (1962)
- "How can you mend a broken heart? How can you stop the sun from shining? How can a loser ever win." The Bee Gees (1971)
- "How much is that doggie in the window, the one with the waggily tail? I hope that doggie's for sale." Patti Page (1953)
- "How important can it be? Why get lost in yesterday? Even foolish hearts can learn." 1955 song recorded by Joni James, Sarah Vaughan, Teresa Brewer
- "How can you expect to be taken seriously? What have I done to deserve this?" Pet Shop Boys (1990)
- "How'd you like to spoon with me?" song hit of 1906
- "Somewhere there's music, I'll paint the tune. How high the moon?" song hit of 1940 (recorded by Benny Goodman, Stan Kenton, Les Paul & Mary Ford)
- "How are you going to keep them down on the farm, after they've seen Paree?" 1919 song hit

If

- "If I fell in love with you, would you promise to be true?" The Beatles (1964)

- "If you leave me now? You'll take away the biggest part of me. How could we let it slip away? How could we end it all this way." Chicago (1976)
- "If I give my heart to you, will you handle it with care? Will you swear that you'll be true to me." Doris Day (1954)

Is

- "Is there still room for me beneath the old apple tree?" song hit of 1916
- "Is you is, or is you ain't my baby? Is my baby still my baby too?" Buster Brown (1960)
- "Is that all there is to a fire, the circus, to love, to life? Let's keep dancing, break out the booze and have a ball." Peggy Lee (1969)
- "Is there any chance that you and I can start all over? Say that you'll try." Marty Robbins (1960)

Isn't

- "Isn't it romantic?" 1920s song classic
- "Isn't it bliss? Aren't we a pair? You here at last on the ground, me in mid-air. Send in the clowns." from "A Little Night Music" (1973)
- "Isn't it a pity? Isn't it a shame? Their eyes can't hope to see the beauty that surrounds them." George Harrison (1970)
- "Isn't it about time?" Stephen Stills (1973)
- "Isn't this a lovely day to be caught in the rain? Long as I can be with you, it's a lovely day." Irving Berlin (1935)

May

- "May I speak with you? May I bring you joy? Girl, I've been searching for someone like you." Maurice Williams & the Zodiaks (1959)

Shall

- "Shall we dance? On a bright cloud of music, shall we fly? Shall you be my new romance?" Richard Rodgers & Oscar Hammerstein, "The King & I" (1951)

What

- "What would you do if I sang out of tune? Would you stand up and walk out on me?" The Beatles (1967)

- "What child is this?" traditional Christmas song
- "What is my life without you by my side? What I feel, I can't say. Then I'll try my best to make everything succeed." George Harrison (1970)
- "What in the world's come over you? Could you ever change your mind? If you do, I'll still be here, longing, waiting for you." Jack Scott (1960)
- "What becomes of the brokenhearted? Who has love that's now departed? I'll be searching everywhere just to find someone to care." Jimmy Ruffin (1966)
- "What'd I say? See the girl with the red dress on? She can dance all night long." Ray Charles (1959)
- "What do you get when you fall in love? A guy with a pin to burst your bubble. I'll never fall in love again." Burt Bacharach & Hal David (1969)
- "What am I living for, if not for you? Nobody else will do." Chuck Willis (1958)
- "What now my love now that you left me? How can I live through another day?" 1966 hit by Sonny & Cher
- "What kind of fool am I, who never fell in love? Why can't I fall in love like any other man? Maybe then I'll know what kind of fool I am." Anthony Newley (1962)
- "What is love? Five feet of heaven in a ponytail, the cutest ponytail that sways with a wiggle when she walks." The Playmates (1958)
- "What are you doing the rest of your life? I have one request, that you spend it with me." Michel Legrand, Alan & Marilyn Bergman (1969)
- "What do I have to do to get the message through?" Kylie Minogue (1987)
- "What'll I do when you are far away? What'll I do, with just a photograph to tell my troubles to." 1920s song by Irving Berlin
- "What kind of girl do you think I am?" Loretta Lynn (1967)
- "What is this thing called? Who can solve its mystery? Why should it make a fool of me?" 1920s song by Cole Porter

What's

- "What's this whole world coming to? Things just aren't the same. Anytime the hunter gets captured by the game." Smokey Robinson (1967)

- "What's he doing in my world? If he's not more than just a friend, then why were you kissing him?" Eddy Arnold (1965)
- "What's new, pussycat? I've got flowers and lots of hours to spend with you. You're so thrilling, and I'm so willing to care for you." Burt Bacharach & Hal David (1965)
- "What's your name? Is it Mary or Sue? Do I stand a chance with you?" Don & Juan (1962)
- "What's love got to do with it? Who needs a heart when a heart can be broken." Tina Turner (1984)
- "What's new? How is the world treating you? How did that romance come through? Seeing you is grand." recorded 1929 by Bing Crosby, 1983 by Linda Ronstadt

When

- "When will I see you again? When will we share precious moments? Will I have to wait forever? Is this my beginning or end." The Three Degrees (1974)
- "When you smile at me, well, I know our love will always be. If you will, I know all will be fine. When will you be mine?" The Kalin Twins (1958)
- "I've been cheated. I've been mistreated. When will I be loved?" recorded 1960 by The Everly Brothers, 1975 by Linda Ronstadt

Where

- "Where have all the flowers gone? Long time passing, long time ago. When will they ever learn?" The Kingston Trio (1962)
- "Where's the playground, Susie? The carousel has stopped us here. What merry-go-round can you ride without me?" Glen Campbell (1969) (composed by Jim Webb)
- "Where do I go? Follow the river. Is there an answer that tells me why I live and die?" Gerome Ragni, James Rado & Galt MacDermot from 1968 Broadway musical "Hair"
- "Where are you? Where have you gone without me? Where's my heart? Where is the dream we started?" Frank Sinatra (1955)
- "Where is the love?" Donny Hathaway & Roberta Flack (1972)

- "Where do I begin to tell the story of how great a love can be? There'll never be another love. She fills my heart with very special things." Carl Sigman & Francis Lai (theme from "Love Story") (1970)

Which

- "Which way are you going, Billy? Can I go too? I have nothing to show if you should go away." Poppy Family (Terry & Susan Jacks) (1970)

Who

- "Who can I turn to when nobody needs me? My heart wants to know, and I must go where destiny leads me. Maybe tomorrow I'll find what I'm after." Anthony Newley (1962)
- "I long to wake up in the morning and find everything has changed. For I have something else entirely free. To question such good fortune, who am I?" Petula Clark (1967)
- "Who put the bomp in the bop shoo bop shoo bop? Who put the ram in the rama lama ding dong?" Barry Mann (1961)
- "Who wrote the Book of Love? I've got to know the answer. Was it someone from above?" The Monotones (1958)
- "Who are you? I want to know." Peter Townshend & The Who (1978)
- "Who will the next fool be?" Bobby Bland (1962)
- "Who can explain it? Who can tell you why? Fools give you reasons. Wise men never try." Richard Rodgers & Oscar Hammerstein, from "South Pacific"
- "Who's sorry now? Who's sad and blue? Who's crying too? Not like I cried over you." Connie Francis (1957)
- "Who do you think you are to take such advantage of me?" Bo Donaldson & the Heywoods (1974)
- "Who's making love to your old lady, while you're out making love?" Johnnie Taylor (1968)
- "Trying to find the sun. Who'll stop the rain?" Creedence Clearwater Revival (1970)
- "Who's zooming who?" Aretha Franklin (1985)

- "Who's afraid of the big bad wolf?" sung by the Three Little Pigs in Walt Disney cartoon classic (1933)
- "Who stole my heart away? Who makes me dream all day the dreams that I know will never come true." Otto Harbach, Oscar Hammerstein & Jerome Kern (1925)

Why

- "Why do birds sing so gay? Why does the rain fall from up above? Why does my heart skip this crazy beat? Why do fools fall in love?" Frankie Lymon & the Teenagers (1955)
- "Why, oh why, do I love Paris? Because my love is near." 1920s song by Cole Porter
- "Why does the sun go on shining? Why does the sea rush to shore? Don't they know it's the end of the world." Sung by Skeeter Davis (1963)
- "Why me, Lord? What have I ever done to deserve even one of the pleasures I've known?" Kris Kristofferson (1973)
- "Why can't we be friends? I've seen you around for a long time. The color of your skin doesn't matter to me, long as we can live in harmony." Sung by War (1975)
- "Why don't you do right, like some other men do? Get out of here and get me some money too." Benny Goodman (1943)
- "Why don't you believe me? It's you I adore. Can I promise more? How else can I tell you? I love only you." Joni James (1952)
- "Why don't you love me like you used to do? How come you treat me like a worn-out shoe? I'm the same old trouble that you've always been through." Hank Williams (1950)

Will

- "Is this a lasting treasure, or just a moment's pleasure? Will my heart be broken when the night meets the morning sun? Will you still love me tomorrow?" Carole King & Gerry Goffin (1961)
- "Will I find my love today? Will I see her smiling face in some quiet magic place? How I wonder where we'll meet. Will she come my way?" Johnny Mathis (1957)

- "What will I be? Will I be pretty? Will I be rich? Will we have rainbows day after day? Que sera, sera, whatever will be will be." Doris Day (1956)

Would

- "Would you lay with me in a field of stone?" Tanya Tucker (1974)
- "Would you like to swing on a star? Carry moonbeams home in a jar. And be better off than you are. If you don't care a feather or a fig, you may grow up to be a pig." Bing Crosby (1944)

Wouldn't

- "Wouldn't anybody like to meet a sweet old-fashioned girl?" Teresa Brewer (1956)
- "Wouldn't it be nice if we were older? Wouldn't it be nice to live in the kind of world where we belong? it might come true." The Beach Boys (1966)

When you ask questions, you get answers. Sometimes, the answers are factual. Others offer reflections into how people think or feel. Still other answers contain nuggets of gold, insights that can transform your organization into a valued success. To get the best answers, one must ask the best questions, think beyond the obvious and stretch the idea process.

Answers: Statements and Affirmations

- "Hey life, look at me. I can see through reality. It's not a dream. It's not a bliss. It happened to me, and it can happen to you." Sung by Diana Ross & the Supremes, (1967)
- "Question me an answer right away. Then, I will answer with a question, clear and bright." Burt Bacharach & Hal David (1972)
- "What goes up must come down. Spinning wheel must go around." Blood, Sweat & Tears (1969)
- "If I loved you, time and again I'd want to say all that I want you to know. Longing to tell you but afraid and shy. I'd let my golden chances pass me by." Richard Rodgers & Oscar Hammerstein, "Carousel" (1946)
- "While you see a chance, take it." Steve Winwood (1981)
- "When I fall in love, it will be forever." 1930s song
- "Whatever Lola wants, Lola gets." From the Broadway musical "Damn Yankees" (1955)

- "When you wish upon a star. Makes no difference who you are. Your dreams will come true." Jiminy Crickett, in 1941 Disney movie classic "Pinnochio"
- "I've looked at life from both sides now. Those bright illusions I recall. I really don't know life at all." Judy Collins (1968)
- "Only love can conquer hate. Find a way to bring some understanding today. Talk to me so you can see what's going on." Marvin Gaye (1971)
- "Don't make me over. Now that I'd do anything for you. I'll always be by your side, whenever you're wrong or right." Burt Bacharach & Hal David (1962)
- "Imagine there's no heaven. It's easy if you try. Above us only sky. Imagine all the people living for today." John Lennon (1971)
- "You must remember this. A kiss is just a kiss. A sigh is just a sigh. The fundamental things apply as time goes by." song popularized in "Casablanca" (1943)
- "The day would surely have to break. It would not be new, if not for you." Bob Dylan (1963)
- "There aren't no good guys or bad guys. There's only you and me, and we just disagree." Dave Mason (1978)
- "When my bankroll is getting small, I think of when I had none at all. And I fall asleep, counting my blessings." 1954 song by Irving Berlin
- "Life goes on, after the thrill of living is gone." John Mellencamp (1982)
- "When it's time to change, you've got to rearrange." The Brady Bunch (1972)
- "I was so much older then. I'm younger than that now." Bob Dylan (1967)
- "It's your thing. Do what you want to do." The Isley Brothers (1969)
- "Kicks just keep getting harder to find. Before you find out it's too late, you better get straight." Paul Revere & the Raiders (1966)
- "And in the end, the love you take is equal to the love you make." The Beatles (1969)

Chapter 3

BEGINNING THE RECORDING
INDUSTRY, 1877–1919

T he first twenty-two years of recorded sound were marked by technological innovation, errors, experiments and rudimentary efforts at musical performances. The original concept of a revolving cylinder found recording of voices for office equipment use. Then came spoken word recordings. Then came operatic performances by singers with piano accompaniment. Twenty years in, the recordings moved to orchestras, singers and newly composed music for twentieth-century audiences.

Sheet music includes the notes and words to songs, utilized for playing piano and singing along. Choirs utilize sheet music, with different parts charted. Orchestras and bands utilize sheet music created by arrangers and composers. Printed music was published in 1473.

Song sheets were prominent in the early twentieth century. They were inventories of tunes, their authors, publishers and copyright information. They set categories of music, including cake walks, hesitations, intermezzos, show tunes, piano roll compositions, dances, folk music, instrumentals, marches, the blues, ballads, apparel songs, Dixie songs, tunes about foreign lands, mother songs, name songs, lullabies, war songs and dance crazes.

Piano rolls carried 88 notes and were engraved to launch songs on player pianos. Piano rolls were introduced in 1896, with 45,000 titles introduced. The first works by Scott Joplin and George Gershwin were available as piano rolls. The recording industry replaced piano rolls with waxed performances of songs by prominent performers.

Edison, Inventor of Music Players

Thomas Alva Edison was America's most prolific inventor. He began inventing as a child. At age twenty-one, he went to work in a stock brokerage firm and promptly made innovations to the ticker machines. He sold rights to that process, setting himself up as a full-time inventor, wearing a chemist's white coat in the laboratory. Over the next five years, he averaged one invention per month. Entire industries evolved from his ideas and innovations.

In 1877, at age thirty, Edison invented the phonograph unintentionally. At the time, Edison was trying to devise a high-speed telegraph machine as a counterpart to the telephone that Alexander Graham Bell had invented a year before.

For his contributions to the telephone, Edison had already become quite wealthy. Edison thought he heard sounds and sought out to track down the phenomena. It occurred to him that he could devise a low-cost machine that would record voices. On a metal cylinder, a needle would move. Once that apparatus was completed, Edison shouted a child's nursery rhyme into the mouthpiece, "Mary had a little lamb." He admittedly was shocked when it reproduced his voice.

Edison received his patent on the cylinder style phonograph in 1878. From 1879–1887, Edison dropped the idea of developing the phonograph and concentrated his energies on developing the electric light.

Meantime, a young German immigrant named Emile Berliner developed the gramophone, which played discs. It was patented in 1887 and involved the making of a reverse metal matrix from the original acid-etched recording. He then used the negative master to stamp positive duplicates. The record player became a huge success.

In 1888, Edison took note of Berliner's invention and retooled his cylinder technology for commercial recording. The first releases also recited poetry. The US

Marine Band recorded marches over and over again, as each consumer cylinder was a master. Only the wealthy could afford cylinders, priced in 1890 at $10 each. The machine on which they played sold for $200.

By the end of the nineteenth century, Berliner's record machine process was out-distancing Edison's cylinder machine. This was similar to the manner in which VHS tapes out-distanced beta-max tapes in the early 1980's, becoming the dominant technology. By 1900, Edison had gotten into the commercial recording business but kept putting out cylinders until 1911, well past the time that Berliner's phonograph record had become the industry standard. The cylinders had more disc space to contain longer performances, but the phonograph records were the preferred medium.

In 1919, experimentation began on electrical recording and reproduction. Until then, the phonographs were cranked by hand. Those developments came from companies other than Edison.

On Nov. 1, 1929, the Edison Company announced that they would cease the production of phonographs and records. The announced reason was so that they could concentrate on the manufacture of radios and dictating machines, which is what Edison's talking horn started out to be in the first place. Thomas Alva Edison was then 82 years old and ceased to be active in the business.

The two oldest record companies, Columbia (founded in 1898) and RCA Victor (founded in 1901) are still with us today. The two oldest record companies developed the next technologies as alternatives to the breakable 78RPM recordings. Though both companies started research and development in 1931, Columbia introduced the long-playing record (LP) in 1948, and RCA Victor introduced the 45RPM single in 1949.

The fortunes and electrical recording techniques of Columbia, RCA Victor, Brunswick and others had years earlier shoved Edison's recording empire into nostalgia. One can still find Edison cylinders in antique shops. Edison died in 1931. By that time, the recording industry had left its infancy and was experiencing the growing pains of youth. Edison saw it all and fathered it all, the industry that he started back in 1877.

The compact disc (CD) is an updated version of Emile Berliner's phonograph record, developed in 1877. CD's were developed by Sony and Philips in the late 1970s. Both companies started the research independently of each other but, learning from Edison's demise, combined as a joint effort in 1979. CDs had their first commercial releases in 1982.

First Superstar, Around Whom the Recording Industry Grew

Enrlco Caruso is the classical and operatic singer to whom others have been compared for 125 years. He was the first major recording star and pioneered acoustical methods. He was the highest paid recording and concert artist of his day, and his earnings, with inflationary considerations, still rank supreme today.

To classical lovers, Caruso is the biggest single star of all time. He performed for kings and commoners. From modest roots himself, Caruso's music struck responses in all segments of the world. As a result, the infant recording industry literally grew around him.

When Enrico Caruso was born on Feb. 25, 1873, he was a scrawny baby with little chance for survival. Delivered by a midwife, his mother had already delivered 17 brothers and sisters, each of them dying from a dreaded Italian fever. He was met-nursed by another woman who had just lost her baby. Caruso grew up in poverty, had problems in school and found recluse in music lessons. He sang in church choirs, then sang professionally. Despite his poverty, the young Caruso voice had exceptional promise.

In 1894, he landed a season in an opera company, where he made mistakes and learned lessons. By the end of 1895, the people of Salerno, Italy, were reveling to his tenor voice. Caruso appeared in Puccini's "La Boheme," with Arturo Toscanini conducting. He became a star in 1897. He toured internationally.

The year 1902 was Caruso's year of destiny. He began recording for the new Victor label. He sang into tin horn, accompanied by a piano. Record sales boosted the opera box office, and Caruso was commanding $1,100 per performance at the Metropolitan Opera. The Caruso recordings made at Carnegie Hall in 1905 sold at $3 per 10-inch disc. In 1905, his annual income was $100,000.

The public flocked to the opera to hear their hero. Crowds gathered outside his New York apartment to catch a glimpse of Caruso.

In 1905, Victor began marketing the Victrola, a horn-shaped phonograph. In 1906, Caruso recorded with orchestras. Under his Victor agreement, he would earn $2 million in royalties over his lifetime.

At the Central Park Zoo, a woman accused Caruso of molesting her. Rather than be horrified, the public was amused, and it added to Caruso's luster. Caruso pursued a reckless romantic life. He feared he would lose his voice and sought medical treatment. A Sicilian mob demanded $15,000, threatening to kill him, but the plot was foiled.

Caruso became a perfectionist at recording and was fascinated with technological developments. He often visited Victor's factory in Camden, New Jersey, to watch the processing. He was on radio in the beginning of that medium. He continually rewarded musicians and recording engineers.

Record sales continued to make Enrico Caruso a cult figure. He often did benefit concerts and made contributions to needy Italians back home. Caruso became an art collector and did sketches himself.

In later years, Caruso was a tired, obese man. He smoked and grieved for the plight of opera stars of other nations who were made political prisoners during World War I. Caruso married a much-younger woman, and they had a daughter in 1919. He exercised little and worked too much, fearing his $400,000 annual income would turn to bankruptcy. He made his last recordings in 1920, including "Dreams of Long Ago," his only pop song in English, which was sung phonetically.

In 1921, Enrico began coughing and experiencing dizziness, to the detriment of his performances. He had developed acute pleurisy, followed by bronchial pneumonia. He lingered between life and death, lapsing in and out of a coma in ensuing weeks. He set sail for Italy and lived out the last painful weeks. Caruso died on Aug. 2, 1921, at age forty-eight. His estate was valued at $9 million.

All through the twentieth century, there have been young tenors publicized as "the next Caruso," but there was only one, and he was the greatest of all time. Enrico Caruso was the record industry's first superstar.

With the invention of cylinder and disc equipment, the demand for more written songs appeared. Tin Pan Alley was a section in New York where songwriters created tunes and music publishers took the songs to market. Tin Pan Alley was fueled by increased demand, a thriving sheet music industry, a growing recording industry and a radio market where more songs could be played.

Composers provided music to Broadway shows, which fueled outlets for sheet music, recording and radio airplay. They included George M. Cohan, Walter Donaldson, Irving Berlin, Paul Dresser, Victor Herbert, Arthur Schwartz, Howard

Dietz, Gus Edwards, Monroe Rosenfeld, James Thornton, Cole Porter and George & Ira Gershwin.

World War I occurred during this period, and it spawned many songs of optimism and patriotism. Tin Pan Alley continued as a hub for music writing and publishing into the 1930s. Growth of other music hubs in the 1920s created an expanded industry. Refinements in recording techniques, record distribution and marketing of product led to the growth years of the 1920s.

Chapter 4
THE ROARING 1920S, RISE OF POP MUSIC

The Roaring Twenties was a time of economic growth, fun times and living life to the extent. There was an air of superficiality in the decade, with turbulence beneath the surface. Widespread prosperity was driven by recovery from wartime devastation and deferred spending, a boom in construction and growth of consumer goods such as automobiles and electricity in America and other developed countries.

This era spanned 1919–1933. It opened in 1919, following World War I and a global pandemic. The influenza epidemic of 1918–1919 resulted in more than 17 million deaths worldwide.

Prohibition of alcohol was one of the biggest disasters in social history. It was pushed on the country by idealists, culminating with the 18th Amendment to the US Constitution in 1920. Sales of liquor was banned, leading to a revolution of bad taste and morals. Cars became portable saloons. People bought alcohol from questionable sources, which fueled the rise of gangsters and organized crime. Throughout the 1920s, the US spent $50 million per year in trying vainly to enforce the highly unpopular Prohibition Act. Bootleggers, racketeers and mobsters made billions of dollars and established footholds in territories that were impossible to retract. An unpopular law spearheaded by a zealous few was never really enforced, and its criminal perpetrators became "folk heroes" to many. The 21st Amendment in 1933 repealed this prohibition.

In 1920, women got the right to vote via the 19th Amendment and spent the decade pursuing independence. Aviator Charles Lindberg became a global hero with his transatlantic flight. Cars dominated the landscape, fueling businesses in their paths. Sound was added to the movies in 1927.

In the 1920s, the public was continually in search of something, while also escaping something. The mantra was to keep things growing, keep moving and being happy. Following the shocks of the pandemic, war and prohibition, excessive consumerism resulted. Many took holidays from thinking and pursued the high life. The feeling was that times were never better and that they would continue forever.

They can't hang you for saying nothing," quipped President Calvin Coolidge in the 1920s. He spent more time doing chores at his farm and taking long naps than taking care of the nation's business. Coolidge prided himself upon doing little, failing to see crises brewing during his presidency. A person once joked to President Coolidge that he could get him to say three or more words, to which Coolidge quipped, "You lose."

Slogans of the era included "back to normalcy," "a chicken in every pot," "the business of America is business" and "everything going one way only." Wall Street speculation grew to dangerous heights. Stocks were sold at dizzying high rates, with fearless speculators buying on margin. It culminated with the stock market crash of Oct. 24–29, 1929, plunging the world into the Great Depression, triggering hardship worldwide.

The Roaring Twenties got its name from the exuberant, freewheeling popular culture. Dancing rose in popularity, in opposition to the mood of World War I. The contributors were jazz bands and flappers.

The Growth of Radio

Radio grew in the 20s, with five stations on the air at the beginning of the decade and more than 600 stations at decade's end. Radio brought music to everyone, with a growing phonograph record industry providing music to compliment what was on the radio.

Samuel F.B. Morse was an artist and opened a studio in Boston, MA, in 1815. While on a voyage to Europe for art studies in 1832, a conversation on discoveries in electromagnetism inspired in him an invention for the transmission of information. While still onboard the ship, he drafted sketches for a telegraph. By 1838, Morse had a working model for translating letters into dots and dashes. In 1843, Congress appropriated funds to build the first telegraph line. In 1844, Morse tapped the first message, "What hath God wrought."

In 1877, at age thirty, Thomas Edison invented the phonograph unintentionally. At the time, Edison was trying to devise a high-speed telegraph machine as a counterpart to the telephone that Alexander Graham Bell had invented a year before.

In the 1880s, Heinrich R. Hertz discovered radio waves. In the 1890s, Guglielmo Marconi developed the first apparatus for long distance radio transmissions. In 1900, the first audio was sent, covering one mile. By 1910, these wireless systems had come to be called radio.

John Wanamaker started working as a delivery boy at age fourteen, entering the clothing business at eighteen. In 1861, with Nathan Brown, he founded Brown and Wanamaker, which became the leading men's clothier in the US within ten years. In 1875, he opened a dry goods and clothing business, inviting other merchants to sublet from him. In 1918, Wanamaker's stores piped music to each other, this innovation giving birth to commercial radio.

In the 1920s, local radio stations broadcast a variety of programming. The "service radio" format had stations offering different shows throughout the day, including music performed by local bands, concert remotes, news and interviews.

David Sarnoff immigrated from Russia to the US when he was nine. He studied engineering and began work in 1906 on wireless communications services. In 1913, he joined the Marconi Radio Company as chief inspector and rose through the ranks to management. Marconi was merged with Radio Corporation of America in 1919. Sarnoff was elected general manager of RCA in 1921, executive vice president in 1929, president in 1930 and chairman of the board in 1947. RCA was the leading manufacturer of radio sets in the 1920s, and Sarnoff championed the founding of the National Broadcasting Company to provide programming.

William S. Paley took a chain of 16 radio stations and grew it into the Columbia Broadcasting System in 1927. Paley grasped the potential of radio, with great programming essential to advertising sales and revenue. He created a major news division that coincided with World War II. CBS was known as the "tiffany network" for its quality in every programming real. CBS excelled in phonograph records with its Columbia label, developing the LP in 1948. CBS expanded into television. In 1976, Paley founded the Museum of Broadcasting.

Lee DeForest was an electrical engineer and inventor. His first patent was for an electrolytic detector that made possible the use of headphones with wireless receivers. In 1906, he invented the triode electron tube, with potential for relaying radio signals. His sound process evolved into radio. In 1919, De Forest developed a sound system for motion pictures. He made important contributions to the electric phonograph, television, radar and diathermy. He made and lost four fortunes in his life and remained committed to the educational potential for radio and TV.

The Jazz Age

In the first two decades of recorded music, all that was available were classical, opera and marching band recordings.

In the 1920s, the market opened for jazz, blues, pop and show tunes. Jazz came out of the South and added regional nuances in centers like Chicago, Kansas City and New York. Blues songs were originally passed along but became institutionalized via Tin Pan Alley published sheet music. Musicians from Harlem took ragtime music into fashionable clubs and Broadway theatres. Revues of contemporary music were embraced by the public, who sought recordings of these fashionable music genres. The merging of multi-cultural music styles was later sophisticated into the Big Band Era of the 1930s and 1940s.

Popular dance bands of the 1920s were led by Paul Whiteman, Nat Shilkret, Ben Bernie, Ben Selvin, Isham Jones, Fletcher Henderson, Leo Reisman, Ted Lewis, Rudy Vallee, Vincent Lopez, Ted Weems and Jacques Renard.

Popular jazz musicians included Louis Armstrong, Duke Ellington, Jelly Roll Morton, Bix Beiderbecke, Benny Goodman, Fats Waller, and King Oliver. Popular blues musicians included Mamie Smith, Ma Rainey, Bessie Smith, Lonnie Johnson, Blind Lemon Jefferson and Victoria Spivey.

Popular Broadway stars who recorded included Eddie Cantor, Sophie Tucker, Fanny Brice, Helen Morgan, Ethel Waters and Al Jolson.

Dance crazes included the Charleston, Black Bottom, fox trots, waltzes, cake walk, swing, ragtime, tango and lindy hop.

Jazz was brought uptown via a concert held on Feb. 12, 1924, at Aeolian Hall in New York City. Paul Whiteman's orchestra presented a jazz program, highlighted by George Gershwin playing piano on his suite "Rhapsody in Blue." The twenty-four pieces on the concert surveyed the scope of 1920s music. The program gained respect for jazz and created a recording market for the panorama of musical styles.

Irving Berlin created musical revues for the theatre. Florenz Ziegfeld created stage shows containing the tunes, plus dancing, comedy stars and an air of spectaculars. Other revues included George White's Scandals, the Grand Street Follies, Greenwich Village Follies, The Shuberts' Passing Shows and Earl Carroll's Vanities.

Top songs of the era included "Ain't We Got Fun," "Singing in the Rain," "Margie," "It All Depends on You," "You're the Cream in My Coffee," "Dardanella," "The Man I Love," "Love Nest," "Makin' Whoopee," "It Had to Be You," "Ma, He's Making Eyes at Me," "Am I Blue," "Give Me a Little Kiss," "Bye, Bye Blackbird," "Deed I Do," "Dinah," "If You Knew Susie," "I'll See You in My Dreams," "Barney Google," "My Buddy," "Look For the Silver Lining," "Running Wild," "Blue Skies," "When You're Smiling," "Sleepy Time Gal," "Yes, We Have No Bananas," "Three Little Words," "Tea For Two," "Limehouse Blues," "Indian Love Song" and "Together."

Top selling records of the 1920s included:

- "Whispering" by Paul Whiteman
- "April Showers" and "Swanee" by Al Jolson
- "Me and My Shadow" by Helen Morgan
- "There'll Be Some Changes Made" and "Some of These Days" by Sophie Tucker
- "Ain't Misbehaving" by Fats Waller
- "Heebie Jeebies" and "St. Louis Blues" by Louis Armstrong
- "Who's Sorry Now" and "Remember" by Isham Jones
- "I'm Looking Over a Four-Leaf Clover" by Jean Goldkette

- "Baby Face" by Ben Selvin
- "That Old Gang of Mine" by Billy Murray
- "My Blue Heaven" and "Ramona" by Gene Austin
- "Yes Sir, That's My Baby" by Blossom Seeley
- "Tip-Toe Thru' the Tulips with Me" by Nick Lucas
- "Painting the Clouds with Sunshine" by Johnny Marvin
- "The Varsity Drag" by Abe Lyman's California Orchestra
- "In the Jailhouse Now" by Jimmie Rodgers
- "My Man" by Fanny Brice
- *Downhearted Blues" by Bessie Smith
- *Sweet Georgia Brown" by Ben Bernie
- "The Prisoners Song" by Vernon Dalhart

Chapter 5

BIG BAND ERA, THE SWING
AND SINGING YEARS

There is a lot of romanticism about the Big Band Era. It made music in all tempos. It was a major innovation on popular music, and its impact on the recording industry continues to be felt. From 1931–1948, master musical groups displayed a virtuosity and technical perfection that no other "sound" has matched since.

The big bands got people dancing, and Victorian inhibitions were lost. The Big Band Era was the first time where adults let their hair down. It was the first era where teenage audiences began developing as consumers for popular music. Stuffed shirts gave way to sweaters, zoot suits, swirling skirts, bobby sox and penny loafers.

And look what people were dancing to relieve their minds of, including the effects of 1920s excesses, the Great Depression, World War II, rebuilding a war-torn world. Big bands spoke to the times around us, and its many styles and variations helped a weary world cope. Those were years of austerity and sacrifice.

Through it all, the 1930s and 1940s seemed romantic. This was the golden age of radio and motion pictures. Music was played everywhere. A cavalcade of songwriters, musicians and song arrangers kept the levels of quantity and quality of great music. Broadway shows created hits that dance bands played in live radio remotes and dance halls.

The result was that popular music figured more prominently into people's lives than any other time in history. Recorded music was the primary source of entertainment. Dozens of bands recorded and performed live. The music is remembered for a long time.

Benny Goodman was credited with kicking off the Big Band Era. He made his first appearance playing the clarinet at age twelve. He made a reputation as a jazz instrumentalist. He took to the position of leading bands with relish and flair. He conducted on Billie Holiday's first recording session and Bessie Smith's last one. By 1934, Goodman had his own national radio show on NBC, entitled "Let's Dance," which became his theme song.

In 1935, the Big Band Era broke loose. A dance at Palomar Ballroom in Los Angeles, CA, proved to be the catalyst. By 1936, America was dancing the jitterbug. Goodman was the King of Swing. Top instrumentalists like Gene Krupa, Harry James, Bunny Berigan, Ziggy Elman, Teddy Wilson and Lionel Hampton made up his super-group.

Benny Goodman broke racial taboos, with Wilson and Hampton as black superstars in his mostly white band. Goodman recognized the elements of jazz and soul, which began in black communities. He offered major concert exposure for black jazz stars, who later organized their own bands and helped get fame for other artists. To keep a balance of the big band sounds, Goodman fronted jazz combos in blockbuster recordings and world tours. His hits included "Bugle Call Rag," "Sometimes I'm Happy," "Jersey Bounce," "Why Don't You Do Right," "Don't Be That Way" and "Sing, Sing, Sing."

The Dorsey brothers presented precedents in big band and jazz contributions. Both Tommy and Jimmy Dorsey were born in Shenandoah, PA, and grew up playing together in bands. They worked together professionally with Jean Goldkette, Red Nichols, Paul Whiteman and other bandleaders of the early 1930s. In the mid-30s, they split up. Tommy Dorsey became the second superstar of the Big Band Era. Among the stellar talents that worked for his band were Charlie Spivak, Louis Bellson, Bunny Berigan, Buddy De Franco and singing talents like Frank Sinatra, Jo Stafford and the Pied Pipers.

Tommy Dorsey's style was perhaps the broadest of the big bands. His theme song was "I'm Getting Sentimental Over You." His sub-unit, with whom he jammed on jazz sets, was The Clambake Seven. His hits included "I'll Be Seeing You," "Boogie Woogie," "Song of India," "Who," "Polka Dots and Moonbeams," "This Love of Mine" and "The Music Goes Round and Round."

Jimmy Dorsey played in many commercial radio bands. When he and brother Tommy had their own orchestra, the players included Glenn Miller and Bob Crosby. Jimmy went onto commercial success on the Decca label, with an orchestra that featured the vocals of Bob Eberly and Helen O'Connell. His hits included "Green Eyes," "Amapola," "The Breeze and I," "Besame Mucho," "Maria Elena," "Pennies From Heaven" and "Tangerine."

In 1953, the Dorsey brothers got their bands back together as one. They headlined their own weekly show on CBS-TV in 1955–56, a show which holds the distinction as giving Elvis Presley his first national exposure. Jimmy continued to lead the band after Tommy died in 1956. Jimmy recorded "So Rare," a hit single that became a Rock & roll classic. Shortly after, in 1957, he died.

Glenn Miller was a top musician with many name bands. He yearned to create his own sound. Himself a trombone player, it was Miller's discovery of the reed section and his placing of clarinets and saxophones together as a solo section that proved the realization of his special sound. It was the rich dance-band sound that was widely received by the broadest possible audiences.

The Glenn Miller sound was sweet, even when it had that swing. In 1939, his orchestra reached the peak in popularity. His hits included "In the Mood," "Moonlight Serenade," "Chatanooga Choo Choo," "Tuxedo Junction," "Kalamazoo," "American Patrol," "A String of Pearls" and "Juke Box Saturday Night." The band appeared in two movies, 1941's "Sun Valley Serenade" and 1942's "Orchestra Wives," which introduced the song "At Last."

Glenn left it all in 1942 to join the service. He was persuaded to organize a touring band for the US Air Force. This kept him busy until his 1944 death while on tour. Miller's sound was widely copied after his death. In fact, it was the prevailing sound of the five years following World War II.

Artie Shaw was a fluent clarinetist. His intensity and depth of expression created a successful band. He started out as a jazz performer, organized one band and had to reorganize again to give the unit more of a commercial edge. At the peak of popularity, in December 1939, Shaw disbanded the group. Six months later, he put it back together. After another two years, he joined the US Navy. Soon, the band with a large string section, was back, entertaining troops. His hits included "Begin the Beguine," "Frenesi," "Moonglow," "Back Bay Shuffle," "Dancing in the Dark," "Nightmare" and "Summit Ridge Drive."

An outspoken critic of the exploitation of music, Artie Shaw left performing to become a writer. His source of nirvana was his jazz unit, The Gramercy Five, formed in 1940 out of his large orchestra. The Five toured off and on, up to the mid-1950s. Shaw next ran a dairy farm, later moving to Spain. He was married eight times. Two of his wives were famous actresses, Lana Turner and Ava Gardner.

If you think Artie Shaw's eight marriages were a record, think again. Charlie Barnet was married 11 times. He was a poll-winning instrumentalist. Charles Daly Barnet studied piano and saxophone as a child, though his wealthy parents tried to persuade him to become a corporation lawyer. He played in bands on cruise ships and formed his own in 1933, at age twenty. His music career was interrupted in 1935–1936 when he became a Hollywood actor. In 1939, his band hit the top, and it had lots of Duke Ellington influence in its style.

From the late-1930s through the 1950s, Barnet lead a successful band, employing music's top arrangers and a host of top black sidemen, many of whom went on to form their own bands, including Dizzy Gillespie, Skip Martin, Roy Eldridge and Clark Terry. Barnet was in the vanguard of Bebop. His hits included "Cherokee," "Pompton Turnpike," "Redskin Rhumba" and "Leaping at the Lincoln."

William "Count" Basie played jazz piano in Kansas City with Bennie Moten's orchestra. In 1936, upon Moten's death, he took over leadership. In 1937, they were the first black band to be taken under the management of Music Corporation of America. Count Basie's band was a sensation on records and on radio. Their Broadway debut was in 1938. They played Carnegie Hall and appeared in movies.

A consistent award winner, Basie incorporated the best of jazz and big bands without losing the integrity of either form. He was the longest survivor of the Big Band Era, touring well into the 1980s. His hits included "One O'Clock Jump," "April in Paris," "Fly Me to the Moon" and "Jive at Five."

The man with the other royal title, Duke Ellington, had flair, magnificence and lasting power. Edward Kennedy Ellington took up the piano as a child. He got the nickname "Duke" as a sandlot baseball player. In his 20s, he formed jazz combos that wowed them up in Harlem. Ellington made jazz chic. Uptown went downtown and vice versa. He is one of the most influential black musicians in the history of pop music. His hits included "Flamingo," "Take the A Train," "It Don't Mean a Thing If It Ain't Got that Swing," "Do Nothing Till You Hear From Me," "I Let a Song Go Out of My Heart," "Sophisticated Lady," "I Got It Bad and That Ain't Good," "Rocking in Rhythm," "Mood Indigo" and "Black and Tan Fantasy."

A prolific composer, Ellington's body of music is impressive. He paralleled the Big Band Era with dreamy ballads and enough swing to give many a musician lessons for life. Dressed elegantly and carrying an aristocratic manner, Duke explained the complexities of music to all audiences. He served it up in impressive and diversified forms. His 1974 death ended a career of fifty-plus years as an innovator, behind whom the others inevitably followed.

At age nine, Woodrow Wilson Herman was billed as the "boy wonder of the clarinet." By age twenty-three in 1936, he was leading his own professional big band. His arrangements fluctuated between swing and Dixieland. From 1939's blockbuster "Woodchopper's Ball," Woody Herman was assured a spot as one of the biggest bands. His hits included "Caldonia," "Blues in the Night," "Bijou," "Four Bothers," "Blue Flame" and "I'll Remember April."

After the decline of the Big Band Era, Woody Herman and his Herd, which at one time included almost every musician of note, took more of a jazz approach. The appearance of the electric piano and other devices has kept Herman's Herd in the forefront of jazz.

Bunny Berigan was perhaps the greatest trumpet player of the 1920s and 1930s. He was raised in a musical family in Wisconsin and learned by jamming with jazz bands. He moved to New York in 1930, at age twenty-three, and became a top session player with Hal Kemp, the Dorsey Brothers, Paul Whiteman and Benny Goodman. In 1937, Berigan organized his own band and recorded what was then the industry's longest record, "I Can't Get Started."

Harry James from Albany, GA, emerged as the superstar of the Benny Goodman band. The precision trumpet solos of Harry James established his esteem. In 1939, at age twenty-three, he formed his own orchestra, and the tunes were more dance-band than jazz. His earliest singer was Frank Sinatra, on their hit "On a Little Street in Singapore." His hits included "Ciribiribin," "You Made Me Love You,"

"It's Been a Long, Long Time," "I Had the Craziest Dream" and "Music Makers." The superb trumpet crackling always came through. James received notoriety by marrying pin-up girl Betty Grable, back when she was Hollywood's biggest box office draw. Throughout the decades since the demise of the Big Band Era, Harry James continued to headline popular bands, mostly working out of Nevada.

Larry Clinton was born in Brooklyn, NY. His mother was a concert soprano. Larry was a self-taught trumpeter. He arranged for the bands of Tommy Dorsey, Glen Gray and Bunny Berigan. He formed his own swing band in 1938, which he led until 1950, interrupted only for military service. His hits included "My Reverie," "Martha," "Dipsy Doodle," "Deep Purple" and "Over the Rainbow." From the 1950s forward, Clinton was a force behind the scenes in the music publishing and recording industries.

Les Brown's first band was the Duke Blue Devils while a student at Duke University. A one-time arranger for Larry Clinton, Brown formed his own group in 1938. Throughout the 1940s and afterward, Les Brown and His Band of Renown developed a fine reputation as a pop band. His hits included "Leap Frog," "Sentimental Journey," "Bizet Has His Day" and "September Song." Les Brown's band was associated with Bob Hope for several decades. Brown played the alto sax and clarinet, though he was never featured as a soloist.

Stan Kenton blended his music in new directions. He was constantly experimenting and always relied on jazz. Although associated with grandiose cathedrals of sound, his band always played a diverse repertoire. Kenton did his first arrangement in 1928, at age sixteen. He formed his first orchestra in 1940. With a movie score feel, the Kenton compositions had classical music embodiments. His hits included "Artistry in Rhythm," "Laura," "Peanut Vendor," "Malagueña" and "Intermission Riff."

The list of talents that have gone through the Kenton organization is staggering, including vocalist June Christy and arrangers Pete Rugolo, Shorty Rodgers and Gerry Mulligan, plus musicians Stan Getz and Bud Shank. Stan Kenton continued as ever throughout the 1950s, 1960s and 1970s. He stood with Woody Herman as innovative and a prime spokesman for modern jazz.

Vaughn Monroe was a vocalist who fronted a big band. He was born in Akron, OH, in 1911. In 1925, at age fourteen, he won a state trumpet playing championship. In 1940, he formed his own band, with solid 1940s hits including

"Ballerina," "Racing with the Moon," "There I've Said It Again," "Riders in the Sky," "Sound Off" and the original version of "Let It Snow! Let It Snow! Let It Snow!" In the 1950s, he had vocal hits and won more acclaim as the advertising spokesman for RCA Victor, for whom he recorded.

Other big bands were led by Blue Barron, Cab Calloway, Frankie Carle, Xavier Cugat, Eddy Duchin, Shep Fields, Erskine Hawkins, Horace Heidt, Eddy Howard, Hal Kemp, Wayne King, Kay Kyser, Johnny Long, Freddy Martin, Clyde McCoy, Ray Noble, Tony Pastor, Jan Savitt, Bobby Sherwood, Claude Thornhill, Tommy Tucker and Ted Weems.

Bands of the previous era who flourished in the Big Band Era included Louis Armstrong, Guy Lombardo, Ozzie Nelson, Russ Morgan, Lawrence Welk, Ben Bernie and Rudy Vallee.

Big Bands who continued in other eras included Count Basie, Woody Herman, Bob Crosby, Ralph Flanagan, Jan Garber, Lionel Hampton, Louis Jordan, Stan Kenton, Sammy Kaye, Gene Krupa, Enoch Light, Louis Prima, Alvino Rey, Victor Young and Glen Gray.

Stars to come out of the Big Band Era as headliners in later years included Frank Sinatra, Doris Day, Jo Stafford, Georgia Gibbs, Merv Griffin, Helen O'Connell, Tex Beneke, Mel Torme, Helen Forrest, Ella Fitzgerald, Hoagy Carmichael, Gene Krupa, June Christy, Billy Eckstine, Peggy Lee and Billie Holiday.

I met many of the bandleaders during the 1970s and 1980s, including Duke Ellington, Count Basie, Woody Herman, Benny Goodman, Harry James and Ozzie Nelson. I talked with singers who had performed with big bands, including Frank Sinatra, Doris Day, Helen O'Connell and Ken Curtis. I interviewed some who arranged for big bands and later fronted their own orchestras, including Nelson Riddle and Ray Anthony. They were a wealth of knowledge and experience.

The Big Band Era is loved and remembered by people of all ages. There was such a wealth of quality recordings and beloved songs. Hearing the music is reminiscent of times past, though the songs have continued to be covered as standards.

Big Band Anthology Playlist of Top Hits
- "A-Tisket/Tasket and Undecided," 1938, Chick Webb band, vocal by Ella Fitzgerald
- "I'm Getting Sentimental Over You" and "Marie," 1935, Tommy Dorsey

- "Take the A Train" and "Perdido," 1941, Duke Ellington
- "Moonlight Serenade" and "In the Mood," 1939, Glenn Miller
- "A String of Pearls" and "Blueberry Hill," 1940, Glenn Miller
- "Daddy," 1941, Sammy Kaye
- "Tonight We Love (Tchaikovsky Piano Concerto #1)," 1941, Freddy Martin
- "Amapola," 1941, Jimmy Dorsey, vocal by Bob Eberly and Helen O'Connell
- "Apple Blossom Time," 1941, The Andrews Sisters
- "Maria Elena," 1941, Wayne King
- "Maybe," 1941, The Ink Spots
- "Cherokee," "Leaping at the Lincoln" "Pompton Turnpike," 1940, Charlie Barnet
- "I Can't Get Started," 1937, Bunny Berigan
- "One O'Clock Jump," 1939, Count Basie
- "Old Man River," 1928, Paul Whiteman, vocal by Bing Crosby
- "Martha" and "My Reverie," 1940, Larry Clinton, vocal by Bea Wain
- "Ciribiribin," 1939, Harry James
- "Honky Tonk Train Blues," 1943, Meade Lux Lewis
- "Sentimental Journey," 1944, Les Brown, vocal by Doris Day
- "Sing, Sing, Sing," 1938, Benny Goodman
- "I'll Be Seeing You," 1944, Bing Crosby
- "G.I. Jive," 1945, Louis Jordan and his Tympany Five
- "Flying Home," 1942, Lionel Hampton
- "St. Louis Blues," 1929, Louis Armstrong
- "Into Each Life Some Rain Must Fall," 1944, Ella Fitzgerald and the Ink Spots
- "Coming In on a Wing and a Prayer," 1945, Song Spinners
- "Frenesi," 1940, Artie Shaw
- "Besame Mucho," 1943, Jimmy Dorsey, vocal by Bob Eberly and Helen O'Connell
- "I'll Walk Alone," 1943, Dinah Shore
- "And the Angels Sing," 1939, Glenn Miller, vocal by Ray Eberle
- "Bugle Call Rag" and "Christopher Columbus," 1936, Benny Goodman

- "Holiday For Strings," 1942, David Rose
- "Oh, Look at Me Now," 1941, Tommy Dorsey, vocal by Frank Sinatra
- "When the Lights Go on Again All over the World," 1944, Vaughn Monroe
- "I Said No," 1945, Alvino Rey, vocal by Yvonne King
- "Blues in the Night," 1944, Woody Herman
- "C-Jam Blues" (Duke's Place), 1940, Duke Ellington
- "Remember Pearl Harbor," 1944, Sammy Kaye
- "Love For Sale," 1939, Hal Kemp
- "Mamselle," 1947, Art Lund
- "Johnson Rag" and "Little Brown Jug," 1940, Glenn Miller
- "Don't Get Around Much Anymore," 1944, Ink Spots
- "Boogie Woogie," 1938, Tommy Dorsey
- "Heartaches," 1947, Ted Weems
- "Time Waits For No One," 1944, Helen Forrest
- "Caldonia," 1945, Louis Jordan and his Tympany Five
- "It Can't Be Wrong" (theme from "Now Voyager"), 1943, Dick Haymes
- "I'm Beginning to See the Light," 1944, Duke Ellington
- "Brazil," 1939, Xavier Cugat
- "Buttons and Bows," 1943, Dinah Shore
- "Prisoner of My Love," 1946, Perry Como
- "Special Delivery Stomp," 1945, Artie Shaw and his Gramercy Five
- "The Music Goes Round and Round," 1936, Tommy Dorsey & his Clambake Seven
- "To Each His Own," 1947, Eddy Howard
- "Woodchopper's Ball," 1946, Woody Herman
- "This Love of Mine," 1940, Tommy Dorsey, vocal by Frank Sinatra
- "You're Breaking My Heart," 1948, Vic Damone
- "Begin the Beguine," "Indian Love Call" and "Back Bay Shuffle," 1938, Artie Shaw
- "Jumpin' Jive," 1945, Cab Calloway
- "Who" and "Song of India," 1937, Tommy Dorsey
- "Laughing On the Outside," 1946, Andy Russell
- "Blueberry Hill," 1949, Louis Armstrong
- "Linda," 1944, Buddy Clark

- "Carle Meets Mozart," 1947, Frankie Carle
- "At Last," 1941, Glenn Miller, vocal by Ray Eberle
- "It's Been a Long, Long Time," 1945, Bing Crosby, with Les Paul
- "Leap Frog," 1945, Les Brown and his Band of Renown
- "Goodnight My Love," 1936, Benny Goodman, vocal by Ella Fitzgerald
- "Accentuate the Positive," 1944, Johnny Mercer and the Pied Pipers
- "Now Is the Hour," 1948 Margaret Whiting
- "The Breeze and I," 1940, Jimmy Dorsey, vocal by Bob Eberly
- "Stomping ar the Savoy," 1936, Benny Goodman
- "Bumble Boogie," 1938, Freddy Martin
- "Ballerina," 1947, Vaughn Monroe
- "To Each His Own" and "The Gypsy," 1946, The Ink Spots
- "Cow-Cow Boogie," 1942, Ella Mae Morse
- "Rippling Rhythm," 1938, Shep Fields
- "Marie," 1937, Tommy Dorsey, vocal by Jack Leonard
- "I'll Buy That Dream," 1945, Dick Haymes and Helen Forrest
- "Bell Bottom Trousers," 1945, Tony Pastor
- "The Prisoner's Song," 1937, Bunny Berigan
- "Why Don't You Do Right," 1942, Benny Goodman, vocal by Peggy Lee
- "Woody Woodpecker Song," 1948, Kay Kyser, vocal by Gloria Wood
- "Racing With the Moon," 1940, Vaughn Monroe
- "Beer Barrel Polka," 1938, Will Glahe
- "On a Little Street in Singapore," 1939, Harry James, vocal by Frank Sinatra
- "Don't Fence Me In," 1944, Bing Crosby and the Andrews Sisters
- "Jumpin' at the Woodside," 1957, Count Basie
- "Candy," 1945, Johnny Mercer, Jo Stafford and the Pied Pipers
- "And the Angels Sing," 1939, Ziggy Elman
- "So Rare," 1937, Guy Lombardo, vocal by Carmen Lombardo
- "Symphony," 1947, Freddy Martin, vocal by Clyde Rogers
- "Anniversary Song," 1947, Tex Beneke
- "Doctor, Lawyer, Indian Chief," 1945, Betty Hutton
- "Let It Snow, Let It Snow, Let It Snow," 1945, Vaughn Monroe
- "On the Atchison, Topeka and Santa Fe," 1945, Judy Garland
- "Personality," 1946 Johnny Mercer and the Pied Pipers

Hank Moore with Duke Ellington

Hank Moore with Ella Fitzgerald

Glenn Miller, Benny Goodman, and the stars of the Big Band Era

Chapter 6
HIT PARADE YEARS, 1948–1956

There was a special period in popular music between the Big Band Era and the birth of rock and roll. The years of 1948–1956 were sweet. They were probably the last show of naïve simplicity that we had. These were the hit parade years.

The early 1950s were the last of the Tin Pan Alley composers. Movie and Broadway music added gems to the repertoire. An exciting generation of recording artists experimented with techniques and music genres.

The public bought their records in phenomenal numbers, mostly because of technological innovations that ushered in this modern era in middle-of-the road contemporary pop. Development of records that played at speeds of 45RPM and 33-1/3RPM, on unbreakable discs with "high fidelity," enabled widespread distribution of the releases.

As the Big Band Era drew to an official close, it became apparent that singers were the most idolized by the public. Bing Crosby and Frank Sinatra caused that. Singers and groups began performing to pre-recorded instrumental tracks. The development of magnetic tape recording in the late 1940s inevitably led to editing and over-dubbing.

The Billboard Hot 100 charts were instituted. To fill radio airwaves, there was the largest volume of recordings issued. Often, the same songs were recorded by several artists, a version on each of the major record labels. This chart action also included instrumental recordings. Record sales were at all-time highs. Pop music appealed to all family members. Juke boxes in restaurants and other retail locales fueled the enthusiasm for middle-of-the-road pop. Portable radio sales grew, and 45RPM record players even appeared in automobiles. Everything that pop music became was nurtured during the 1950s.

Musically, the early 1950s set standards for all time of what middle-of-the-road contemporary pop should and could be.

Recording Stars of the Hit Parade

Perry Como was always at the top of the charts in the 1950s. The epitome of the song stylist, Como's choice of material always seemed right. One of thirteen children in Canonsburg, PA, Perry Como became a barber at age fourteen to support his family. At age twenty-one, he got his first job singing with a band. He was a major star of radio beginning in 1942 and television beginning in 1948. He was a major recording artist on RCA Victor Records from 1944 through the next five decades.

Perry Como's hits included "Till the End of Time," "Prisoner of Love," "When You Were Sweet Sixteen," "Because," "A, You're Adorable," "A Dreamer's Holiday," "No Other Love," "Wanted," "Papa Loves Mambo," "Home For the Holidays," "Hot Diggity," "Round and Round," "Catch a Falling Star," "Magic Moments," "Kewpie Doll," "Dream On Little Dreamer," "It's Impossible," "And I Love You So" and "I Think of You."

One of eleven children in Tulsa, OK, Clara Ann Fowler sang in a church choir. At age nineteen, she was a staff singer on radio. She chose her name from one of the station's sponsors, the Page Milk Company and was renamed Patti Page. In 1948, she signed with a new label, Mercury Records. The Singing Rage, Miss Patti Page blazed trails for female vocalists over the decades. She was the first to overdub her voice several times in multi-part harmony. Her hits included "Tennessee Waltz," "Cross Over the Bridge," "Let Me Go Lover," "Allegheny Moon," "Old Cape Cod," "Left Right Out of Your Heart," "Most People Get Married" and "Hush Hush Sweet Charlotte."

Tony Bennett enjoyed the longest tenure of stars from that era. Anthony Dominick Benedetto first appeared in church choirs at age seven in his native New York City. While serving in the US Army during World War II, he sang for the troops. Bob Hope discovered Tony Bennett and made him part of his traveling cast.

Tony's first two hits for Columbia Records in 1951 hit Number One within a month of each other, "Because of You" and "Cold, Cold Heart." Tony Bennet has sung every major dreamy ballad and jazz vocal. Other hits included "Blue Velvet," "Rags to Riches," "Stranger in Paradise," "In the Middle of an Island," "Firefly," "Just in Time," "I Left My Heart in San Francisco," "The Best is Yet to Come," "The Good Life," "If I Ruled the World" and "When Joanna Loved Me."

Rosemary Clooney first sang in her native Kentucky to help her grandfather run for mayor. She and her sister Betty won an amateur contest and jobs fronting Tony Pastor's orchestra.

Clooney appeared in 1954's "White Christmas" with her friend Bing Crosby. One of the durables of the 1950s was her appearance on variety shows of Ed Sullivan and others. She appeared "in the family way," as pregnancy was then known. She and husband Jose Ferrer had six children throughout the 1950s. Her hits included "Tenderly," "Beautiful Brown Eyes," "Half as Much," "Hey There," "This Ole House," "Memories of You," "Mangos," "Love Eyes" and "I've Grown Accustomed to Your Face."

Frank Sinatra was the major musical phenomenon of the 1940s. He was discovered on the "Major Bowes Amateur Hour" on radio in 1935. In 1939, he sang with Harry James' band. He reached superstardom as the singer with the Tommy Dorsey Band, 1940–1942. A bobby sox idol, Sinatra's career flourished in the 1940s, extending into the movies. His career dipped late in the decade. Sinatra switched record labels from Columbia to Capitol.

In the 1950s, he was a hip swinger, with recordings featuring arrangements by Nelson Riddle, Gordon Jenkins and Billy May. Sinatra evolved into the image of the international playboy, the prototype of the debonair gentleman. In the 1960s, he was Chairman of the Board of the Rat Pack, the in-crowd of top singers and actors. For three more decades, he was the elder statesman of pop music, the benchmark to which others aspired.

The Sinatra hits included "All or Nothing at All," "Sunday, Monday or Always," "Dream," "Nancy," "The Coffee Song," "Castle Rock," "Young at

Heart," "Three Coins in the Fountain," "Love and Marriage," "Learning the Blues," "The Tender Trap," "Hey6 Jealous Lover," "All the Way," "Witchcraft," "Mr. Success," "High Hopes," "Pocketful of Miracles," "Strangers in the Night," "That's Life," "Summer Wind," "The World We Knew," "My Way," "New York, New York" and "Cycles."

Teresa Brewer also appeared on the "Major Bowes Amateur Hour," as a regular for five years, from ages seven to twelve. After high school graduation at age sixteen, she became a popular nightclub singer. She was the little lady with the bubbly voice.

Known for happy, peppy songs, Teresa Brewer became a major recording star at age eighteen, on Coral Records. Her hits included "Music, Music, Music," "Till I Waltz Again with You," "Ricochet Romance," "Bell Bottom Blues," "Jilted," "Let Me Go Lover," "Pledging My Love," "Sweet Old Fashioned Girl," "Mutual Admiration Society," "Bo Weevil," "Empty Arms," "You Send Me," "A Tear Fell" and "Heavenly Lover."

Nat King Cole was a preacher's son. A piano player since childhood, he gained fame for his King Cole Trio, the classiest jazz set at the top supper clubs in Los Angeles. He joined Capitol Records at its founding in 1942. One of his jazz hits was "Straighten Up and Fly Right," based upon one of his father's sermons.

From 1946's "The Christmas Song" forward, Nat King Cole was identified with dreamy ballads, with lush arrangements by Nelson Riddle. Cole was one of the greatest voices of the century for pop music. He was the first black to have his own network TV show and was until his death the top paid entertainer in Las Vegas. He died of lung cancer in 1965. His daughter Natalie Cole continued his stellar legacy.

The hit Capitol recordings of Nat King Cole included "For Sentimental Reasons," "Nature Boy," "Too Young," "Mona Lisa," "Orange Colored Sky," "Red Sails in the Sunset," "Unforgettable," "Walking My Baby Back Home," "The Ruby and the Pearl," "Pretend," "Answer Me My Love," "Darling Je Vous Aime Beaucoup," "A Blossom Fell," "Ask Me," "Night Lights," "Raintree County," "Madrid," "Looking Back," "Nothing in the World," "I Must Be Dreaming," "Rambling Rose," "Lazy Hazy Crazy Days of Summer," "Dear Lonely Hearts," "LOVE" and "Cat Ballou."

Les Paul could not read music but developed the techniques of overdubbing on magnetic tape, which was then a new medium. While Les Paul invented guitars and simulated an army of instruments via his overdubbing, his wife Mary Ford sang the enchanting vocals.

The hits of Les Paul and Mary Ford included "Tennessee Waltz," "Mocking Bird Hill," "How High the Moon," "The World is Waiting For the Sunrise," "Just One More Chance," "I'm Confessing," "In the Good Old Summertime," "Smoke Rings," "Bye, Bye Blues," "I'm Sitting on Top of the World," "Vaya Con Dios," "I Really Don't Want to Know," "I'm a Fool to Care," "Hummingbird" and "Cinco Robles."

Eddie Fisher was discovered singing in the Catskills Mountains by entertainment legend Eddie Cantor. Fisher was that clean-cut guy who made the girls squeal in the early 1950s. He launched a long string of hits on RCA Victor and continued to record while serving in the US Army. In the mid-1950s, Fisher headlined two 15-minute music variety shows per week on NBC-TV, alternating with Perry Como and Dinah Shore on various nights.

Eddie Fisher married actress Debbie Reynolds in 1955. It was like the boy and girl next door getting married. They had a baby girl, Carrie Fisher, later of "Star Wars" fame. Carrie's godmother was movie superstar Elizabeth Taylor. Carrie's brother, Todd Fisher, was named for Elizabeth's husband, Michael Todd. Michael died in a plane crash, leaving Liz a widow. Eddie Fisher made headlines in 1958 by leaving Debbie for Liz, who later left Eddie for actor Richard Burton. Since leaving Debbie, Eddie's hits and TV shows dried up. He remained a nightclub entertainer for the remaining thirty years of his life.

The hits of Eddie Fisher included "Thinking of You," "Bring Back the Thrill," "Turn Back the Hands of Time," "Any Time," "Tell Me Why," "Forgive Me," "I'm Yours," "Wish You Were Here," "Lady of Spain," "Down Hearted," "I'm Walking Behind You," "With These Hands," "Many Times," "Oh My Papa," "A Girl," "I Need You Now," "Count Your Blessings," "A Man Chases a Girl," "Heart," "Song of the Dreamer," "Dungaree Doll," "On the Street Where You Live," "Cindy Oh Cindy," "Tonight," "This Nearly Was Mine," "Games That Lovers Play" and "People Like You."

Dinah Shore was seemingly a major media star forever, always vivacious and bubbly. Frances Rose Shore was also a protégé of Eddie Cantor. She started recording for RCA Victor in 1941 at the age of twenty-four. Throughout the 1950s, she was a major television star, throwing kisses to viewers at the end of each show, while inviting them to, "See the USA in your Chevrolet." She continued through the 1960s, 1970s and 1980s as a major TV star.

Dinah Shore scored such hits as "I Hear a Rhapsody," "Blues in the Night," "Miss You," "One Dozen Roses," "Dearly Beloved," "Why Don't You Fall in Love With Me," "You'd Be So Nice to Come Home To," "Murder, He Says," "I'll Walk Alone," "Along the Navajo Trail," "Laughing on the Outside," "The Gypsy," "For Sentimental Reasons," "Anniversary Song," "Buttons and Bows," "Lavender Blue," "Far Away Places," "My Heart Cries For You," "Changing Partners," "Blues in Advance" and "I'll Never Say Never Again."

Songwriter Hoagy Carmichael discovered Frank LoVecchio singing in nightclubs. Frankie Laine was signed to the new Mercury Label in 1947 and had one major hit after another. He moved over to Columbia in 1951 and continued to be one of pop music's biggest stars.

Frankie Laine always sang with drama. He was known as Mr. Rhythm. His voice always was powerful enough to fill an auditorium without a microphone. The greatest hits of Frankie Laine included "That's My Desire," "Shine," "That Lucky Old Sun," "Mule Train," "Cry of the Wild Goose," "Dream a Little Dream of Me," "Jezebel," "Rose I Love You," "Jealousy," "High Noon," "I Believe," "Hey Joe," "Someday," "Humming Bird," "Moonlight Gambler," "Love Is a Golden Ring," "Rawhide," "I'll Take Care of Your Cares," "Making Memories," "Laura What's He Got," "You Gave Me a Mountain," "Dammit is Not God's Last Name," "The Meaning of It All" and "Blazing Saddles."

Doris Day was a singer who went on to become a movie star. Unlike others who have gone that route, Doris continued to progress her recording career just as diligently as her film glory. She was Doris Kappelhoff when she was a singer with Les Brown's band in the mid-1940s. She chose her name from the song "Day by Day," at the suggestion of Frank Sinatra. Always on screen as the freckle faced blonde with unswerving virtues, Doris Day's singing reflected good taste, crisp delivery and the finest writings of composers.

The Doris Day catalog includes such hits as "It's Magic," "Again," "Canadian Capers," "Bewitched," "A Bushel and a Peck," "Shanghai," "A Guy is a Guy," "Mister Tap Toe," "Secret Love," "If I Give My Heart to You," "I'll Never Stop Loving You," "Whatever Will Be Will Be," "Teacher's Pet," "Everybody Loves a Lover," "Tunnel of Love," "Any Way the Wind Blues," "Lover Come Back," "Move Over Darling" and "Do Not Disturb."

Dean Martin was a singer who teamed with comedian Jerry Lewis in 1946. They performed in nightclubs, on radio and starred in a series of movies. Dean sang in the act, and naturally he was offered a recording contract. With Capitol Records, Dean had many hits from 1950-1962, including "I'll Always Love You," "If," "You Belong to Me," "That's Amore," "Sway," "Memories Are Made of This," "Return to Me," "Volare," "Angel Baby" and "On an Evening in Roma."

Martin switched to Reprise Records in 1962 and had a host of hits, including "Everybody Loves Somebody," "The Door is Still Open to My Heart," "You're Nobody Till Somebody Loves You," "Send Me the Pillow You Dream On," "Remember Me, I'm the One Who Loves You," "Houston," "I Will," "Come Running Back," "A Million and One," "In the Chapel in the Moonlight," "Little Ole Wine Drinker Me" and "I Take a Lot of Pride in What I Am." Most of these 1960s Reprise hits were up-tempo covers of country songs and oldies remakes. Martin headlined a TV series on NBC and continued to act in movies. In the 1970s, Martin hosted TV celebrity roasts and headlined nightclubs.

The longest running TV telethon has been the annual Muscular Dystrophy Association Labor Day spectacular. It was hosted for many years by Jerry Lewis, who invited the biggest stars to appear. One momentous entertainment event occurred on 1976 MDA telethon, when Frank Sinatra brought a friend to see Jerry and perform. It was Dean Martin, who was Jerry's former show business partner, and this appearance marked the reunion of Martin and Lewis after a twenty-year hiatus.

Bing Crosby was a major force during this pop hit parade period. He hit the music scene in the late 1920s, singing with bands. In 1932, Crosby became a headlining solo recording artist and was the major singing sensation of the 1930s. Crosby reigned throughout the 1940s, as a major movie star and radio star. During the period covered here, Crosby elevated to elder statesman status, the role model of other singers. His Christmas TV specials up through 1977 were must-see events.

Bing Crosby recordings during this period included "Ballerina," "Riders in the Sky," "Sam's Song," "Changing Partners," "Y'all Come," "Dear Hearts and Gentle

People," "True Love," "Now You Has Jazz," "Around the World," "Do You Hear What I Hear," "Say One for Me" and "How Lovely is Christmas."

The Cover Phenomenon

One of the most influential producers of hit records during this era was Mitch Miller. To the public, Miller was best known for "Sing Along with Mitch" in the 1960s. A decade earlier, he set the tone for the commerciality of the recording industry.

Miller was a Julliard trained musician, playing the oboe on classical music performances. He loved jazz and pop music too. As the Big Band Era of the 1930s and 1940s wound down, the solo singers took the limelight, and the bands hence became their accompaniment. Miller saw the dawning of the pop music era in 1948. As director of Artists and Repertoire for Columbia Records, he began signing talent to the label: Frankie Laine, Tony Bennett, Rosemary Clooney, Vic Damone, Johnny Mathis, Sarah Vaughan, Mahalia Jackson, Jerry Vale and others. Miller developed a stable of new recording artists, including Jimmy Boyd, Champ Butler, Mindy Carson, Don Cherry, The Four Lads, Peggy King, Johnny Mathis, The New Christy Minstrels, The Brothers Four, Eileen Rodgers and Joan Weber.

Mitch Miller knew that radio stations were looking for records to give wide airplay. He believed in two concepts that were fresh ground and not like anything during the Big Band Era. One of the concepts was novelty songs, for which there was a large public appetite. The other was pop covers of songs originally done by country and rhythm & blues artists.

Rosemary Clooney was a ballad singer. Mitch Miller gave her a song to record called "Come On-a My House," written by Ross Bagdasarian and William Saroyan and featured in a Broadway musical "The Son." Clooney hated the song, but Miller insisted, saying that heightened radio airplay would stimulate sales of her ballad recordings. Miller led a four-musician combo on the recording, including harpsichordist Stan Freeman. Miller's instincts were right, and the record was a smash hit. This stimulated Clooney recording other novelty songs later, including "This Ole House," "Botch-A-Me" and "Mambo Italiano."

Other novelty songs which Miller produced were:

- "Mama Will Bark" by Frank Sinatra and Dagmar
- "Children's Marching Song" and "Yellow Rose of Texas" by Mitch Miller
- "Ma Says, Pa Says" by Doris Day and Johnnie Ray
- "Mack the Knife" by Louis Armstrong
- "The Battle of New Orleans" by Johnny Horton
- "Istanbul, Not Constantinople," "Skokiaan," "The Mocking Bird" and "Two Ladies in the Shade of the Banana Tree" by The Four Lads
- "The Little White Cloud That Cried" by Johnnie Ray
- "Strange Things are Happening" by Red Buttons
- "A Guy Is a Guy," "Shanghai," "Let It Ring" and "Mister Toe Tap" by Doris Day
- "Daddy," "Doing What Comes Naturally" and "The Egg and I" by Dinah Shore

In 1950, country music was only played on rural radio stations in small markets. Same for black groups performing R&B, which was known at the time as "race music." Miller realized the opportunity to get further exposure for the creators of C&W and R&B music. He asked his stable of stars to record some of those songs in their distinctive pop styles, complete with orchestras, lush arrangements and appealing sounds.

Among Columbia's covers of country tunes were:

- "Cold, Cold Heart," "There'll Be No Teardrops Tonight" and "Candy Kisses" by Tony Bennett
- "Your Cheating Heart," "High Noon" and "Hey Joe" by Frankie Laine
- "Half as Much" and "This Ole House" by Rosemary Clooney
- "You Win Again" and "Kaw-Liga" by Champ Butler
- "Jambalaya" by Jo Stafford
- "Setting the Woods on Fire" by Jo Stafford and Frankie Laine
- "The Roving Kind," "Singing the Blues," "Knee Deep in the Blues" and "Heartaches by the Numbers" by Guy Mitchell
- "Too Old to Cut the Mustard" by Marlene Dietrich and Rosemary Clooney

The other major labels followed suit, featuring popular music artists doing cover versions. The Chords had the R&B version of "Sh-Boom," and The Crew Cuts had the pop version on Mercury. Slim Willet had the country version of "Don't Let the Stars Get in Your Eyes" on Columbia, and Perry Como scored with the pop version on RCA Victor. The country version of "Seven Lonely Days" was by Bonnie Lou on King and The Pinetoppers on Coral, with the pop version by Georgia Gibbs on Mercury.

Red Foley had the country version of "Chattanooga Shoeshine Boy" on Decca, and Frank Sinatra had the pop version on Capitol. Both the country version of "Anytime" by Eddy Arnold and the pop version by Eddie Fisher were both on RCA Victor. Eddy Arnold had "Take Me in Your Arms and Hold Me" on RCA Victor, and Les Paul & Mary Ford had the pop version on Capitol. Hank Williams had "My Bucket's Got a Hole in It" on MGM, and Ricky Nelson did the pop cover on Imperial.

As for R&B covers, the original of "Blue Velvet" by The Clovers on Atlantic was covered by Tony Bennett on Columbia and Bobby Vinton on Epic. The Dominoes had the R&B version of "Learning the Blues" on King, and Frank Sinatra had the pop version on Capitol.

Georgia Gibbs was a pop singer whose range was expansive. She recorded several covers of R&B songs: "Tweedle Dee" (by Ruth Brown), "Dance With Me Henry" (by Etta James), "I Want You to Be My Baby" (by Lillian Briggs) and "Tra La La" (by LaVerne Baker).

Another innovation was to pair up label mates on perform duets. This custom was a recording industry answer to the duets which occurred on radio and TV variety shows. Duets of the 1950s included:

- "Baby It's Cold Outside" by Margaret Whiting and Johnny Mercer on Capitol
- "Civilization" by The Andrews Sisters and Danny Kaye on Decca
- "Aba Daba Honeymoon" by Debbie Reynolds and Carlton Carpenter on MGM
- "Watermelon Weather" by Perry Como and Eddie Fisher on RCA Victor
- "Undecided" by The Ames Brothers and Les Brown on Coral

- "Water Can't Quench the Fire of Love" by Helen O'Connell and Giselle Mackenzie on Capitol
- "Open the Doghouse" and "Long Ago" by Dean Martin and Nat King Cole on Capitol
- "Tell Me a Story" by Frankie Laine and Jimmy Boyd on Columbia
- "Wimoweh" by The Weavers and Gordon Jenkins on Decca
- "A Bushel and a Peck" by Perry Como and Betty Hutton on RCA Victor
- "Dearie" by Ray Bolger and Ethel Merman on Decca
- "A Penny a Kiss" by Dinah Shore and Tony Martin on RCA Victor
- "You'll Never Get Away" by Teresa Brewer and Don Cornell on Coral
- "Mutual Admiration Society" by Eddy Arnold and Jaye P. Morgan on RCA Victor
- "True Love" by Bing Crosby and Grace Kelly on Capitol
- "Up Above My Head" by Frankie Laine and Johnnie Ray on Columbia
- "She Wore a Yellow Ribbon" by The Andrews Sisters and Russ Morgan on Decca
- "Orange Colored Sky" by Nat King Cole and Stan Kenton on Capitol
- "Bibbidi-Bobbidi-Boo" and "You're Just in Love" by Perry Como and The Fontane Sisters on RCA Victor
- "Two Lost Souls" by Perry Como and Jaye P. Morgan on RCA Victor
- "Nice Work If You Can Get It" by Frank Sinatra and Peggy Lee on Capitol
- "Nothing in Common" and "How Are You Fixed For Love" by Frank Sinatra and Keely Smith on Capitol
- "Melody of Love" and "I'm Gonna Live Until I Die" by Frank Sinatra and Ray Anthony of Capitol
- "Yes Indeed" and "Apple for the Teacher" by Bing Crosby and Connie Boswell on Decca
- "In the Cool of the Evening" by Bing Crosby and Jane Wyman on Decca
- "Young at Heart" by Bing Crosby and Guy Lombardo on Decca
- "A Penny a Kiss" by Dinah Shore and Tony Martin on RCA Victor
- "You're My Sugar" by Tennessee Ernie Ford and Kay Starr on Capitol
- "No Two People" by Danny Kaye and Jane Wyman on Decca
- "My Heart Cries For You" by Jo Stafford and Gene Autry on Columbia

Groups of the era included the Ames Brothers, Crew Cuts, Dinning Sisters, Four Aces, Four Coins, Four Freshmen, Four Knights, Four Lads, Gaylords, Hilltoppers, Ink Spots and McGuire Sisters. Record companies developed stables of stars, including Charlie Applewhite, Kay Armen, Don Cornell, Alan Dale, Johnny Desmond, Rusty Draper, Sunny Gale, Richard Hayes, Betty Johnson, Denise Lor, Betty Madigan, Bob Manning, June Valli and Vicki Young.

Chapter 7
1950S ROCK AND ROLL, 1955–1959

There were two distinct aspects to the 1950s, so important that they have two chapters in this book. This chapter covers the rock n' roll innovation that dominated the second half of the 1950s, with implications to succeeding decades.

The pop and easy listening years in the decade paved the way for a combining and coalescing of styles, which came to be known as rock and roll. The art form took musicianship and lyric impact from the Big Band era. It added commerciality to make maximum impact on the public, as advocated by the hit parade era gurus. Add in guts and power from country music. Add moving activity and driving dance power from rhythm and blues. Pepper in the interrelationship of the various styles, and you have rock and roll.

To many, the 1950s were the carefree era of Happy Days. Images of the 1950s were of teenagers dancing, sporting the latest fashions, sharing "youth culture" experiences and driving the economy by their newly found buying power. Factor in the youth of the performers, the flair of the music and the impact on other generations, then the 1950s set the tone for the avalanche of pop culture in succeeding decades.

Radio was the heartbeat of the 1950s, and it was in homes, cars, at the beach, in diners, in stores and on the go. Where teens gathered, there were jukeboxes dispensing the music, serving as popularity polls for the records most chosen by the fans to hear.

The first jukebox automatic-change phonograph was introduced in 1928. Justus P. Seeburg, combined an electrostatic loudspeaker with record player that was coin-operated, allowing patrons to select records. Jukeboxes were popular in the 1940s-1960s. 75% of records went into jukeboxes. The top jukebox hits included "Hound Dog/Don't Be Cruel" by Elvis Presley, "Crazy" by Patsy Cline, "Old Time Rock and Roll" by Bob Seger, "I Heard It Through the Grapevine" by Marvin Gaye, "Rock Around the Clock" by Bill Haley & his Comets, "Hey Jude" by The Beatles, "Dock of the Bay" by Otis Redding, "Lady" by Kenny Rogers, "Satisfaction" by The Rolling Stones. Video jukeboxes came in the 1960s, evolving to MTV, music videos and streaming services for hit songs.

Those 1950s teenagers that ruled the culture as fans of rock n' roll became the adults, parents and grandparents of later decades. In 1958, I met Elvis Presley, the King of Rock and Roll. I asked him about kids' music and its lasting impact. He said to me very prophetic words: "They won't always be kids."

In 1958, Danny & the Juniors sang it: "Rock and roll is here to stay." The kids that loved 50s music went to work, thus infusing society with energy and contributions that went far past diners and malt shops. Rock n' roll music was a social influence and a major motivational factor on broadening the pop music scope.

Roots of Rock N' Roll Music

Rock and roll evolved from several American music forms of the 1940s, including the blues, jazz, Rhythm and Blues, gospel, hillbilly, country, bluegrass and jump tunes. Elements of origin go back to blues songs in the 1920s.

The earliest roots of the new music sensation were found is early recordings, most by rhythm and blues artists:

- "Sweet Home Chicago" by Robert Johnson, 1936
- "Rock It For Me" by Chick Webb and Ella Fitzgerald, 1938
- "Roll Them Pete" by Big Joe Turner.

- "Rocking Rollin' Mama" by Buddy Jones, 1939
- "Rock Me" by Sister Rosetta Thorpe, 1942
- "That's Alright Mama" by Arthur Crudup, 1946
- "Caldonia" and "Choo Choo Boogie" by Louis Jordan & his Tympany Five, 1946
- "Move It On Over" by Hank Williams, 1947
- "Bobby Sox Blues" by T-Bone Walker, 1947
- "We're Gonna Rock and Roll" by Wild Bill Moore, 1947
- "Good Rockin' Tonight" by Wynonie Harris, 1948
- "Old Man River" by The Ravens, 1948
- "Texas Hop" by Pee Wee Crayton, 1948
- "Drinking Wine Spo-Dee-Oo-Dee" by Sticks McGhee, 1949
- "The Fat Man" by Fats Domino, 1950
- "Shotgun Boogie" by Tennessee Ernie Ford, 1951
- "Sixty Minute Man" by Billy Ward and the Dominoes, 1951
- "Rocket 88" by Jackie Brenston, 1951
- "Hound Dog" by Big Mama Thornton, 1952
- "One Mint Julep" by The Clovers, 1952
- "Lawdy Miss Clawdy" by Lloyd Price, 1952
- "The Clock" by Johnny Ace, 1953
- "Mystery Train" by Little Junior's Blue Flames, 1953
- "Crying in the Chapel" by The Orioles and June Valli, 1953
- "Honey Hush" by Big Joe Turner, 1953
- "Such a Night" and "Money Honey" by Clyde McPhatter & the Drifters, 1953
- "Work With Me Annie" by Hank Ballard and the Midnighters, 1954
- "Crazy, Man, Crazy" by Bill Haley and his Comets, 1954
- "Good Lovin" and "Ting-a-Ling" by The Clovers, 1954
- "Sh-Boom" by The Chords and The Crew Cuts, 1954
- "Hoochie Coochie Man" by Muddy Waters, 1954
- "Ling Ting Tong" by The Five Keys, 1954
- "Riot in Cell Block #9" by The Robins and Vicki Young, 1954
- "Don't Be Angry" by Nappy Brown and The Crew Cuts, 1955
- "Smoky Joe's Café" by The Robins, 1955

- "House of Blue Lights" by Ella Mae Morse, 1955

Rockabilly

To some people, mention of the early rock and roll era brings to minds motorcycles, blue suede shoes and a combed-up hairstyle known as the pompadour. To some, the late 1950s were an era of leather and studs. To others, it meant flattop haircuts and skirts made full by metal petticoats and lots of hoops.

Styles of dress varied. There was no typical 1950s teenager. What rock and roll did was to serve as an outlet for young people. The placid and conservative decade was tinged by the mistrust of the blacklist era, a weariness from World War II, an economy plagued by recession and the Cold War. Teenagers were at first shamed by adults because of their temporary physical status. Teens learned how to express themselves. The biggest influence was pure and unadulterated rock and roll music.

To say that 1950s rock and roll was invented is a mistake. There were techniques borrowed from many forms of music. The early purveyors found a middle ground between country & western music and swing. In the beginning, it was rockabilly. Radio stations became aware of the huge teen buying public. Many entrepreneurs cashed in on the trend.

The first rock and roll entertainer was Bill Haley, a country performer who was the first white artist to record rock and roll. His 1954 release "Rock Around the Clock" was not a big hit but was picked to open the 1955 movie "Blackboard Jungle." It introduced a new artform to the public. Instantly, "Rock Around the Clock" became an anthem for the young. The song came to be an awakening for most pop music fans, as their medium was never again to be the same.

Within three years, Bill Haley's status diminished, as the fortunes of Elvis Presley, Jerry Lee Lewis, Little Richard and others rose. He was fondly known as the father of rock and roll along with disc jockey Alan Freed. Haley became a solid act on the Oldies but Goodies circuit. In fact, he initiated the circuit as his hit-making days were gone as others enjoyed chart topping careers.

Sun Records of Memphis, TN, originally specialized in the blues. In 1954, they began recording Elvis Presley. By the time that RCA Victor purchased his contract from Sun in late 1955, Elvis was a mild sensation. After the legend was born, his music was polished. And performances from "Love Me Tender" forward lost their rockabilly edge. Elvis developed his ballad style of music, inspired by Teresa Brewer's 1952 recording "Till I Waltz Again with You."

Carl Perkins was at Sun recording at the same time as Elvis, hoping to match the Presley magic. Carl was a more accomplished musician that Elvis, but he did not have the same charisma. His career was stalled by a 1957 auto accident and a later bout with drugs. A decade later, he was back with the country troupe of Johnny Cash.

Johnny Cash was a product of the Sun rockabilly factory. His releases took a decided country turn. Like Perkins, his career dipped because of drugs. By the mid-1960s, Cash had achieved country superstar status.

Charlie Rich was another 1950s rockabilly performer at Sun to later find his niche in the country style. Hits like 1973's "Behind Closed Doors" became huge pop crossovers.

Jerry Lee Lewis was the other important Sun artist. He came from country music, banged out several hits on his pumping piano and later returned to country music in the late 1960s.

Buddy Holly was from Lubbock, TX, and figured he should record country music. He flopped at it and realized that the steel guitar form of rock and roll was his strength. Holly attracted legions of fans during his brief career, one that is credited with inspiring such later trailblazers of music as The Beatles. Don McLean's 1971 hit "American Pie" dramatized "the day the music died." That day was Feb. 3, 1959, when Holly's plane crashed over Mason City, IA. Holly's versatility in styles (rhythms and ballads) was a major influence on decades of other performers.

Other promising stars were casualties of the Holly plane crash. J.P. Richardson was a Beaumont, TX, radio disc jockey, known as The Big Bopper. Ritchie Valens, from Los Angeles, CA, was the first Hispanic rock star.

Another great talent went to his death in an auto accident just as his career was taking off. Eddie Cochran was the first rock and roll artist to overdub tracks, using the best of jam sessions and his own work on several instruments.

Gene Vincent and his group The Blue Caps were just as fine sounding in concerts ass on recordings. Handicapped and quite underweight, Vincent's stage presence was that of a stark, tragic figure. This unusual quality attracted many fans, including the British, who kept him a star until his 1971 death, long after America had forgotten about him. The Blue Caps got their name from the golf hat worn by President Dwight D. Eisenhower.

There were Don and Phil Everly, whose harmonies inspired two 1960s groups, The Beatles and Simon & Garfunkel. Smash artists, The Everly Brothers were among the first to record in Nashville and to use strings with their rock and roll arrangements.

Groups like Ronnie Hawkins and The Hawks were not just popular in the 1950s. They were copied by the likes of Creedence Clearwater Revival in the 1960s. As the trend in the 1970s turned from acid rock and back to the simplistic style of 1950s rock, The Hawks were a part of that movement as The Band.

Another Sun Records alumnus was Roy Orbison, who became the master of the crying and hurting ballads in his Monument record releases. His material dwelt on such downbeat themes as loneliness, rejected love and contemplated suicide. His voice, inflections and approach fit the melancholy themes of the songs.

Chuck Berry, from St. Louis, MO, was the first guitar hero of rock. He enjoyed success with teen-themed rockers. He got some of the first TV exposure to whites via Dick Clark's "American Bandstand." Berry as regarded, along with Buddy Holly, as most influential on the styles of 1960s and 1970s rock stars, most noticeably The Beatles, The Rolling Stones and Eric Clapton.

Chicago recording artist Bo Diddley was inspired to play the blues guitar by John Lee Hooker. His real name was Ellas McDaniel, and the nickname came from his amateur boxing career. He played blues rock on a rectangularly shaped guitar. When he worked Harlem's Apollo Theatre in the mid-1950s, a young man named Elvis Presley used to come and watch Bo Diddley work, carefully studying his style and stage presence.

Antoine Fats Domino played the blues in New Orleans, LA. He got ideas for his songs from everyday expressions. The banning of his "Blueberry Hill" record in 1956 only added to his star status. He remained in demand over the next decades as any other 1950s artist.

Little Richard Penniman, from Macon, GA, was the first scream rocker. His frantic paces and outrageous dress made his piano-pumping rock and roll a model for so many others. It was during the recording of "Keep a Knocking" in 1957 that Richard walked out and joined the church as a minister. He saw the spacecraft

Sputnik as a sign from above. After a decade in the ministry, Richard Penniman returned to rock and roll as a concert artist. He appeared in movies and TV shows as a personality artist.

After the innovators, rock and roll music had its stars who borrowed portions of styles, adding their style to come up with solid hits. Such was the case with Ricky Nelson, promoted in his singing career by a long, successful TV situation comedy, "The Adventures of Ozzie & Harriet." Rick appeared as an actor in movies and TV shows.

In 1972, Nelson appeared on an oldies concert at Madison Square Garden in New York City. When he showed up with long hair and sang contemporary songs, fans booed him for straying from the old hits. Reflecting on the experience, he wrote "Garden Party," which became his biggest hit record in the 1970s.

So many rock and roll performances came flowing. Many of the groups were "one hit wonders," a concept explored in another chapter in this book. The late 1950s was the era of the steel guitar and the screaming saxophone.

R&B

Rhythm and blues was the embodiment of black music. Years later, the term "soul music" evolved. The pop and rock scene owes more to R&B than perhaps any other element. R&B grew out of jazz, gospel and the blues. It was a far cry from the 1940s and early 1950s from the pop songs that dominated the pre-Elvis pop charts. Rock and roll evolved when whites sought out black music and bought recordings of it.

A handful of themes dominated early R&B, including tales of woe, money troubles, crime and dangerous situations. Drinking, virility, fast cars and a party life were often proclaimed.

The early practice was for white artists to cover R&B. 1954's "Work with Me Annie" by Hank Ballard & the Midnighters became stylized as "Dance with Me Henry" by Georgia Gibbs. Other hits transitioned from R&B included "Sh-Boom" (from The Chords to The Crewcuts), "Sincerely" (from The Moonglows to the McGuire Sisters), "Fever" (from Little Willie John to Peggy Lee) and "Devil or Angel" (from The Clovers to Bobby Vee). Hits by white artists were often recut with a R&B slant.

A few black artists were regularly played on white radio stations, where the chart rankings originated. They included Nat King Cole, Ella Fitzgerald, The Mills Brothers, Billy Eckstine, The Platters, The Drifters and Sarah Vaughan.

By the mid-1950s, R&B hits often crossed to the pop charts, as did some country records. Elvis Presley took some R&B tunes, adding to them his brand of country music, creating rockabilly, which became designated as rock and roll.

The rock and roll boom dictated that the inimitable styles of Chuck Berry, Little Richard, Bo Diddley, Fats Domino and others could only come from the originals. By the end of the decade, the practice of white cover versions of R&B was minimized.

Doo-Wop

The rhythm and blues style of the ballad had a moderate tempo. It had enchanting and driving backgrounds. As blues was incorporated into rock and roll, it stood to reason that the black ballad would be as well. When whites incorporated these ballads, it was named the Doo-Wop sound.

Doo-wop groups numbered three, four or five. Their "street corner" style included three-part harmony. As the lead vocalist crooned in front of the group, a mesmerizing showmanship went on in the back. Soul groups of later decades continued the doo-wop tradition as a singing and dancing chorus line. Doo-wop sounds could be any tempo.

Many of the doo-wop groups had superlative and grandiose names. There were The Rays, whose hit "Silhouettes" was written on a train, as composer Bob Crewe, later of Four Seasons fame, watched the outline of two young lovers. In Pittsburgh, The Skyliners sang "Since I Don't Have You," the first time that a rock song had strings and brass. There was the group from Staten Island, NY, The Elegants, whose 1959 hit "Little Star" was based upon Mozart's first composition at age five, "Twinkle Little Star."

The Tune Weavers got their name when an emcee at a dance mistakenly identified them. They got airplay from their record "Happy, Happy Birthday Baby" when a radio disc jockey put it on by mistake. The record hit the top, and they were not heard from again.

Five Air Force buddies formed the Dell Vikings after their discharge. Their record "Come Go with Me" was written in five minutes. It was recorded in the basement of a disc jockey's house. They were one of the first groups with both white and black members.

James Sheppard formed The Heartbeats in 1956. When his girlfriend moved, he wrote "A Thousand Miles Away." In 1961, he formed another doo-wop group, Shep & the Limelights. "Daddy's Home" was an answer to "A Thousand Miles Away."

The Belmonts got their name from a street in the Bronx. They formed with Dion DiMucci while in high school. Dion left the Belmonts to go solo in 1960. By the end of the decade, he scored as a message singer, with his biggest hit "Abraham, Martin & John" in 1968.

There were The Moonglows, whose membership at one time included Marvin Gaye. The Flamingos featured Joe Jackson, whose kids comprised the Jackson Five. Lead singer of The Falcons in the 1950s was Wilson Pickett, who became a top soul singer in the 1960s.

The doo-wop trend ended in 1963, and the harmonies and stage techniques remained with 1960s and 1970s soul groups.

Easy Listening in the Early-Rock Era

Pop music stars from the previous Hit Parade era continued to record solid hits. They were joined by younger pop stars, who flourished in the late 1950s, throughout the 1960s and into the 1970s. These included Andy Williams, Paul Anka, Bobby Darin, Steve Lawrence, Eydie Gorme, Matt Monro, Gogi Grant, Pat Boone, the Kirby Stone Four, Sam Cooke, Della Reese and Johnny Nash.

As rock and roll grew from a rebel form of expression, lots of repertoire was updated to keep up with the times. Even establishment pop singers made recordings to appeal to the rock n' roll fans. Kay Starr, who used to be a singer with the Glenn Miller orchestra, let parents get interested in their kids' music. Her "Rock N' Roll Waltz" was one of 1955's top hits.

Perry Como, the mellow crooner, recorded several novelty tunes with high-chart success. They included "Round and Round," "You're Following Me," "My Peculiar Way," "Magic Moments," "Hot Diggity," "Ko Ko Mo," "Tina Marie" and "Juke Box Baby."

Rosemary Clooney performed "Love Eyes" with a rock n' roll beat. Song diva Vikki Carr belted "He's a Rebel." Frank Sinatra sang "Lean Baby" to the penny loafer set. Eddie Fisher, another popular crooner, had a hit with "Dungaree Doll."

Core 1950s Hits

Elvis Presley: "Hound Dog," "Don't Be Cruel," "Heartbreak Hotel, "Love Me Tender," "All Shook Up," "Love Me," "Too Much," "Teddy Bear," "Jailhouse Rock," "Don't," "Wear My Ring Around Your Neck," "Hard Headed Woman," "One Night," "I Got Stung," "Fool Such As I," "Big Hunk of Love."

Buddy Holly: "That'll Be the Day," "Peggy Sue," "Oh, Boy," "Maybe Baby," "Rave On," "Heartbeat," "Think It Over," "Early in the Morning," "It Doesn't Matter Anymore," "Raining in My Heart."

Chuck Berry: "Maybellene," "Roll Over Beethoven," "School Day," "Oh Baby Doll," "Rock and Roll Music," "Sweet Little Sixteen," "Johnny B. Goode," "Carol," "Almost Grown," "Little Queenie," "Back in the USA."

Fats Domino: "Blueberry Hill," "Ain't It a Shame," "I'm in Love Again," "Blue Monday," "I'm Walking," "Whole Lotta Loving," "Valley of Tears," "I Want to Walk You Home."

Carl Perkins: "Blue Suede Shoes," "Matchbox," "Boppin' the Blues," "Your True Love," "Everybody's Trying to Be My Baby," "Glad All Over," "Pink Pedal Pushers."

The Everly Brothers: "Bye, Bye Love," "Wake Up Little Susie," "All I Have to Do Is Dream," "Bird Dog," "Till I Kissed You," "Poor Jenny," "Devoted to You," "Claudette."

Little Richard: "Tutti Frutti," "Long Tall Sally," "Keep a Knocking," "Lucille," "The Girl Can't Help It," "Jenny, Jenny," "Good Golly Miss Molly," "Baby Face," "Kansas City."

Bill Haley and his Comets: "Rock Around the Clock," "See You Later Alligator," "Dim the Lights," "Razzle Dazzle," "Rip It Up," "Skinny Minnie," "Burn That Candle."

Jerry Lee Lewis: "Whole Lot of Shakin' Going On," "Great Balls of Fire," "Breathless," "High School Confidential," "Break-Up," "I'll Sail My Ship Alone."

The Platters: "Only You," "The Magic Touch," "The Great Pretender," "I'm Sorry," "Twilight Time," "I Wish," "Smoke Gets in Your Eyes," "Enchanted."

Other key rock and roll songs from 1955–1959 included:

- "Why Do Fools Fall in Love" by Frankie Lymon & the Teenagers, 1955
- "I Hear You Knocking" by Smiley Lewis and Gale Storm, 1955

- "Bo Diddley" by Bo Diddley, 1955
- "Be-Bop-A-Lula" by Gene Vincent, 1956
- "The Fool" by Sanford Clark, 1956
- "Let The Good Times Roll" by Shirley & Lee, 1956
- "Shake, Rattle and Roll" by Joe Turner, 1956
- "Love is Strange" by Mickey and Sylvia, 1956
- "Green Door" by Jim Lowe, 1956
- "At the Hop" by Danny & the Juniors, 1957
- "Young Love" by Sonny James, 1957
- "Party Doll" by Buddy Knox, 1957
- "Little Darlin'" by The Diamonds, 1957
- "Love Potion #9" by The Clovers, 1957
- "Short Shorts" by The Royal Teens, 1957
- "Honeycomb" and "Kisses Sweeter Than Wine" by Jimmie Rodgers, 1957
- "Buzz-Buzz-Buzz" by The Hollywood Flames, 1957
- "Mr. Lee" by The Bobbettes, 1957
- "Peanuts" by Little Joe & the Thrillers, 1957
- "Rocking Robin" by Bobby Day, 1958
- "Get a Job" by The Silhouettes, 1958
- "When" by The Kalin Twins, 1958
- "Do You Want to Dance" by Bobby Freeman, 1958
- "Summertime Blues" by Eddie Cochran, 1958
- "La Bamba," "Donna" and "Come On, Let's Go" by Ritchie Valens, 1958
- "Rock and Roll is Here to Stay" by Danny & the Juniors, 1958
- "Little Bitty Pretty One" by Thurston Harris, 1958
- "Charlie Brown" by The Coasters, 1958
- "Stagger Lee" by Lloyd Price, 1958
- "Big Man" and "26 Miles" by The Four Preps, 1958
- "Summertime" by The Jamies, 1958
- "Chantilly Lace" by The Big Bopper, 1958
- "Willie and the Hand Jive" by the Johnny Otis Show, 1958
- "Don't Let Go" by Roy Hamilton, 1959
- "Lipstick on Your Collar" by Connie Francis, 1959
- "Kansas City" by Wilbert Harrison, 1959

- "Tall Paul" by Annette Funicello, 1959
- "Lonely Teardrops" by Jackie Wilson, 1959
- "Sorry, I Ran All the Way Home" by The Impalas, 1959
- "I'm a Man," "Turn Me Loose" and "Tiger" by Fabian, 1959
- "Queen of the Hop" and "Mack the Knife" by Bobby Darin, 1959

Key ballad song hits from 1955–1959 included:

- "This is My Story" by Gene and Eunice, 1955
- "Sincerely" by The McGuire Sisters, 1955
- "In the Still of the Night" by The Five Satins, 1956
- "Since I Met You Baby" by Ivory Joe Hunter, 1956
- "The Wayward Wind" by Gogi Grant, 1956
- "Love Letters in the Sand" and "April Love" by Pat Boone, 1957
- "Could This Be Magic" by The Dubs, 1957
- "Old Cape Cod" by Patti Page, 1957
- "Tammy" by Debbie Reynolds, 1957
- "Deep Purple" by Billy Ward and the Dominoes, 1958
- "Who's Sorry Now" by Connie Francis, 1958
- "Dream Lover" by Bobby Darin, 1958
- "Out of Sight, Out of Mine" by The Five Keys, 1958
- "Little Star" by The Elegants, 1958
- "My True Love" by Jack Scott, 1958
- "Tears on My Pillow" by Little Anthony & the Imperials, 1958
- "To Know Him is to Love Him" by The Teddy Bears, 1958
- "Susie Darlin'" by Robin Luke, 1958
- "The End" by Earl Grant, 1958
- "Teenager in Love" by Dion & the Belmonts, 1958
- "One Summer Night" by The Danleers, 1958
- "Come Softly to Me" and "Mr. Blue" by The Fleetwoods, 1959
- "Venus" by Frankie Avalon, 1959
- "Hushabye" by The Mystics, 1959
- "Lonely Street" by Andy Williams, 1959
- "Tragedy" by Thomas Wayne, 1959

- "Pretty Blue Eyes" by Steve Lawrence, 1959
- "I Only Have Eyes for You" by The Flamingos, 1959
- "See You in September" by The Tempos, 1959
- "Sleep Walk" by Santo and Johnny, 1959
- "The Big Hurt" by Toni Fisher, 1959
- "Charlie Brown" by The Coasters, 1959

Novelty hits of the era included:

- "The Naughty Lady of Shady Lane" by The Ames Brothers, 1954
- "The Ballad of Davy Crockett" by Fess Parker and Bill Hayes, 1955
- "Transfusion" by Nervous Norvus, 1956
- "Flying Saucers" by Buchanan and Goodman, 1956
- "Stranded in the Jungle" by The Jayhawks, 1956
- "The Auctioneer" by Leroy Van Dyke, 1956
- "I Put a Spell on You" by Screaming Jay Hawkins, 1956
- "Witch Doctor" and "The Chipmunk Song" by David Seville, 1958
- "Purple People Eater" by Sheb Wooley, 1958
- "Black Denim Trousers and Motorcycle Boots" by The Cheers, 1958
- "The Blob" by The Five Blobs (Burt Bacharach), 1958
- "Beep Beep" by The Playmates, 1958
- "Lucky Ladybug" by Billie and Lillie, 1958
- "Splish Splash" by Bobby Darin, 1958
- "Little Red Riding Hood" by The Big Bopper, 1958
- "Charlie Brown" and "Yakety Yak" by The Coasters, 1959
- "Pink Shoe Laces" by Dodie Stevens, 1959

Johnny Cash and Elvis Presley

Jukeboxes, Nostalgia of the Happy Days

Chapter 8
TV SHOWS SHOWCASING MUSIC

To most people, music is the soundtrack to our lives, on radio and jukeboxes. Music had a wider berth on television. Rock stars and shows were part of TV's search for young viewers, who have continued to show their loyalty. From specials to variety shows to music videos, the visualization of music has further stimulated record and concert sales.

Top variety shows featuring musical guest stars were hosted by Ed Sullivan, Milton Berle, Steve Allen, Arthur Godfrey and Garry Moore. There was also "Shower of Stars" and "Hollywood Palace."

Music stars hosted variety shows, including Perry Como, Dinah Shore, Bing Crosby, Eddie Fisher, Nat King Cole, Frank Sinatra, Dean Martin, Sammy Davis Jr., Jo Stafford, Liberace, Tennessee Ernie Ford, Frankie Laine, Rosemary Clooney, Patti Page, Roy Rogers & Dale Evans, Lawrence Welk, Ray Anthony, Judy Garland, Spike Jones, Andy Williams, Sonny & Cher, Donny & Marie Osmond, Danny Kaye, Jimmy Dean, Lulu and Tom Jones.

Comedy shows featuring musical guest stars included "Saturday Night Live," "Broadway Open House" and those hosted by Jackie Gleason, Carol Burnett, Jim Nabors, Red Skelton and Flip Wilson.

Late-night shows featuring musical guest stars included "The Tonight Show," hosted by Steve Allen, Jack Paar, Johnny Carson, Jay Leno and Jimmy Fallon. Other shows were hosted by Joey Bishop, Dick Cavett, Arsenio Hall, Joan Rivers, David Letterman, Jimmy Kimmel and Conan O'Brien.

Daytime shows featuring musical guest stars included "Don McNeill's Breakfast Club" and "Art Linkletter's House Party." Other daytime variety shows were hosted by Kate Smith, Merv Griffin, Mike Douglas, Betty White, Vicki Lawrence, Rosie O'Donnell, Ricki Lake, Ellen Degeneres, Kelly Clarkson and Drew Barrymore.

Music showcase shows on TV included "Your Hit Parade," "American Bandstand," "The Dick Clark Beechnut Show," "Where the Action Is," "Happening '68," "Dick Clark's Rockin' New Year's Eve," "Dick Clark's Golden Greats," "Dick Clark's Live Wednesday," "Soul Train," "Hullabaloo," "Oh, Boy," "The Music Scene," "Showtime at the Apollo," "Kraft Music Hall," "Playboy After Dark," "Sing Along with Mitch," "The Brady Bunch Variety Hour," "Solid Gold," "The Mancini Generation," "In Concert," "The Midnight Special," "Shindig," "Shivaree," "Something Else," "8-Track Flashback," "Arthur Murray Party," "Malibu U.," "Fabian's Goodtime Rock N' Roll," "Art Ford's Greenwich Village Party," "Austin City Limits," "Great Performances," "PBS Oldies Concerts" and "MTV Unplugged."

Teen music local bandstand shows were hosted by Lloyd Thaxton, Alan Freed, Murray the K, Art Laboe, Dewey Phillips, Paul Whiteman, Brian Henderson, Milt Grant, Larry Kane, Buddy Deane, Ron Chapman, Jack Spector and Rik Turner. Others included "Teenarama," "Hit Scene," "Teenage Barn," "The Beat," "Teen Town," "Swinging Time," "Coke Dance Party," "Hi-Fi Club," "The Upbeat Show," "Barris Beat" and "Teen a Go-Go."

Country music shows included "Grand Old Opry," "Ozark Jubilee," "Louisiana Hayride," "Porter Wagoner with Dolly Parton," "Hee Haw," "Don Messer's Jubilee," "National Barn Dance," "Big Red Shindig, "Community Jamboree" and "Tex Ritter's Ranch Party." Plus, those hosted by Johnny Cash, The Wilburn Brothers, Don Reno & Red Smiley, Jimmy Wakely and Eddy Arnold.

Summer replacement TV shows were hosted by Tony Bennett, Bob Crosby, Ray Stevens and The Everly Brothers, plus "Summer Chevy Show" and "Glenn Miller Time."

TV music specials were hosted by Doris Day, Guy Lombardo, Fred Astaire, Herb Alpert & the Tijuana Brass, Lynda Carter, Leonard Bernstein, Julie London, Nancy Sinatra, Olivia Newton-John, Adele and Burt Bacharach.

Music is always performed on the Grammy Awards, American Music Awards, Kennedy Center Honors, Country Music Awards, BET Awards, Academy Awards and Tony Awards.

Music game shows included "Name That Tune," "Juke Box Jury," "Songland," "American Song Contest" and "That's My Jam."

Talent Contest TV Shows

Talent contests have been held for centuries in communities, schools and performing venues. With the advent of broadcasting came shows accenting talent discovery. From 1948 forward, TV talent contests have been venerable sources of stars and are popular with the public.

In the 1940s, Clara Ann Fowler began singing on a radio station in Tulsa, OK. Another singer was billed as "Patti Page," on a show sponsored by the Page Milk Company. When that singer left, Clara took her place and her name. For the next fifty years, Patti Page was a prominent singer, with countless hits, including "Tennessee Waltz," "Cross Over the Bridge," "Old Cape Cod," "Allegheny Moon" and "Hush, Hush, Sweet Charlotte."

Josephine Cottle, from Houston, TX, was the winning contestant on a radio show in 1939, winning the name "Gale Storm." She became an actress in the 1940s and starred in two prominent TV shows in the 1950s, "My Little Margie" and "The Gale Storm Show/Oh, Susanna." In the 1950s and 1960s, she was a recording artist, with hits including "I Hear You Knocking," "Dark Moon," "Ivory Tower" and "Memories Are Made of This."

One of the winners on "Major Bowes Amateur Hour" on radio in 1935 was The Hoboken Four, with Frank Sinatra as lead singer. Sinatra then sang with the big bands of Harry James and Tommy Dorsey. He became a hit solo singer in the 1940s and starred in numerous movies. His concerts and chairmanship of The Rat Pack heightened his luster as one of the greatest entertainers of the century.

Johnny Tillotson became a local radio star at age nine on "Young Folks Revue" in Florida. In the 1950s, he became a popular recording artist. His teen ballad hits included "Dreamy Eyes," "Talk Back Trembling Lips," "Why Do I Love You So," "Send Me the Pillow You Dream On," "It Keeps Right on Hurting" and "Jimmy's Girl."

Music TV talent shows included "Ted Mack's Original Amateur Hour," "Arthur Godfrey's Talent Scouts," "Star Search," "American Idol," "The Voice" and "America's Got Talent."

Stars launched on Ted Mack's Original Amateur Hour included Gladys Knight, Pat Boone, Ann-Margret, Jose Feliciano, Irene Cara, Nick Carter, Beverly Sills, Robert Merrill, Joey Dee, Jim Stafford and Maria Callas.

Stars launched on Arthur Godfrey's Talent Scouts included Patsy Cline, Rod McKuen, Jose Melis, The Chordettes, The McGuire Sisters, Carmel Quinn, Tony Bennett, Rosemary Clooney, The Blackwood Brothers, Roy Clark, Florian Zabach, Vic Damone, The Diamonds, Eddie Fisher, Connie Francis, Steve Lawrence, Al Martino, Barbara McNair, Marian McPartland, Johnny Nash and Leslie Uggams. Among those who were auditioned but not chosen to appear included Elvis Presley, Buddy Holly and The Four Freshmen.

Stars launched on "Star Search" included Britney Spears, Justin Timberlake, Usher, Alanis Morissette, Christina Aguilera, Tiffany, Sawyer Brown, Sam Harris, Jessica Simpson, The Backstreet Boys, Destiny's Child and Alison Porter, who later won "The Voice."

Stars launched on "American Idol" included Kelly Clarkson, Carrie Underwood, Katharine McPhee, Jennifer Hudson, Fantasia Barrino, Adam Lambert and Jordin Sparks.

"X Factor" launched the career of Leona Lewis. "Pop Stars" winner was Nicole Scherzinger. "Nashville Star" winner was Miranda Lambert. "Canadian Idol" winner was Carly Rae Jepsen. "Britain's Got Talent" launched Susan Boyle. "Sweden's Got Talent" launched Zara Larsson.

At the dawning of TV, Ed Sullivan launched a variety show on CBS-TV. It ran until 1974, reruns are still running.

Dick Clark hosted "American Bandstand" from 1956–1987

Chapter 9
CHRISTMAS MUSIC

Holiday music first began being written in the 4th Century. It came into popular usage in the thirteen century. Carols in the English language first appeared in 1426, as balladeers traveled from town to town, and choirs sang outside neighbors' houses.

The sixteenth century brought classics still being sung: "God Rest Ye Merry Gentlemen," "O Christmas Tree" and "The Twelve Days of Christmas." Carols and symphony suites in the 19th century, including "O Holy Night," "O Little Town of Bethlehem" and "Silent Night."

"Greensleeves" is a traditional English folk song, dating back to 1580. Holiday songs with the same tune began circulating in 1686. The most popular adaptation was "What Child is This," written in 1865.

In 1892, Pyotr Ilyich Tchaikovsky composed a musical symphony to accompany ballet, "The Nutcracker Suite." This remains the most performed holiday extravaganza.

Saint Nicholas and Santa Claus began appearing in early twentieth century holiday songs. These were introduced at the dawning of recorded music. Popular early songs included "Jolly Old Saint Nicholas" and "Up on the Housetop." Older Christmas hymns and carols were translated into English, becoming rediscovered in the twentieth century.

During the 1880 Christmas season, Thomas Edison introduced the first outdoor electric Christmas light display to the world. He displayed the lights outside of his laboratory compound, which sat near a railway where many people could see it each night. This was the first official outdoor Christmas display that was separate from decorating just the Christmas tree.

Edward Johnson, who was an inventor under the supervision of Thomas Edison, created the first string of Christmas lights a couple of years later. The string of lights was made out of 80 small electric light bulbs. In 1890, strings of lights were manufactured, and department stores began displaying them in Christmas displays in their stores. Public displays of Christmas lights in retail stores and buildings became popular in the US at the turn of the twentieth century. This inspired outdoor displays on homes when the electric lights became more affordable.

Songs of American origin began appearing in the 1930s, many serving as spirit songs during the Great Depression. Many focused upon children, including "Rudolph the Red-Nosed Reindeer" and "Santa Claus is Coming to Town."

From the 1930s forward, historic holiday carols have been recorded and performed in concerts. The most popular ones include "Good King Wenceslas," "Adeste Fidelis/O Come All Ye Faithful," "Away in a Manger," "Deck the Halls," "While the Shepherds Watched Their Flocks," "We Three Kings," "O Come Emmanuel," "The First Noel," "Angels We Have Heard on High," "We Wish You a Merry Christmas," "Joy to the World," "I Saw Three Ships" and "Hark! The Herald Angels Sing."

These older songs are in the public domain and are not covered by copyrights. Thus, they are recorded and performed widely. Recording artists faithfully perform these songs, adding their own touches and modern arrangements. The same songs performed by hundreds of artists still find enchantment and favor with every generation.

Happy novelty songs were not of a secular nature and appealed to wider audiences.

Top 25 Christmas Songs

These are the top twenty-five holiday songs, according to number of times played and recorded. This is the official tabulation of the American Society of Artists, Composers and Publishers (ASCAP):

1. "The Christmas Song" (Chestnuts Roasting on an Open Fire) was written in 1945 by Robert Wells and Mel Torme. It was first recorded by Nat King Cole, with strings added by Nelson Riddle. This was the first time that Cole emerged from a jazz combo into being a balladeer with full orchestral accompaniment.

2. "Have Yourself a Merry Little Christmas" was written in 1944 by Ralph Blane and Hugh Martin. It was first sung by Judy Garland in the movie "Meet Me in St. Louis."

3. "Winter Wonderland" was written in 1934 by Felix Bernard and Richard B. Smith. The lyrics by Smith were inspired by his time spent in a sanitarium in Pennsylvania, dream sequences during his treatment for tuberculosis. In 1946, Johnny Mercer and Perry had the biggest hits with the song.

4. "Santa Claus is Coming to Town" was written in 1934 by J. Fred Coots and Haven Gillespie. Major hits were in 1951 by Perry Como and Gene Autry.

5. "White Christmas" was written in 1940 by Irving Berlin. It was popularized by Bing Crosby in the 1942 movie "Holiday Inn." The movie included a collection of other Berlin tunes. In 1954, "White Christmas" became the title of a second collection of Berlin songs, that movie starring Bing Crosby, Danny Kaye, Rosemary Clooney and Vera-Ellen.

6. "Let It Snow! Let It Snow! Let It Snow!" was written in 1945 by Sammy Cahn and Jule Styne. It was written in California during a July heatwave. It was first recorded by Vaughn Monroe.

7. "Jingle Bell Rock" was written in 1957 by Joseph Beal and James Ross Boothe. It was first recorded by Bobby Helms. This was the first rock n' roll Christmas hit.

8. "The Little Drummer Boy" was written in 1941 by Katherine K. Davis, Kenneth V. Onorati and Harry Simeone. Its most famous recording was in 1958 by The Harry Simeone Chorale.

9. "Sleigh Ride" was written in 1948 by Leroy Anderson and Mitchell Parish. Anderson recorded the instrumental version, still played on radio stations. The vocal version has been performed by many artists, the most famous rendition by Johnny Mathis.

10. "Rudolph the Red-Nosed Reindeer" was written in 1939 by Johnny Marks. The most famous version was recorded in 1949 by Gene Autry.

11. "It's the Most Wonderful Time of the Year" was written in 1963 by Edward Pola and George Wyle. The most famous version was the original by Andy Williams in 1963.

12. "I'll Be Home for Christmas" was written in 1943 by Walter Kent, Kim Gannon and Buck Ram. The original Bing Crosby version remains the top one. The flip side was "Danny Boy." The song resonated in 1943 as a World War II spirit song.

13. "Silver Bells" was written in 1950 by Jay Livingston and Ray Evans. It first appeared in the movie "The Lemon Drop Kid," performed by Bob Hope and Marilyn Maxwell. The first recorded version was by Bing Crosby and Carol Richards."

14. "Rockin' Around the Christmas Tree" was written in 1958 by Johnny Marks, first recorded by Brenda Lee. It was the second major rock n' roll Christmas hit.

15. "Feliz Navidad" was written in 1970 by Jose Feliciano, who recorded it, with a masterful arrangement by Perry Botkin Jr. This stands as the most digitally downloaded Christmas song, at 808,000.

16. "Blue Christmas" was written in 1948 by Billy Hayes and Jay Johnson. The original hit versions were in 1949 by Ernest Tubb and Russ Morgan. The 1957 remake by Elvis Presley stands as the definitive version.

17. "Frosty the Snowman" was written in 1950 by Steve Nelson and Walter "Jack" Rollins. The lasting hit was the first, in 1950 by Gene Autry. Frosty headlined a TV special in 1969, which has aired annually ever since.

18. "A Holly Jolly Christmas" was written in 1962 by Johnny Marks. It was featured in the holiday special "Rudolph the Red-Nosed Reindeer," voiced by Burl Ives.

19. "It's Beginning to Look a Lot Like Christmas" was written in 1951 by Meredith Willson, while he was staying at a hotel in Nova Scotia. Perry

Como had the first hit with the song. He rode to greater glory as composer of the hit Broadway musical "The Music Man" in 1957. Willson incorporated his Christmas hit into his 1963 Broadway show "Here's Love."

20. "I Saw Mommy Kissing Santa Claus" was written in 1952 by Tommie Connor. It was recorded by 13-year-old Jimmy Boyd on Columbia Records, launching a whole genre of holiday novelty songs recorded by kids.

21. "Here Comes Santa Claus" was written in 1947 by Gene Autry and Oakley Haldeman. It was inspired by Autry's appearance in the 1946 Hollywood Christmas Parade.

22. "Carol of the Bells" was written in 1914 by Peter Wilhousky and Mykola Leontovych. It was based on a Ukranian folk chant "Shchedryk" and has remained a popular chorale performance number.

23. "Do They Know It's Christmas?" (Feed the World) was written in 1984 by Bob Geldof and Midge Ure. It led the genre of records benefiting charitable endeavors, feeding the starving globally.

24. "Home for the Holidays" was written in 1954 by Bob Allen and Al Stillman. The definitive recording was the first one by Perry Como, released as the flip side to his pop hit "Silk Stockings."

25. "Santa Baby" was written in 1953 by Joan Ellen Javits, Philip Springer, Tony Springer and Fred Ebb. It was a major hit for Eartha Kitt, following her pop hit "C'Est Si Bon." Cover versions since then have been by Madonna, Kylie Minogue, Gwen Stefani and Ariana Grande.

Packaging of Christmas Songs

With the advent of record albums in the 1940s, collections of holiday songs were produced and marketed. In 1947, Bing Crosby recorded a complete Christmas album on Decca Records. That included a re-recording of his 1942 release "White Christmas," which he had performed in the movie "Holiday Inn."

Gene Autry recorded a succession of holiday singles, which were compiled into an album. Other artists of the 1940s made Christmas albums. Crosby made another one with The Andrews Sisters, his label mates on Decca. Crosby took Christmas music to his radio show, setting the trend for Christmas specials over the decades. By the 1950s, Crosby became known as the "voice of Christmas.," with Perry Como as the next honoree.

LP records and 45RPM record box sets took over the recording industry in the 1950s. The technology was lighter and offered greater listening clarity than the old 78RPM records. Much material from past catalogs was reprocessed and released on new albums. This included compilations of singles and newly recorded albums.

By the late 1950s, Christmas albums were very popular. Current recording artists recorded holiday songs in their own styles, including Elvis Presley, Johnny Mathis, Brenda Lee, Andy Williams, Burl Ives and Bobby Helms. In the 1960s, thematic Christmas albums were made by Phil Spector and The Beach Boys. The Beatles made 45RPM special holiday greeting records for their fan clubs and media. Record labels recorded voiced greetings from their stars for radio stations to play along with the music. In the 1960s and 1970s, each genre had holiday records released, played on the radio and collected by fans.

In the 1960s, record companies produced compilation albums for commercial clients. Firestone dealers distributed "Great Songs of Christmas by the Great Artists of our Time," produced for years by Columbia, which also had "A Rocking Christmas" and comparable albums of patriotic music.

RCA Victor had its "Christmas Is" and "Many Moods of Christmas" series. Capitol had the "Boy of Christmas" and "It's the Happiest Time of the Year" series. Decca-MCA had "We Wish You a Merry Christmas," with tracks from the Bing Crosby albums.

These albums featured stars on their labels, which stimulated interest in buying complete albums by artists. These custom record albums were great for dealer sales, as well as stimulating further interest in holiday recordings.

Other retailers launched their own holiday premium records, licensing recordings from various major labels, augmented by newly recorded tracks by other artists. Companies distributing Christmas LPs included, Sears, Western Union, Radio Shack, Lazy-Boy Recliners, Magnavox, RCA Victor and Goodyear.

As Christmas albums became more popular and grew in numbers, the repertoire expanded to include songs that were not written for holidays but which were compatible with them. Many of these songs became part of the holiday playlists that are still on the radio, including:

- "Baby It's Cold Outside," a duet by Esther Williams and Ricardo Montalban in the 1949 movie "Neptune's Daughter." That year, there were eight duet recordings made of the song.
- "It's a Marshmallow World," a song about winter that was recorded by Bing Crosby, Vaughn Monroe and others in 1949.
- "Let It Snow" was written in 1945 by Sammy Cahn and Jule Styne. It did not mention holidays and carried a winter theme. In the Southern hemisphere, it is played in summer months.
- "Count Your Blessings Instead of Sheep," written by Irving Berlin and featured in the 1954 movie "White Christmas," starring Bing Crosby, Danny Kaye, Rosemary Clooney and Vera-Ellen.
- "Ave Maria," the traditional Christian prayer.
- "Pachelbel's Canon," written in the 18th Century and also played at weddings.
- "My Favorite Things" was written by Richard Rodgers and Oscar Hammerstein for their Broadway musical "The Sound of Music." Coinciding with the 1965 movie version, Herb Alpert & the Tijuana Brass put the song on its holiday album. Other artists followed suit by including it on their Christmas collections.
- "Let There Be Peace on Earth (And Let it Begin with Me)" was a religious song written in 1955 and performed by a children's choir in 1967. World festivals featured the song performed by singers and dancers. The song was first recorded by John Gary, then by Gladys Knight & the Pips, Vince Gill, Sandi Patti, The Harlem Boys Choir, Carlos Santana and others.

Goodyear sponsored "Great Songs of Christmas," an annual holiday album produced by Columbia Records, featuring tracks by its artists. The album was sold in Goodyear stores.

Firestone sponsored "Your Christmas Favorites," an annual holiday album produced by RCA Victor Records, featuring tracks by its artists. The album was sold in Firestone stores.

Other companies manufacturing and distributing holiday promotional albums included Magnavox, Sears, Radio Shack, Carling Black Label Beer, Lazyboy

Recliners, Central Trust Company, Southwest Airlines, Schlitz Beer, Coca-Cola, Hallmark, Remington Typewriters, American Airlines, etc.

Compilations by various artists in the CD era carried titles such as "Now That's What I Call Christmas," "Motown Christmas," "Cool Yule," "Christmas Through the Years," "A Very Special Christmas," "A Rocking Christmas," "1940s Christmas," "Arista Pop Holiday Sampler," "The Beauty of Christmas," "It's the Happiest Time of the Year," "Christmas Through the Years," "The Joy of Christmas," "Austin Rhythm and Blues Christmas," "Epitome of Cool at Christmas," "The Many Moods of Christmas," "A Reggae Christmas," "Soap Opera Christmas" and "Billboard's Greatest Christmas Hits."

Just as retailers had with Christmas compilation LPs in the 1960s and 1970s, other stores and companies produced CD sets with Christmas music. Those included Dillard's, Pottery Barn, M.D. Anderson Cancer Center and St. Jude's Children's Hospital.

These are the top selling Christmas albums of all time, as compiled by Billboard and the Recording Industry Association of America:

1. Elvis Presley's 1957 "Christmas Album."
2. "Miracles: The Holiday Album" by Kenny G in 1994.
3. Nat King Cole's "The Christmas Song" from 1957.
4. "Mannheim Steamroller Christmas" from 1984.
5. "A Fresh Aire Christmas" by Mannheim Steamroller in 1988.
6. Josh Groban's "Noel" from 2007.
7. Mariah Carey's "Merry Christmas" from 1994.
8. "These Are Special Times" by Celine Dion in 1998.
9. Barbra Streisand's 1967 "Christmas Album."
10. "Merry Christmas" by Johnny Mathis in 1958.
11. "Merry Christmas" by Bing Crosby, 1945.
12. "A Charlie Brown Christmas" by the Vince Guaraldi Trio in 1965.
13. "The Gift" by Susan Boyle in 2010.
14. Kenny G's "Faith, A Holiday Album" in 1999.
15. "Christmas Eve and Other Stories" in 1996 by the Trans-Siberian Orchestra.

16. "When My Heart Finds Christmas" in 1993 by Harry Connick Jr.
17. "Beyond the Season" from 1992 by Garth Brooks.
18. Amy Grant's "Home For Christmas" in 1992.
19. "December" by George Winston in 1982.
20. From 1971, "Elvis Presley Sings the Wonderful World of Christmas."
21. From 2014, "That's Christmas to Me" by Pentatonix.
22. "My Christmas" by Andrea Bocelli in 2009.
23. "The Lost Christmas Eve" in 2004 by the Trans-Siberian Orchestra.
24. "Christmas Interpretations" in 1993 by Boyz II Men.
25. "Let There Be Peace on Earth" by Vince Gill in 1993.
26. Neil Diamond's "The Christmas Album" in 1992.
27. "Merry, Merry Christmas" in 1989 by New Kids on the Block.
28. "Merry Christmas to You" by Reba McEntire in 1987.
29. George Strait's 1986 LP, "Merry Christmas Strait to You."
30. 1985's "Alabama Christmas."
31. "Once Upon a Christmas" from 1984 by Kenny Rogers and Dolly Parton.
32. Anne Murray's "Christmas Wishes" in 1981.
33. "Christmas" by Kenny Rogers in 1981.
34. "A Pentatonix Christmas" from 2016.
35. "Because It's Christmas" by Barry Manilow in 1990.
36. "Andy Williams Christmas Album" from 1963.
37. "Mario Lanza Sings Christmas Songs" from 1951.
38. "The Jackson 5 Christmas Album" from 1970.
39. "That Christmas Feeling" in 1968 by Glen Campbell.
40. "Hymns and Carols" by the Robert Shaw Chorale in 1952.
41. John Denver's "Rocky Mountain Christmas" in 1975.
42. "Merry Christmas From Lawrence Welk & His Champagne Music" in 1956.
43. "Little Drummer Boy" by the Harry Simeone Chorale in 1958.
44. From 1982, "Christmas" by The Oak Ridge Boys.
45. From 2004, "Merry Christmas With Love" by Clay Aiken.
46. "Christmas" by Michael Buble from 2011.
47. "Christmas With Arthur Godfrey & All the Little Godfreys" from 1953.

48. Mitch Miller's 1958 LP "Christmas Sing-A-Long With Mitch."

49. "Ray Conniff Christmas Album" from 1958.

50. "Partridge Family Christmas Card" from 1971.

51. "Selections From White Christmas" by Bing Crosby, Danny Kaye and Peggy Lee.

52. "Christmas Portrait" from 1970 by The Carpenters.

53. "Christmas Jollies" from 1975 by the Salsoul Orchestra.

54. From 2006, "Wintersong" by Sarah McLachlan.

55. From 1997, "Snowed In" by Hanson.

56. From 2000, "Dream a Dream" by Charlotte Church.

57. "That Christmas Feeling" by Bing Crosby in 1957.

58. "Chipmunk Christmas" from 1959 by David Seville & The Chipmunks.

59. "Wrapped in Red" from 2013 by Kelly Clarkson.

60. "A Christmas Together" from 1979 by John Denver and The Muppets.

61. "Jim Nabors' Christmas Album" from 1969.

62. "Waltons Christmas Album" from 1974.

63. "Star Wars Christmas Album" by Meco in 1980.

64. "Merry Christmas, Baby" by Rod Stewart in 2012.

65. "Harry For the Holidays" by Harry Connick Jr. in 2003.

66. From 1981, "Pretty Paper" by Willie Nelson.

67. From 1963, "Happy Holiday" by Steve Lawrence and Eydie Gorme.

68. "A Merry Mancini Christmas" from 1966 by Henry Mancini.

69. "Perry Como Sings Merry Christmas Music" from 1952.

70. "Christmas Present" by Andy Williams in 1974.

71. "Now is the Caroling Season" by Fred Waring & his Pennsylvanians in 1955.

72. "For Christmas This Year" in 1962 by The Lettermen.

73. "Christmastime in Carol and Song" from 1969 by Leontyne Price, Arthur Fiedler, Steve Lawrence and Eydie Gorme.

74. "Hallmark Presents Songs For the Holidays" from 1987.

75. "Sing We Now of Christmas" by the Harry Simeone Chorale in 1961.

76. "Seasons Greetings" by Perry Como in 1959.

77. "Ella Wishes You a Merry Christmas" from 1962 by Ella Fitzgerald.

78. "Sinatra Family Wishes You a Merry Christmas" from 1967.

79. "Christmas with the Trapp Family Singers" from 1953.

80. James Brown's "Santa's Got a Brand New Bag" from 1965.

81. From 1967, "Happy Holidays" by Sandler & Young.

82. "Sending You a Little Christmas" from 1976 by Johnny Mathis.

83. "Christmas Wonderland" by Bert Kaempfert from 1962.

84. "Frank Sinatra Christmas Album" on Columbia

85. "Frank Sinatra Christmas Album" on Capitol

86. "Frank Sinatra Christmas Album" on Reprise

87. "Christmas Album" by Bobby Sherman from 1970.

88. "Phil Spector's Christmas Album" from 1963.

89. "Christmas Album" by Harry Belafonte from 1958.

90. From 1952, "Christmas For Children" by Frank Luther.

91. "Christmas, What's It Gonna Be, Santa" from 1999 by Chicago.

92. "Silent Night, Gospel Christmas With Mahalia Jackson" from 1960.

93. From 1993, "It's Christmas Time" by Kathie Lee Gifford.

94. From 1959, "Christmas Songs" by the Obernkirchen Children's Choir.

95. From 1962, "A Very Merry Christmas" by Bobby Vinton.

96. From 1962, "Christmas With Kate Smith."

97. "Twas the Night Before Christmas" by Fred Waring from 1950.

98. "O Tannenbaum" by Werner Mueller from 1961.

99. "Christmas Sing Song" by Woody the Woodchuck from 1959.

100. "Christmas For Kids From One to Ninety-Two" by Nat King Cole.

Chapter 10

RECORD LABELS

The first record label was Columbia, founded in 1898. To serve oldies after-markets, the label established Columbia House Special Products, whose compilations included "Swinging the Classics," "Italian Love Songs," "The World's Most Beautiful Music," "Remember How Great," "Best of the Hit Parade," "Good Times in Country Music," "Million Dollar Country."

Columbia introduced the Greatest Hits LP record series. In 1958, Johnny Mathis was at his peak, and there was not enough material yet for a new album. Mitch Miller, head of Artists and Repertoire for Columbia, decided to put together Johnny's first few singles with B-sides and issued "Johnny's Greatest Hits." That album holds the record for longest stay on Billboard's Top Albums chart, nine and one-half years. After that, Greatest Hits by other Columbia artists ensued, followed by second and third volumes still later. Columbia also launched its Harmony series for reissuing recordings at budget costs. This set the precedent for other record labels to follow suit with Greatest Hits albums and budget record series.

The second record label was RCA Victor, founded in 1901. RCA Victor had the largest inventory of Big Band era recordings, which spawned an endless supply of reissues in the LP, cassette tape and CD eras. Victor's budget record series was named RCA Camden, after the location of the record production plant, in Camden, NJ.

The third record label was Brunswick, founded in 1916 by Brunswick-Balke-Collender, a company based in Dubuque, IA since 1845, which manufactured farming and sporting equipment. Brunswick was sold to Warner Bros. Pictures in 1930, to Decca UK in 1932, to Columbia Records in 1939, with Vocalion established as the second label to press reissues.

The fourth record label was Decca Records, founded in 1932. The first superstar was Bing Crosby, initially recorded by Brunswick and from 1934-1957 by Decca. In 1943, Brunswick and Vocalion were both sold to Decca, which then added the Coral, Kapp and Uni labels. All Decca labels were combined as MCA Records in 1973. Vocalion became the reissue label in the UK, and MCA began reissuing everything from the catalog in 1973, the same year that Elton John and Neil Diamond were turning out new hit records.

The fifth record label was Capitol, founded in 1942 by songwriters Johnny Mercer and Buddy DeSylva and record store owner Glenn Wallichs. Mercer supervised early recording sessions, wrote songs and recorded many of his own. Capitol was the first major West Coast label to compete with others based on the East Coast. Capitol had a country music division, produced children's records and streamlined distribution mechanisms. Capitol created a Library Production Music division, the Capitol Hi-Q series being recognizable soundtracks and themes songs on 1950s and 1960s TV shows and movies.

In 1955, British music empire EMI acquired Capitol records and built the famous Capitol Tower in Hollywood to complement its famous Abbey Road studios in London. Capitol released many international recordings plus EMI's Angel label, thus paving the way to Capitol's dominance in the 1960s British invasion recordings by The Beatles, Peter & Gordon and other groups.

Capitol-EMI released such hit compilations as "Do You Wanna Dance," "The Way We Were," "Death, Glory & Retribution," "Rock N' Roll at the Capitol Tower," "Only in America," "Unforgettable," "Happy Trails, Songs of the Great Singing Cowboys," "Great Country Stars Singing Their Biggest Hits," "Hillbilly Heaven."

Mercury Records was founded in Chicago in 1945. It aimed primarily at juke boxes, had plants to issue recordings within twenty-four hours and rose the pop charts throughout the 1950s and 1960s. Mercury signed Patti Page as a top talent on the rose. Patti recorded many of her hits with her own voice on second, third and fourth harmonies. This followed the recording process of Les Paul and Mary Ford on Capitol, who sang all the voices and overdubbed all the instruments. Andy Williams later recorded many multi-part harmony hits on the Cadence and Columbia labels.

Mercury began putting out greatest hits LPs in the 1950s, with titles like "Vocal Group Collection," "Original Golden Hits of the Great Groups." Mercury's budget label was Wing, and its jazz label was Emarcy. It had country, classical and children's divisions.

In the 1960s and 1970s, Mercury was a major label, with stars such as Brook Benton, Dinah Washington, Ray Stevens and Sarah Vaughn. In the rock era, recording artists included Manfred Mann, Spanky & Our Gang and John Cougar Mellencamp. R&B stars on Mercury included Kool & the Gang. After 2000, Elton John's albums and reissues were on Mercury.

Warner Bros. Pictures established a record label in 1957, as one of their top stars Tab Hunter was having hits on the Dot label. Warner Bros. actively recorded actors in their stable as singers with a teen pop bent. Warner Bros. also recorded soundtracks. In the 1960s, the label became a major source of hit recordings for the Top 40 and rock markets. Warner Special Products released many compilation sets in the 1970s, 1980s and 1990s.

Randy Wood owned radio station WHIN in Gallatin, TN. In the early 1950s, he founded Dot Records, doing the recording in the station's production studio in the evenings, with early artists including The Hilltoppers, Johnny Mattox and Billy Vaughn. In 1955, Dot moved to Hollywood, CA, and recordings by Pat Boone, The Fontane Sisters, Gale Storm and others were backed by Billy Vaughn's orchestra. Vaughn also had a twenty-year string of hit 45RPM singles and albums. Its subsidiary was Hamilton Records.

Cover record labels included Value, Tops, Broadway, 18 Big Hits, Bravo, Hit, Gateway, Gilmar, Promenade and Waldorf. Reissue record labels included Eric, Collectables and Underground. Discount record labels included Royale,

Hallmark, Silvertone, Vocalion, RCA Camden, Columbia Harmony, Pickwick and Metro.

Record Label Slogans

ABC Paramount: Full Color Fidelity.

Blue Note: Hits a New Note.

Brunswick: Records You'll Want to Own.

Capitol: From the Capitol of the World, Starline Series.

CBS: Individuals for and by Individuals.

Columbia: Hall of Fame, Microgroove, Finest Name on Record.

Decca: Music Wherever You Go.

Dot: Nation's Best-Selling Records.

ECM: Most Beautiful Sound Next to Silence.

Era: Finest Sound in Recorded Music.

Island: Just Off the Coast of PolyGram.

Liberty: Personality Sound of the Sixties, First in the Foreground of Sound.

Mercury: Music for Every Mood, Established in 1947 on a Sound Basis.

Monument: Name is Artistry.

Motown: The Sound of Young America, Hitsville USA.

Parlophone: The Stars Turn on Parlophone.

Philadelphia International: The Sound of Philadelphia, A Message in the Music.

Philips: One World of Great Music on One Great Label.

Philles: Tomorrow's Sound Today.

RCA Victor: His Master's Voice, New Orthophonic Sound, Gold Standard Series.

Steed: With an Ear to the Future.

Tabu: The Earth Has Music for Those Who Listen.

United Artists: Proudest Name in Entertainment, Silver Spotlight Series.

Record labels and picture sleeves from the 1940s–1970s

Chapter 11
1960S MUSIC, 1960–1963

There was more music available to the public in the 1960s than in any other decade before or since. The emphasis was on youth. The growth of rock n' roll in the 1950s accentuated the potential for young people as consumers and culture leaders. In the 60s, it challenged and changed social conventions. It remains, through golden oldies, remakes of the songs, nostalgia and love of the music.

1960s music influenced films, TV, fashions and social mores. Those who grew up in the decade witnessed changes that cascaded into succeeding decades. It changed the way music sounded and the manners in which it was sold to the public.

To understand music output and availability on the market is to understand radio. In the 1950s, radio was enjoyed by all the family. By the 1960s, there were stations programming to the teen and youth markets.

The Billboard Top 100 charts governed what was played on the radio. Stations developed their own formats and played songs off most of the Top 100. That allowed disc jockeys to have "picks to click," those songs entering the charts which had potential as popular hits. That allowed records on the way down the time to usher in new releases by the same artists. Radio playlists were big and broad, the programming allowed for up to six hours without repeats. Playlists included instrumentals, local records, novelty songs and more. Newscasts were shorter and less frequent, thus allowing for continuous music, with DJ banter.

Records in the late 1950s and early 1960s were shorter, with average running times being two minutes. This allowed radio stations to play more songs per hour. Some sped up turntable speeds to give the records more of a competitive edge.

In the early 1950s, radio stations had "service radio" formats, meaning that different kinds of music could be played in different dayparts. The 1960s brought more formats, including country, R&B/soul, easy listening and classical.

Markets for the Music

To understand the appetite for so many records is to understand how the markets were created and sustained. The major record labels released huge amounts of records. The number of independent labels started with a handful in the mid-1950s and increased to hundreds in the 1960s. Music was everywhere in the 1960s.

More stores sold records than ever before. You could go into the neighborhood grocery store and find racks of the hits. You could find bargain bins of records that had gone off the charts, at reduced prices and often in grab bags with others. Records were sold at convenience stores, Western Auto, clothing shops, department stores, pharmacies, jewelry stores, roller rinks, diners, five-and-dime stores, and more.

There was an industry of sound-alike records, sold at reduced prices. Cover record labels included Value, Tops, Broadway, 18 Big Hits, Bravo, Hit, Gateway, Gilmar, Promenade and Waldorf.

All families had phonographs, and music was going into cars via radio, thus stimulating record sales and thus encouraging other technologies to bring music into cars (emerging as meccas in our mobile society).

Used record stores came into being. When the music industry introduced LPs and 45RPM singles in 1949, it was inevitable that 78RPM records would be phased out. These records included major hits from the 1930s and 1940s, and I remember finding these gems for 10-cents at the Austin Army-Navy Store, which grew into Academy Super Surplus. That concept of after-market sales grew in the 1960s to used record stores and retailers such as Half Price Books, Records and Tapes. That concept grew by the 2000s to online marketplaces such as Ebay.

LP records came of age, and legions more were made than in the 1950s. Contemporary 1960s artists put out hit singles, as well as concept albums. Many artists covered hits by others, offering their takes on the most popular songs of the era. There were live concert albums, children's records, spoken word recordings, classical compilations and more.

The 1960s was the heyday for custom pressed EPs and LPs. The major labels (RCA, Columbia, Capitol and MCA) issued compilation albums, containing samples of new album releases. These special records were available to the public through advertising incentives, returned box-tops, coupons, seasonal retail sales and in-store promotions.

In the 1960s, every major label put out its own reissue series, most of them back-to-back hits, re-enhanced for stereo, digitally re-mastered for better quality sound. Those include Columbia's "Hall of Fame," RCA Victor's "Gold Standard Series," Epic's "Memory Lane," Capitol's "Starline Series," Mercury's "Celebrity Series," Warner Bros. Records' "Back to Back Hits," United Artists' "Silver Spotlight," Musicor's "Startime," A&M "Forget Me Not," Arista "Flashback," Buddah "Radioactive Gold," Motown "Yesteryear Series," MGM "Golden Circle Series," Roulette "Golden Goodies Series," Philips "Double-Hit Series," King/Federal "Golden Treasures, Gusto and Old Gold" series, Stax "Double-Hitter Series." These were prominent in record stores and in mail-order catalogs.

Reader's Digest started compiling great music and began releasing LP box sets. The first releases featured Big Band Era recordings, known for their high fidelity and greater sound quality than the previous scratchy 78RPM records from which they were re-mastered. Next came classical music box sets, easy listening compilations and Christmas collections.

Time-Life got into music compilations in the rock era. Their compilation sets included "Singers & Songwriters," "The Rock N' Roll Era," "Smooth Soul," "Instrumental Favorites," "Lifetime of Romance" and "Legends Do It Again."

The 1960s brought TV record offers to the marketplace. K-tel was founded in Canada in 1962 by Philip Kives. He named the company K-tel, as his record reissues were sold via television commercials, with viewers directed to phone numbers and mailing addresses to buy. In addition to records, Kives sold the Beg-O-Matic, Miracle Brush and Feather Touch Knife, with the tagline "Wait there's more." K-tel record offers were compilations of the latest hits by the original artists, with titles such as "Summer Cruisin," "20 Power Hits," "Disco Rocket," "Goofy Greats" and "Super Bad."

The 1960s brought many other distribution channels to the marketplace:

- Jukeboxes.
- Greatest hits albums.
- Record clubs.
- Records as giveaway prizes via radio stations and retailers.
- Music videos, played on TV and in movie theatres.
- Movies and TV shows showcasing music and its performers.
- Exports of American records to international marketplaces.
- The practice of using name hits on radio and TV commercials, a practice that continues today.
- Music played on sound systems for ambiance.

There were distinct aspects to 1960s music, Teen Pop, The Motown Sound, The British Invasion, Soul, Rock and Hybrid Pop, with implications to succeeding decades.

Teen Pop

Teen idols became prominent in the late 1950s. They were young singers who were close in age to the teenage audiences. Teen idols of that era included Elvis Presley, Tommy Sands, Sal Mineo, Cliff Richard, Frankie Avalon, Annette Funicello, Fabian, Bobby Rydell, Pat Boone, Tab Hunter, Paul Anka and Ricky Nelson.

In the late 1950s, rock and roll appealed to audiences as raw and fresh. Some things occurred at the end of the decade, affecting rock. Elvis Presley was drafted into the US Army. He stockpiled two years' worth of recordings to cover his absence. Elvis served in the Army and was a positive role model for soldiers.

On Feb. 3, 1959, the fastest rising rock superstar, Buddy Holly, was killed in a plane crash in IA. He had been touring the Midwest, and other fatalities on the plane included two others with promising futures, Ritchie Valens and J.P. Richardson (The Big Bopper).

Little Richard, the exponent of shock rock abruptly quit music and joined the ministry. He had seen spacecraft Sputnik as a sign from above and traded his music lifestyle for the church. He would not return to rock and roll until 1963.

Chuck Berry, the guitar hero and singer with an attitude, had his own nightclub in St. Louis, MO. In 1962, he was convicted for violations of the Mann Act, having transported a fourteen-year-old girl across state lines for purposes of sexual activities. By the time he got out of prison, he had more record hits but none with the same power as his 1950s records. He became known as a nostalgia performer. I emceed Chuck Berry in a 1980 concert.

The trend in 1960 shifted to more mellow songs, teen pop recording artists and a more serene time. In the early 1960s, the next breed of teen idols dominated charts. They included Bobby Vee, Lou Christie, Neil Sedaka, Connie Francis, Brian Hyland, Jimmy Clanton, Johnny Tillotson, Jimmy Rodgers, Mark Dinning, James Darren, Shelley Fabares, Johnny Crawford, Dion, Brenda Lee, Johnny Burnette, Chubby Checker, Rod Lauren and Ray Peterson.

Meanwhile, Over in Great Britain

The British loved American rock and roll and consumed all the import records they could get. In the 1950s and early 1960s, the UK had record import quotas, to stimulate the British recording industry. American artists that could be covered by British artists did not get import sales. Artists that could not be covered by British counterparts got the radio airplay and record store distribution.

Young aspiring British singers and musicians carefully watched and were inspired by US stars. Teenagers John Lennon and Paul McCartney copied their harmonies from The Everly Brothers. They modeled their stage presence and energy of recordings from Buddy Holly, Elvis Presley and Little Richard. George Harrison and Eric Clapton got their guitar prowess channeled from Chuck Berry.

Cliff Richard was called the UK version of Elvis, but he was still a teenager and had massive appeal. He and fellow teen idols Marty Wilde, Billy Fury headlined a UK music series, "Oh, Boy!" Adam Faith was a popular teen idol, with traits from US teen idols and charisma to appeal to UK youths. Other British teen pop singers of the 1960-1963 era included Craig Douglas, Helen Shapiro, Tommy Steele, Lance Fortune, Alma Cogan, Garry Mills, Frankie Vaughan and Ricky Valance.

Some British pop records made it to the US and placed on the charts. Records paving the way for what was about to come included "I Remember You" by Frank Ifield, "Cara Mia" by David Whitfield, "Silver Threads and Golden Needles" by The Springfields (featuring Dusty Springfield), "He's Got the Whole World in His Hands" by Laurie London, "Living Doll" by Cliff Richard, "Does Your Chewing Gum Lose Its Flavor on the Bedpost Overnight" by Lonnie Donegan, "Petite Fleur" by Chris Barber, "Stranger on the Shore" by Acker Bilk, "From Russia With Love" by Matt Monro, "Midnight in Moscow" by Kenny Ball and "When" by the Kalin Twins. These records held their own with American releases and proved that Great Britain was a viable resource for creative music.

Girl Group Sound

The girl group rise started in the 1930s. The Andrews Sisters started in 1937 with "Bei Mir Bist Du Schon." The hits kept coming, including "Boogie Woogie Bugle Boy," "Don't Sit Under the Apple Tree," "Beer Barrel Polka," "Rum and Coca-Cola," "Beat Me Daddy Eight to the Bar," "In Apple Blossom Time," "I Can Dream, Can't I" and "A Bushel and a Peck." They recorded with Bing Crosby many times and appeared on his radio show.

In the early 1930s, the Gumm Sisters performed in vaudeville shows. In 1935, Frances Gumm was signed by MGM to a studio contract as a solo artist. Her name was changed to Judy Garland, and she became movie royalty.

Other girl groups during the Big Band Era included the Boswell Sisters, Dinning Sisters and King Sisters. In the 1950s came the McGuire Sisters, Fontane Sisters and DeJohn Sisters.

In the 1960s, the Girl Group Sound hit its heyday. Stars included the Ronettes, Shangri-Las, Shirelles, Angels, Exciters, Supremes, Orlons, Chiffons, Crystals, Jelly Beans, Marvelettes, Raindrops, Secrets, Toys, Ribbons, Dixie Cups, Jaynetts, Girlfriends, Cupcakes, Essex, Butterflys, Ad-Libs, Mermaids, Cookies, Chantels, Reparta & Delrons, Martha & Vandellas, Bonnie & Treasures and Patti Labelle & the Bluebells. Solo singers included Lesley Gore, Mary Wells, Dee Dee Sharp, Darlene Love, Little Eva, Claudine Clark, Betty Everett, Peggy March, Tracey Dey and Evie Sands.

The Girl Group Sound had high energy, quality production and a vibrant appeal to youths. Girl groups were ideals as friends. They sang teen music, with relatable themes. Singers had attitude and swagger, a step forward from demure ballad singers of previous decades. Many of these hits stand as all-time classics.

Top Girl Group Hits

- "It's My Party," "Judy's Turn to Cry," "She's a Fool," "You Don't Own Me," "That's the Way Boys Are," "Maybe I Know," "Hey Now," "The Look of Love," "Sunshine, Lollipops and Rainbows," "My Town, My Guy and Me," "I Won't Love You Anymore" and "California Nights" by Lesley Gore
- "I Won't Tell," "Get Along Without You Now," "Teenage Cleopatra," "Jerry I'm Your Sherry," "Blue Turns to Grey," "Long Time, No See" and "Here Comes the Boy" by Tracey Dey
- "Will You Love Me Tomorrow," "Soldier Boy," "Baby It's You," "Dedicated to the One I Love," "Mama Said," "Boys," "Foolish Little Girl" and "Big John" by The Shirelles
- "The Wah-Watusi," "Don't Hang Up," "South Street," "Crossfire" by The Orlons
- "The Kind of Boy You Can't Forget" by The Raindrops
- "Tell Him," "Do-Wah-Diddy" and "He's Got the Power" by The Exciters
- "The Boy Next Door" by The Secrets
- "I Will Follow Him," "I Wish I Were a Princess" and "Hello Heartache, Goodbye Love" by Peggy March
- "My Boyfriend's Back" and "I Adore Him" by The Angels
- "Home of the Brave" by Bonnie and the Treasures
- "Easier Said Than Done" and "A Walking Miracle" by The Essex
- "Sally Go Round the Roses" by The Jaynetts
- "Lover's Concerto" and "Attack" by The Toys
- "Oh No, Not My Baby" by Maxine Brown
- "He's So Fine," "One Fine Day" and "Sweet Talking Guy" by The Chiffons
- "I Can't Let Go" by Evie Sands
- "Nothing But a Heartache" by The Flirtations
- "I'm into Something Good" by Earl-Jean
- "Our Day Will Come," "Hey There Lonely Boy" and "Young Wings Can Fly" by Ruby & the Romantics

- "Needle in a Haystack" and "He Was Really Saying Something" by The Velvelettes
- "Ain't Gonna Kiss You" by The Ribbons
- "Chains" and "Don't Say Nothing Bad About My Baby" by The Cookies
- "You're No Good" and "The Shoop Shoop Song" by Betty Everett
- "Chapel of Love," "People Say" and "Iko Iko" by The Dixie Cups
- "I Wanna Love Him So Bad" by The Jelly Beans
- "Remember, Walking in Sand," "Leader of the Pack" and "Give Him Great Big Kiss" by The Shangri-Las
- "He's a Rebel," "He's Sure the Boy I Love," "Then He Kissed Me" and "Da Doo Ron Ron" by The Crystals
- "Be My Baby," "Best Part of Breaking Up," "Walking in the Rain" by The Ronettes

Folk Music

Folk music always represented integrity and the voice of the people. Its 1940s and 1950s purveyors were the mavericks of the recording industry. Pete Seeger came out of the blacklist era to be the big daddy of the hootenannies.

In the 1950s, folk music was performed in coffee houses all around America. The Weavers recorded on Decca, mentored by bandleader Gordon Jenkins. The Kingston Trio became major recording artists on Capitol, followed by The Brothers Four and Bob Dylan on Columbia Records. Warner Bros. recorded a folk trio named Peter, Paul & Mary. Harry Belafonte had solid calypso folk hits on RCA Victor.

Folk music became a national craze in 1962, featured on TV shows like "Hootnanny." That craze made stars of the Chad Mitchell Trio, whose membership at one time included John Denver. Also in the era were Pete Seeger, Joan Baez, Arlo Guthrie, Judy Collins, Lonnie Donegan, the New Christy Minstrels, Smothers Brothers, Serendipity Singers, Clancy Brothers, Burl Ives, Tom Paxton, Buffy Saint-Marie, Tom Rush, Joni Mitchell, Theodore Bikel, Gordon Lightfoot and Phil Ochs.

Factors that brought the folk boom to a close included the British Invasion, the intertwining of folk into rock and the ever-present dawning of the "next new thing."

Top Folk Hits

- "Lemon Tree," "500 Miles," "Puff the Magic Dragon," "Rock My Soul," "Blowing in the Wind," "Don't Think Twice, It's Alright," "Stewball," "Tell It on the Mountain" and "Early Morning Rain" by Peter, Paul & Mary
- "Tom Dooley," "Scotch and Soda," "Tijuana Jail," "A Worried Man," "M.T.A.," "It Was a Very Good Year," "Greenback Dollar," "Reverend Mr. Black," "Olly Oxen Free" and "Seasons in the Sun" by The Kingston Trio
- "On Top of Old Smoky," "Goodnight, Irene," "Wimoweh" and "The Roving Kind" by The Weavers
- "John Henry" by Odetta
- "This Land is Your Land," "Joshua Fit the Battle" and "Little Boxes" by Pete Seeger
- "Midnight Special" by Leadbelly
- "Both Sides Now" by Judy Collins
- "Big Rock Candy Mountain" and "Blue Tail Fly" by Burl Ives
- "House of the Rising Sun" and "Gypsy Davy" by Woody Guthrie
- "Michael Roy the Boat Ashore" and "Cotton Fields" by The Highwaymen
- "Time" by The Pozo-Seco Singers
- "Green-Green," "Today" and "Saturday Night" by The New Christy Minstrels
- "I'll Never Find Another You" and "World of Our Own" by The Seekers
- "I'd Like to Teach the World to Sing" by The New Seekers
- "Baby the Rain Must Fall" and "She" by Glenn Yarbrough
- "Banana Boat Song" and "Jamaica Farewell" by Harry Belafonte
- "We'll Sing in the Sunshine" by Gale Garnett
- "Rock Island Line" by Lonnie Donegan
- "The Unicorn" by The Irish Rovers
- "The Night They Drove Old Dixie Down" and "Diamonds and Rust" by Joan Baez
- "Marianne" by Terry Gilkyson & the Easy Riders
- "Walk Right In" by The Rooftop Singers
- "Mr. Bojangles" by Jerry Jeff Walker
- "Gotta Travel On" by Billy Grammer
- "Simple Song of Freedom" by Tim Hardin

Bossa Nova

It grew from the samba. Add in unconventional chords and innovative syncopation, and you have the Brazilian Bossa Nova. It synthesized rhythm on the classical guitar. The Term Bossa Nova means new trend and new wave.

"Manha de Carnavel" was introduced in the soundtrack of the 1959 movie "Black Orpheus." Key Bossa Nova songs included "Desafinado" by João Gilberto, "Mas Que Nada" by Sergio Mendes & Brasil '66, "One Note Samba" by João Gilberto and "Summer Samba" by Walter Wanderley. Antônio Carlos Jobim's hits included "Wave," "Meditation," "Felicidade," "Outra Vez" and "Chega de Saudade."

"The Girl From Ipanema" by Stan Getz & Astrud Gilberto was originally titled "Menina que Passa" ("The Girl Who Passes By"). It won the Grammy Award for Record of the Year for 1964. In 2004, the record was chosen by the Library of Congress to be one of fifty to be added to the National Recording Registry. In 2009, Rolling Stone Magazine named it as the greatest Brazilian song.

The trend even inspired pop songs, such as "Blame It on the Bossa Nova" by Eydie Gorme, "Bossa Nova USA" by Dave Brubeck, "Big Band Bossa Nova" by Quincy Jones and "Bossa Nova Baby" by Elvis Presley.

A bossa nova song won the Oscar for Best Song of 1965. It was "The Shadow of Your Smile," from the movie "The Sandpiper," starring Elizabeth Taylor, Richard Burton, Eva Marie Saint and Charles Bronson. Tony Bennett's recording won the Grammy Award for Song of the Year.

Beach Music

The coastal lifestyle has long been a source of manifestation among the young. The atmosphere of waves, breezes, sun, parties and the freedom of expression created musical forms to mirror the attraction.

The west coast surfer sound originated in and gloried California. It talked about finding waves, enjoying the sun, meeting girls, dancing, fast cars and partying.

Top west coast beach songs included:

- "Surfin' Safari," "I Get Around," "Surfer Girl," "Little Deuce Coupe," "Be True to Your School," "409, "Fun, Fun, Fun," "Help Me Rhonda," "California Girls," "Good Vibrations" and "Kokomo" by The Beach Boys

- "Surf City," "Honolulu," "Drag City," "Dead Man's Curve," "Little Old Lady From Pasadena," "Sidewalk Surfing" and "Ride the Wild Surf" by Jan & Dean
- "Little Honda," "My Buddy Seat" and "Younger Girl" by The HondellsCustom Machine" and "Summer Means Fun" by Bruce & Terry
- "California Sun" by The Rivieras
- "I Live for the Sun" and "Andrea" by The Sunrays
- "Surfing Bird" by The Trashmen
- "Papa-Oom Mow Mow" by The Rivingtons
- "Hey Little Cobra," "Three Window Coupe" and "Here I Stand" by The Rip Chords

In 1963 alone, there was a treasure trove of surfing instrumentals, including "Wipe Out" by The Surfaris, "Let's Go" by The Routers, "Pipeline" by The Chantays, "Misirlou" by Dick Dale & the Daletones, "Apache" by The Shadows, "Rumble" by Link Wray, "Surfer's Stomp" by The Markets and "Bulldog" by The Fireballs. The super instrumental group was The Ventures, with hits including "Walk, Don't Run," "Perfidia," "Slaughter on Tenth Avenue," "Balboa Blue" and "Hawaii Five-0."

East coast beach music was soulful. It was most popular in the Carolinas, Georgia, Florida and Illinois. The Carolina shag was the primary dance. It encompassed Northern Soul hits from the 1960s and 1970s, plus Motown hits. It was the upbeat brand of rhythm and blues.

Top east coast beach songs included:

- "39-21-46 Shape: by The Showmen
- "Build Me Up Buttercup" by The Foundations
- "Cool Jerk" by The Capitols
- "Double Shot of My Baby's Love" by The Swinging Medallions
- "The Horse" by Cliff Nobles & Co.
- "Working in a Coal Mine" by Lee Dorsey
- "What Kind of Fool Do You Think I Am" and "I've Been Hurt" by Bill Deal
- "Backfield in Motion" by Mel & Tim

- "Girl Watcher" by The O'Kaysions
- "But It's Alright" by J.J. Jackson
- "Get On Up" by The Esquires
- "Love Makes a Woman" by Barbara Acklin
- "Give Me Just a Little More Time" by the Chairmen of the Board
- "The Cheater" and "The Teaser" by Bob Kuban and the In-Men
- "Hold Back the Night" by The Trammps
- "Be Young, Be Foolish, Be Happy" by The Tams
- "Shake a Tail Feather" by The Five Du-Tones
- "K-Jee" by The Nite-Liters
- "Mama Didn't Lie" by Jan Bradley
- "Hey Baby" by Bruce Channel
- "She's Not Just Another Woman" by The 8th Day
- "It's Alright" and "Woman's Got Soul" by The Impressions
- "Soulful Strut" by Young-Holt Unlimited
- "Party Lights" by Claudine Clark
- "Baby Come Back" by The Equals
- "Shame, Shame" by The Magic Lanterns
- "Westbound #9" by The Flaming Ember
- "Want Ads" and "One Monkey Don't Stop No Show" by The Honey Cone
- "Gimme Little Sign" and "Oogum Boogum Song" by Brenton Wood
- "Twine Time" by Alvin Cash & the Crawlers
- "Express Yourself" and "Love Land" by Charles Wright & the Watts 103rd Street Rhythm Band

The Motown Sound

The Detroit sound was revving motors, the city being the automobile capitol of the world. In the 1960s, the Motown Sound became soul, a slickened form of rhythm and blues, with sophisticated production and a youthful appeal that sold records into the multi-millions.

The Motown sound had a formula: a danceable lead, incredible base lines and double percussion. The fact that it sold so spectacularly came from cross-ethnic appeal. The formula for Motown worked, and it was strictly adhered to.

The label was founded in Detroit in 1959 by a part-time songwriter who was moonlighting from his assembly line job at Ford. Berry Gordy Jr. came up with a formula that achieved his dream. His wish was that his stable of stars would one day headline New York's Copacabana nightclub. Some achieved even higher stellar fame.

Motown had its own writers, arrangers and a house band known as The Funk Brothers. They worked out artists' routines onstage, dances, singing styles and manners. Some like William "Smokey" Robinson were multi-talented, as a singer, writer, producer and actor. When Diana Ross left The Supremes and got an Oscar nomination for "Lady Sings the Blues," the Motown dominance in records extended to other forms of show business.

The Detroit sound came from rhythm and blues and pop. The Motown catalog is a perfect capsule of feel-good pop in the 1960s and 1970s.

These were the stars and songs that made Motown sound that everybody loved and admired.

Stevie Wonder: "Fingertips," "Hey Harmonica Man," "Blowing in the Wind," "A Place in the Sun," "Traveling Man," "I Was Made to Love Her," "I'm Wondering," "Alfie," "For Once in My Life," "My Cherie Amour," "Signed, Sealed, Delivered I'm Yours," "Heaven Help Us All," "If You Really Love Me," "Superstition," "You Are the Sunshine of My Life," "Higher Ground," "Living For the City," "Boogie on Reggae Woman," "Sir Duke," "Master Blaster," "I Just Called to Say I Love You," "Part-Time Lover," "Overjoyed."

The Temptations: "The Way You Do the Things You Do," "My Girl," "It's Growing," "Since I Lost My Baby," Get Ready," "Ain't Too Proud to Beg," "Beauty is Only Skin Deep," "I'm Losing You," "I Wish It Would Rain," "Cloud Nine," "Ball of Confusion," "Just My Imagination," "Papa Was a Rolling Stone," "Masterpiece."

Marvin Gaye: "Stubborn Kind of Fellow," "Hitch Hike," "Pride and Joy," "Can I Get a Witness," "How Sweet It Is to be Loved by You," "I'll Be Doggone," "Ain't That Peculiar," "I Heard It Through the Grapevine," "Too Busy Thinking About My Baby," "What's Going On," "Mercy Me," "Inner City Blues," "Trouble Man," "Let's Get It On," "Come Get to This," "I Want You," "Got to Give It Up."

Diana Ross & the Supremes: "Where Did Our Love Go," "Baby Love," "Come See About Me," "Stop in the Name of Love," "Back in My Arms Again," "Nothing But Heartaches," "I Hear a Symphony," "My World is Empty Without You," ":Just

Like an Itching in My Heart," "Can't Hurry Love," "You Keep Me Hanging On," "Love is Here and Now You're Gone," "The Happening," "Reflections," "In and Out of Love," "Forever Came Today," "Some Things You Never Get Used to," "Love Child," "I'm Living in Shame," "The Composer," "No Matter What Sign You Are," "Someday We'll Be Together."

The Contours: "Do You Love Me," "Shake Sherry" and "Just a Little Misunderstanding."

The Four Tops: "Baby I Need Your Loving," "I Can't Help Myself," "It's the Same Old Song," "Something About You," "Reach Out I'll Be There," "Standing in the Shadows of Love," "Bernadette," "7 Rooms of Gloom," "Still Water."

The Marvelettes: "Please Mr. Postman," "Twisting Postman," "Playboy," "Beechwood 4-5789," "As Long as I Know He's Mine," "He's a Good Guy," "You're My Remedy," "Too Many Fish in the Sea," "I'll Keep Holding On," "Danger Heartbreak Dead Ahead," "Don't Mess with Bill," "The Hunter Gets Captured by the Game," "When You're Young and in Love," "My Baby Must Be a Magician."

Kim Weston: "Take Me in Your Arms" and "It Takes Two" (with Marvin Gaye).

The Jackson Five: "1 Want You Back," "ABC," "The Love You Save," "I'll Be There," "Mama's Pearl," "Never Can Say Goodbye," "Maybe Tomorrow," "Sugar Daddy," "Little Bitty Pretty One," "Corner of the Sky," "Hallelujah Day," "Get It Together," "Dancing Machine," "Whatever You Got, I Want," "I Am Love," "Forever Came Today."

Smokey Robinson & the Miracles: "Shop Around," "What's So Good About Goodbye," "I'll Try Something New," "You've Really Got a Hold on Me," "Mickey's Monkey," "That's What Love is Made Of," "Ooh Baby," "Tracks of My Tears," "Going to a-Go-Go," "More Love," "I Second That Emotion," "If You Can Want," "Yester Love," "Special Occasion," "Point It Out," "Tears of a Clown," "I Don't Blame You at All."

Eddie Kendricks: "Keep on Trucking," "Boogie Down," "Son of a Sagittarius."

Jr. Walker: "Shotgun," "Do the Boomerang," "Shake and Finger Pop," "Cleo's Back," "Road Runner," "How Sweet It Is," "Shoot Your Shot," "What Does It Take," "These Eyes," "Hold onto This Feeling."

Mary Wells: "My Guy," "The One Who Really Loves You," "Two Lovers," "You Beat Me to the Punch," "Once Upon a Time."

Gladys Knight & the Pips: "I Heard It Through the Grapevine," "The End of Our Road," "The Nitty Gritty," "If I Were Your Woman" and "Neither One of Us."

David Ruffin: "My Whole World Ended," "Walk Away from Love," "Heavy Love."

Jimmy Ruffin: "What Becomes of the Brokenhearted," "I've Passed This Way Before," "Give Her All the Love I've Got," "Stand by Me" (with David Ruffin).

Martha & the Vandellas: "Come and Get These Memories," "Heat Wave," "Quicksand," "Live Wire," "In My Lonely Room," "Dancing in the Street," "Wild One," "Nowhere to Run," "Love Makes Me Do Foolish Things," "My Baby Loves Me," "I'm Ready for Love," "Jimmy Mack," "Love Bug Leave My Heart Alone."

Chapter 12
1960S MUSIC, 1964–1969

The British Invasion

The British invaded America in 1964. The world of pop music has not been the same ever since. In the 1950s, England admired American rock and roll, just as did the rest of the world. There were some early British imports, hit records fashioned much in the American style. They were good and, thus, they were worldwide hits.

The people who were to revolutionize music in the mid-1960s paid their dues and did cover versions of American hits. The Beatles covered twenty American songs, and The Rolling Stones did several.

The groups put bits and pieces together from several American acts. The result became the famous Liverpool sound. They borrowed harmony from The Everly Brothers, purist rock and roll from Chuck Berry, progressive melodies from Buddy Holly, soul from Little Richard and The Isley Brothers and solid instrumental work from pickers like Duane Eddy. The singing stars were the ones most idolized in Britain. Instrumental handiwork onstage became a must, as the newly emerging sound had to be just as good on the concert stage as in the recording studio. The result became the famous Liverpool sound.

What made The Beatles, Dave Clark Five and the others unique was that they combined styles for the modern era. When the Beatles first invaded America, the impact brought so many others in on their coattails. Collectively, they made that extra difference, one which revolutionized pop music.

There were Mick Jagger and The Rolling Stones, still a survivor from that era. The Stones were never imitations of the mop-top four. They were not the first English group to do blues, but they were the most magnificent one.

The Dave Clark Five were the biggest Beatle imitation. They met in a gymnasium and played together to raise money for Dave's football club. Their style was admittedly borrowed from the soul sound of America's Motown.

The Animals' early works were adaptations of blues and folk material. They were originally a jazz group, the Alan Price Combo. It was the hard, raspy voice of Eric Burdon that set The Animals apart.

The Kinks were straight-out rock and roll. Their musicianship is held in high esteem by the other British groups. The Kinks' later releases were satirical putdowns of the straight world.

Manfred Mann's sound was inspired by the 1950s Chicago blues of Bo Diddley and Muddy Waters. They experimented with blues-rock, which British pop was later to become.

Much in the same bag were Eric Clapton and other polished instrumentalists. His group The Yardbirds were rivals to The Rolling Stones. Eric Clapton went into a harder sound later with Blind Faith and Cream. Another Yardbird, Jeff Beck, organized his own group.

The Zombies came up with a subtle style of minor-mood tunes. They were unlike anything that crossed the Atlantic Ocean with The Beatles.

If The Beatles could not be everywhere, their proteges could. John Lennon and Paul McCartney wrote songs for Peter Asher and Gordon Waller. Peter was the brother of Paul's girlfriend, Jane Asher. Billy J. Kramer & the Dakotas were also awarded the honor of original Lennon-McCartney material, intended for that group and not for The Beatles.

Mick Jagger's girlfriend in the mid-1960s was Marianne Faithfull, who became a singing sensation of her own. Her gentle style was in the tradition of English folk music. Drugs and the too-frantic pace led to her downfall.

The Searchers took American songs and gave them added luster. "Needles and Pins" was a minor hit for Jackie DeShannon. The Searchers made it a major British Invasion charter. Chad & Jeremy were folk rockers and also appeared in American TV situation comedies.

There was a trio of brothers named Gibb, who sang romantic ballads through their noses. The Bee Gees came on like The Beatles three years later. In the 1970s, they were the white superstars of the disco craze.

The Beatles were from Liverpool, England, as were Gerry & the Pacemakers. English bubblegum evolved from groups like Freddie & the Dreamers and The Hollies featuring Graham Nash.

Herman's Hermits had perfect timing. Mothers could call them sons when they could not bestow the honors on The Beatles. The pre-teen record market was opened up to such other luminaries as Paul Revere & the Raiders, Bobby Sherman, John Travolta and The Partridge Family. Peter Noone, the Herman of the group, was so clean that he was the only pop superstar that Ed Sullivan could cope with painlessly.

Girl singers were an important phase of the British sound. They were mostly demure and with that subtle English charm. There was Petula Clark, who hits were written and conducted by Tony Hatch. There was Dusty Springfield, whose career began with her family, The Springfields, doing country-folk songs. Sandie Shaw did the music of Burt Bacharach and Hal David.

Lulu was one of many who did movie title songs, thus signifying the British influence on motion pictures, a trend that gave Hollywood its first shock since the advent of television. Mary Hopkin was another protégé of The Beatles, having been introduced to them by fashion model Twiggy. There was Cilla Black, under management of Brian Epstein.

Olivia Newton-John was in the same bag but blossomed later than the others. She became one of the hottest successes in the 1970s and 1980s.

There were other groups riding the crest of Beatles fame. They included the You-Know-Who Group, Unit Four Plus Two, Nashville Teens and Swinging

Bluejeans. There was goodtime rock from Georgie Fame, the Walker Brothers, Wayne Fontana & the Mindbenders, Spencer Davis Group and the Troggs. Donovan Leitch was one of the first to mirror changes in the world, like flower power, drugs and psychedelics.

The Moody Blues demonstrate the ups and downs of the entertainment business. They really were hot, then were ripped off by their supposed mentor. Their comeback was a most dramatic one. The Moody Blues were the first to combine rock with classical overtones.

The Who grew out of the mid-1960s British Invasion and into their own innovative group. Their rock opera "Tommy" travelled new ground and established pop as legitimate in the leagues of operetta, Broadway and traditional concert forms.

Heavier groups came along as the 1960s concluded. There was Rod Stewart, whose voice signified the transition to the 1970s. As hard rock and progressive sounds emerged, the styles simply could not be counted in the column of one country or another. The Beatles did creative things and broke up in 1970. Then came Elton John.

The Stones and others in the British Invasion were strong in the 1970s. Their rock is not of one country anymore and is of the world. That merging, exchanging and inter-mingling is a result of the trendy years of 1964–1969. Looking back, the innovative sound from England was an amalgamation of sounds from 1950s America. Music is indeed very cyclical.

Soul

It started as blues in the 1920s. It merged into swing music during the 1930s and 1940s. It evolved into rhythm & blues in the 1950s. Soul became mega-popular and mainstream in the 1960s. The rhythm side had the Motown sound (covered in the last chapter). In the 1960s, soul went uptown.

One of the most durable R&B groups of the 1950s was The Drifters. Their 1953 version of "White Christmas," arranged in the style of their other 1953 hit "Such a Night," is still played on the radio.

In 1959, producers Jerry Lieber and Mike Stoller got Stan Applebaum to arrange and conduct new releases for The Drifters. He was the first to add full string orchestra to rock n' roll songs. "There Goes My Baby" in 1959 had classical segues from the 1812 Overture. The label Atlantic hated the arrangement, but once they saw the record climbing charts to new heights, they changed their tune. Then came "Dance with Me," "This Magic Moment," "Lonely Winds," "Save the Last Dance for Me," "I Count the Tears," "Sweets for My Sweet" and "Up on the Roof." The Drifters rode high with these lush Applebaum productions. Lead singer Ben E. King decided to leave The Drifters and go solo. He debuted on the charts with two iconic Applebaum records, "Spanish Harlem" and "Stand by Me."

Soul was the pinnacle of music. It was chic, cool and motivated record buyers of all ages and ethnic groups.

Atlantic Records boasted a string of soul music singers and hits in the 1960s. Aretha Franklin grew up and sang in the church, where her father was pastor. After the death of Billie Holliday, Columbia Records signed Aretha to carry forward a comparable repertoire of ballads, blues, standards and show tunes. For five years, she recorded solid singles and albums. My favorite of hers during the 1960–1965 period was "Friendly Persuasion," a soulful remake of Pat Boone's 1956 hit.

Aretha Franklin then moved to Atlantic Records, where she became the Queen of Soul. Her hits included "Respect," "You Make Me Feel Like a Natural Woman," "Think," "Until You Come Back to Me," "Chain of Fools," "Do Right Woman," "See Saw," "Call Me," "Angel" and "Spirit in the Dark." Aretha's Arista Records era was from 1980-2007, with the hits including "Jump to It," "Freeway of Love," "Jimmy Lee," "Jumping Jack Flash," "Love All the Hurt Away" and "Everyday People."

Atlantic's soul artists included Barbara Lewis, with "Hello Stranger" and "Puppy Love." Barbara Mason sang "Baby I'm Yours" and "Make Me Your Baby." Booker T. & the MGS scored soul instrumental hits like "Green Onions" and "Time is Tight." Archie Bell & the Drells recorded "Tighten Up," "Showdown" and "I Can't Stop Dancing."

Wilson Pickett had "In the Midnight Hour," "Funky Broadway," "Land of 1,000 Dances," "Mustang Sally," "She's Looking Good" and "Soul Dance Number Three." Sam & Dave scored with "Hold On, I'm Coming," "Soul Man" and "T Thank You." Eddie Floyd recorded "Knock on Wood," "I've Never Found a Girl" and "Bring It on to Me."

The Chicago sound came from Veejay, Mercury and Brunswick Records, with artists including Jerry Butler, Gene Chandler, Dee Clark, Betty Everett and The Chi-Lites.

The Philadelphia soul of the 1960s included The Orlons, Deedee Sharp, Patti Labelle & the Bluebells, Jay & the Techniques, Madeline Bell and Cliff Nobles. In the 1970s, the Philly sound grew to rival Motown.

Southern soul featured stars like Otis Redding, Lee Dorsey, James Brown, Toussaint McCall, Johnny Taylor, Lightning Hopkins, Fats Domino, Al Green, Carla Thomas, Rufus Thomas, Buster Brown, Ann Peebles and The Dramatics.

Rock

Rock progressed out of formulas in the mid-1960s. To say that when The Beatles got serious was the turning point is not enough. When rock and roll went progressive, it lost the roll. The 1960s were years of musical experimentation.

Some think that rock and roll matured. It progressed from the early fad styles. Rockabilly had been commercialized into Top 40 music. The old crooners were no longer appealing to teen and young adult record buyers.

Several terms apply to the music that emerged in the handful of years afterward: folk rock, psychedelic rock, garage rock, blues rock, roots rock, progressive rock, party music and hybrid pop. Also emerging were the inevitable commercial expansions of each niche and the whole of rock.

Robert Zimmerman worshipped folksinger Woody Guthrie. As Bob Dylan, the poet laureate of the beat generation, he has told us, in many tempos, of depravity around us. Leonard Cohen and Paul Simon wrote poets' music.

Why not add electronics and make it folk rock? Many felt that the purity of folk and the image of rock were counter-productive. It was not so for kingpin Bob Dylan, adding electronics with "Like a Rolling Stone" in 1965. The Byrds were the first to rock Dylan songs. They made 1965 the year of folk rock.

Paul Simon and Art Garfunkel tried to make it in rock and roll in 1957 as Tom & Jerry. They had Everly Brothers harmony, which they kept in the 60s as Simon & Garfunkel. In 1965, they were doing soft, poetic melodies when tracks of folk rock were added. For the next five years, they were successful with both styles.

There was Barry McGuire, former lead singer with the New Christy Minstrels. He recorded the first rock protest song, "Eve of Destruction." The Lovin' Spoonful was Liverpool in New York. The mop-top group headed by John Sebastian took on their native flavors, combining folk-rock country and the jug-band happiness that the British groups could not conceivably have. The Lovin' Spoonful sang of good times and good climbs.

The Mamas and the Papas were the royal family of American rock, not because their music kept progressing but because they were the first to do their thing. They were the first really big group since The Beatles. They came from Greenwich Village, and they made albums in addition to Top 40 singles. They were the first hippies to strike it rich and live in luxury.

Flower Power meant gentle things, and it meant San Francisco, CA. It meant groups like Eric Burdon & the Animals, after their British sound faded. It meant The Band, the Buffalo Springfield, Scott McKenzie, Spanky & Our Gang, The Rascals and Donovan Leitch.

The New Left had its up-tempo groups, with lots of electricity. There were The Doors, featuring Jim Morrison, Tommy James & the Shondells, T-Rex, Strawberry Alarm Clock, Easybeats, Yardbirds and the Steve Miller Band.

If rock and black music were not married enough, there became even closer ties with rock-blues and rock-soul. Sly & the Family Stone were the epitome of the psychedelic soul movement. Several people would sing lead, with the whole raving apparatus onstage making the concert become an electronic happening rather than a sing-song. The group demonstrated what happens to music as the established things break down, with members being black and white, male and female, soulful and freaky.

There were the Chambers Brothers, Buddy Miles, Santana, Otis Redding, B.B. King and Bobby Bland, many of them becoming more progressive rock than R&B let them be.

The British sound of 1969–forward became synonymous with rock-blues, soul-rock, soul-blues and combinations. Stars included Eric Clapton, the Spencer Davis Group, Canned Heat, Joe Cocker, Fleetwood Mac, Savoy Brown Band, Deep Purple and Ritchie Havens.

Blue-eyed soul-rock during this period came from Laura Nyro and The Righteous Brothers. Rock merged with symphony, thanks to The Moody Blues and Procol Harum. There was jazz-rock, courtesy of Ten Years After, Chicago and Blood, Sweat & Tears.

American pop competed with the British Invasion. Stars included the Fifth Dimension, Spanky & Our Gang, Outsiders, Gary Puckett & the Union Gap, Turtles, Rascals, Isley Brothers, who combined the best of pop, soul and rock.

Much of what those years when rock grew into something more than rock and roll affects us today. Progressive rock was born as an alternative, though many see it as a stereotypical way of conforming to a mold. Progressive rock made the album the thing, contrary to 45RPM singles in the early 1960s.

These enlightening years of 1964–1969 brought us mirror music, looking at times we had, quests we made and feelings for the plights of ourselves and others. All the while, rock made it all seem so exciting.

Superstars for all-time: Dean Martin with Frank Sinatra, The Beatles

Chapter 13
EASY LISTENING MUSIC

Middle-of the Road Pop and Ballads that Live for All-Time

Easy Listening music evolved during the Hit Parade years of 1948–1955. It was the dominant music played on the radio, including ballads, perky rhythm and novelty tunes. That music extended from 1956–1979, being played on contemporary hit radio formats.

As the years progressed, Easy Listening music went from being your parents' music to the backbone of pop, country and R&B playlists on the radio. It included hit ballads, covers of older songs, instrumentals, show tunes and a platform for non-rock artists. There were some stations that programmed just Easy Listening music, calling it "good music," "adult contemporary" and "mellow moods." A later moniker for this genre was "lounge music revival."

Rock stars also recorded ballads. The result was that the ballads, along with the rhythms of rock resulted in making a Pop Hybrid that enriched radio playlists, sold compilation albums and rounded out the repertoire of talented singers.

Some of the top singers were also known as crooners, divas and music legends. They included Frank Sinatra, Tony Bennett, Doris Day, Bing Crosby, Rosemary Clooney, Nat King Cole, Dean Martin, Sammy Davis Jr., Jo Stafford, Frankie Laine, Patti Page, Johnnie Ray, Perry Como, Vic Damone, Georgia Gibbs, Billie Holiday, Sarah Vaughan, Billy Eckstine, Carmen McRae, Joni James and Mel Torme.

The rock era brought Easy Listening recording stars, including Barbra Streisand, Johnny Mathis, Brook Benton, Bobby Darin, Peggy Lee, Sam Cooke, Nancy Wilson, Steve Lawrence, Eydie Gorme, Andy Williams, Jerry Vale, Connie Francis, Pat Boone and Della Reese. The 1960s and 1970s added stars like Neil Sedaka, Cher, The Carpenters, Dinah Washington, Matt Monro, Esther Phillips, Frankie Randall, Dionne Warwick, Marilyn Maye, Cleo Laine, Bobby Vinton, B.J. Thomas, Liza Minnelli, Kenny Rogers, Frankie Vaughan, Neil Diamond and Linda Ronstadt.

Pop-rock stars of the 1980s and 1990s kept feet in both genres and established the hybrid of popular music that continues to this day. Those stars included Michael Jackson, Bette Midler, Kenny Loggins, Richard Marx, Howard Jones, Phil Collins, Cyndi Lauper, Gloria Estefan, Paul McCartney, Madonna, Whitney Houston, Billy Joel, Tina Turner, George Michael, Lionel Richie, Debbie Gibson, Elton John, Laura Branigan and Barry Gibb.

In the twenty-first century, along came singers that embraced Easy Listening music and channeled songbook standards to younger audiences. They included Harry Connick Jr. and Michael Buble. Top pop stars in the 2000s include Mariah Carey, Beyoncé, Alicia Keys, Tori Amos, Miley Cyrus, Kelly Clarkson, Sheryl Crow, Taylor Swift, John Legend, Mary J. Blige, Alanis Morissette, Gwen Stefani, Sinead O'Connor, Rihanna and John Mayer.

Noteworthy Pop Superstars

Frank Sinatra was the best-selling recording artist worldwide. In 1935, his mother persuaded a singing group, The Three Flashes, to join him. They became the Hoboken Four and won "Major Bowes' Original Amateur Hour" on radio. Bandleader Harry James hired Frank as a solo singer, and the hits included "On a Little Street in Singapore," "My Buddy" and "Willow Weep for Me."

Tommy Dorsey hired Frank as the singer for his band, recording over forty songs the first year, including "Polka Dots and Moonbeams," "Stardust," "Everything

Happens to Me," "Oh Look at Me Now" and "This Love of Mine." Sinatra went solo in 1943 and became a matinee idol. His 1940s hits included "Night and Day," "The Song is You," "Saturday Night," "Dream," "Nancy," "Day by Day," "How Deep is the Ocean," "Five Minutes More" and "They Say It's Wonderful."

In the 1950s, Frank Sinatra moved to Capitol, with hits including "Witchcraft," "All the Way," "One for My Baby," "I've Got the World on a String," "Mr. Success," "Three Coins in the Fountain," "Learning the Blues," "Angel Eyes," "My Funny Valentine," "The Lady is a Tramp," "Love and Marriage" and "High Hopes." He recorded theme albums, many with that "ring-a-ding" swinging style. He headlined concerts, Las Vegas and hosted two TV series.

In the 1960s, Sinatra founded Reprise, whose roster included Dean Martin, Sammy Davis Jr., Nancy Sinatra, Trini Lopez and Neil Young. Sinatra's Reprise hits included "Strangers in the Night," "Theme from New York, New York," "My Kind of Town," "Softly as I Leave You," "I'll Be Seeing You," "Pocketful of Miracles," "That's Life," "My Way," "Cycles," "It Was a Verry Good Year," "The World We Knew" and "Something Stupid," duet with daughter Nancy.

Perry Como was a positive and friendly constant for sixty years, having hit records and hosting TV shows. A barber in Pennsylvania, he was discovered by bandleader Ted Weems. In 1943, Como signed a recording contract with RCA Victor. He became, along with Frank Sinatra, a favorite among young record buyers. The hits continued for decades.

He became one of the first show hosts in 1948. He hosted fifteen-minute shows, alternating with Eddie Fisher, Dinah Shore and others. By 1955, NBC trod new ground and launched the pioneer one-hour weekly variety series, starring Perry Como.

It became a trademark in the 1950s and 1960s: "Sing to Me, Mr. C." Como became known in the music industry as the "dean of the jukeboxes." His weekly show ended in 1967, and he continued to host TV specials for thirty more years. His penchant for choosing good material was well known, recording ballads plus happy perky rhythms and novelties.

Nat King Cole was the son of a Baptist minister and began playing the family piano at age four. At seventeen, he turned professional musician. His first record was "Straighten Up and Fly Right," based on one of his father's sermons.

The year 1946 was a turning point. Nat King Cole appeared in four movies and was Bing Crosby's summer replacement on radio. Twenty-one-year-old songwriter Mel Torme brought Nat "The Christmas Song." A string arrangement was added over the record company's objections. The record was a hit, and strings were no longer an intrusion on his jazz style. Cole became established as a ballad singer, with hit after hit.

One night, a yogi named Eden Ahbez came backstage to present Nat a song he had written, "Nature Boy," which became a 1948 hit. From the song "Unforgettable" forward, Nat King Cole had a nice association with arranger-conductor Nelson Riddle, the same man who scored swinging and soft hits for Frank Sinatra.

In 1956, Cole signed the highest-salary contract for Las Vegas stage appearances. NBC signed him to host a TV variety show, the first black to do so. Stations in the South would not air it. NBC struggled to get sponsors. Top guest stars (white and black) appeared, working for minimum scale. Regretfully, NBC had to cancel the show after a year and a half. Cole continued to have hit recordings until his 1965 death.

Tony Bennett has been the "singer's singer" since his first two 1951 hits, "Because of You" and "Cold, Cold Heart." The 1950s hits included "Rags to Riches," "Blue Velvet," "Cinnamon Sinner," "King of Broken Hearts," "Not as a Stranger," "Firefly," "In the Middle of an Island," "One For My Baby" and "Climb Every Mountain." My favorite Tony Bennett record of the era was 1954's "There'll Be No Teardrops Tonight," with a swinging band arrangement, a departure from the original by Hank Williams.

Bennett's 1960s hits included "I Left My Heart in San Francisco," "I Wanna Be Around," "The Good Life," "This is All I Ask," "When Joanna Loved Me," "A Taste of Honey," "If I Ruled the World," "Fly Me to the Moon," "Shadow of Your Smile," "Who Can I Turn To," "The Very Thought of You," "Song From the Oscar" and "Yesterday I Heard the Rain."

Tony Bennett covered top hits of the era. The Beatles loved his cover of "Something." Stevie Wonder adored his cover of "For Once in My Life." Barbara Streisand admired his cover of her hit "People." His first jazz album was 1955's "Cloud 7," and the decades saw many more. He continued to record popular recordings for seven decades. Younger singers respected him and performed duets with him in later years, notably Lady Gaga.

Ella Fitzgerald was called the Queen of Song, First Lady of Jazz, an inventor of soul and top female vocalist in the US She was one of the most respected, decorated and award-laden performers of the twentieth century.

Ella was one of the first artists to release albums, in the era of 78RPM singles. She began singing with Chick Webb's band. She had solid record hits with Decca Records from 1938–1954. In 1955, Ella recorded with Verve Records, resulting in the Songbook series. These were definitive collections of Cole Porter, Richard Rodgers & Lorenz Hart, George Gershwin, Johnny Mercer, Duke Ellington, Irving Berlin, Harold Arlen and Jerome Kern. Ella teamed with Louis Armstrong, Duke Ellington, Nelson Riddle and Billie Holiday.

Ella Fitzgerald sang mellow, and she swinged on rhythm tunes, punctuated with jazz scat-singing. She headlined concerts at every major public venue, including Philharmonic in New York and the Hollywood Bowl. I had the pleasure of introducing her in concert twice. She thrived on keeping the audiences delighted and made it look so easy.

Steve Lawrence and Eydie Gorme were the powerhouse couple of pop music. Both came on the music scene in the 1950s, as regulars on "The Tonight Show Starring Steve Allen." Both recorded for Coral Records, then ABC Paramount, United Artists, Columbia and RCA Victor. Their repertoire included standards, teen ballads, show tunes and swinging pop.

The Steve Lawrence hits included "Banana Boat Song," "Party Doll," "Many a Time," "Fraulein," "Pretty Blue Eyes," "Footsteps," "Portrait of My Love," "My Clair De Lune" and "The Drifter." The Eydie Gorme hits included "Too Close For Comfort," "I'll Take Romance," "Love Me Forever," "Your Kisses Will," "You Need Hands," "Gotta Have Rain" and "Tonight I'll Say a Prayer."

In 1962, Steve and Eydie signed with Columbia Records, who recorded them doing teen pop records. Their hits were written by the best, including Carole King, Gerry Goffin, Barry Mann and Cynthia Weil. Steve's hits included "Go Away Little Girl," "Don't Be Afraid Little Darling," "Poor Little Rich Girl," "Walking Proud," "Everybody Knows" and "Yet I Know." Eydie's hits included "Blame It On the Bossa Nova," "Don't Try to Fight It Baby," "Everybody Go Home," "I Want You to Meet My Baby" and "Where Are You Now." The Steve & Eydie duets included "We Got Us," "I Want to Stay Here," "I Can't Stop Talking About You," "That Holiday Feeling" and "We Can Make It Together."

Mel Torme was a band singer in the 1940s, known as "the velvet voice." In the 1950s, he recorded consistently high-quality pop music records, evolving as a jazz singer in the 1960s. His crowning achievement was a song that he wrote in 1945. "The Christmas Song" (Chestnuts Roasting on an Open Fire) was first recorded by Nat King Cole, with strings added by Nelson Riddle. This was the first time that Cole emerged from a jazz combo into being a balladeer with full orchestral accompaniment. Mel Torme's jazz hits stand as classics, notably "Comin' Home Baby" and "Cast Your Fate to the Wind."

Bobby Darin was a multi-faceted talent that scored in every genre of pop music. His first three hits were early rock and roll classics, including "Splish Splash," "Dream Lover" and "Plain Jane." He then took to the genre of his idol, Frank Sinatra. Darin had swinging classics like "Mack the Knife," "Beyond the Sea" (based on the French song "La Mer"), "Multiplication," "Lazy River," "Nature Boy," "Artificial Flowers" and "Clementine." Concurrently, his albums had ballads, show tunes and original compositions.

Darin married actress Sandra Dee, appeared in movies and headlined nightclubs and Las Vegas. He next had country-influenced hits, including "Things," "18 Yellow Roses" and "Treat My Baby Good." Then, more show tunes and standards. In the late 1960s, Bobby Darin recorded folk songs, including "Reason to Believe," "If I Were a Carpenter," "Baby May," "Simple Song of Freedom" and "Long Line Rider."

James Brown, the Godfather of Soul, was known for high-energy performances. Brown recorded a few ballads, including "It's a Man's World," "Prisoner of Love," "These Foolish Things," "If I Ruled the World," "Guess I'll Have to Cry" and "Make This Christmas Mean Something."

The Beatles were the world's most popular group. They recorded easy listening ballads. The second song they performed on the "Ed Sullivan Show" was "Till There Was You," from Broadway's "Music Man." "Yesterday" was covered by 3,000 other artists, making it the most-covered song of all time. Other mellow Beatles songs included "I Will," "A Taste of Honey," "The Long and Winding Road," "If I Fell," "Let It Be," "Julia," "And I Love Her" and "Hey Jude."

Elvis Presley sang ballads, inspired to his ballad style by Teresa Brewer's 1952 hit "Till I Waltz Again with You." Elvis ballads that scored as easy listening hits included "Can't Help Falling in Love," "Love Me Tender," "Fame and Fortune," "It's Now or Never," "Surrender," "Crying in the Chapel," "Peace in the Valley,"

"Are You Lonesome Tonight," "You Don't Have to Say You Love Me," "Don't Cry Daddy" and "American Trilogy."

Mellow songs by rocking stars included:

- "Beth" by Kiss
- "Only Women Bleed" by Alice Cooper
- "Candle in the Wind" by Elton John
- "As Tears Go By," "Heart of Stone," "Angie," "Lady Jane" by The Rolling Stones
- "Tears in Heaven," "Bell Bottom Blues" and "Wonderful Tonight" by Eric Clapton
- "Bridge Over Troubled Water" by Simon & Garfunkel
- "Imagine" by John Lennon
- "Knocking on Heaven's Door" by Bob Dylan
- "Love Hurts" by Nazareth
- "Love Reign Over Me" by The Who
- "I Do for You" and "Heaven" by Bryan Adams
- "True Love Ways" and "Raining in My Heart" by Buddy Holly
- "Wind Cries Mary" by Jimi Hendrix
- "One" and "With or Without You" by U2
- "Babe" by Styx
- "It Must Have Been Love" by Roxette
- "Save Me" and "The Love of My Life" by Queen
- "Oh Sherry" by Steve Perry

Two prominent country stars took decided easy listening turns in their records. Eddy Arnold was known as "the Tennessee Plowboy," and his country hits of the 1940s and 1950s included "Cattle Call," "Anytime," "Prisoner's Song," "It's a Sin" and "Bayou Baby." In the 1960s, Eddy's hits with strings and full orchestral arrangements included "Make the World Go Away," "Turn the World Around," "Somebody Like Me," "What's He Doing in My World" and "The Last Word in Lonesome is Me."

Ray Price had honky-tonk hits like "City Lights," "My Shoes Keep Walking Back to You," "Hey Joe," "Crazy Arms," "Heartaches by the Number" and "Release

Me." In the 1960s and 1970s, he scored on the pop charts with "For the Good Times," "That's All That Matters," "The Night Life," "You're the Best Thing That Ever Happened to Me" and "I Won't Mention It Again."

Two other country singers scored on the pop charts with crossover hits. Marty Robbins had pop songs, backed by Ray Conniff's orchestra and chorus. They included "A White Sport Coat," "Sitting in a Tree House," "The Hanging Tree" and "The Story of My Life." His next records crossed to the pop charts, including "El Paso," "Big Iron," "Ballad of the Alamo," "Don't Worry," "Devil Woman," "Ruby Ann" and "It's Your World."

Jim Reeves started with country hits like "According to My Heart," "Bimbo," "Mexican Joe," "Drinking Tequila," "Hillbilly Waltz," "Four Walls" and "My Lips Are Sealed." He evolved into an easy listening singer, scoring higher on the pop charts with "He'll Have to Go," "Am I Losing You," "The Blizzard," "I Missed Me," "Is It Really Over," "The Storm" and "Distant Drums."

Other country singers with crossover pop hits included Skeeter Davis, Patsy Cline, Faron Young, Sonny James, Dolly Parton, Roger Miller, Charlie Rich, Crystal Gayle, Eddie Rabbitt, Shania Twain, Taylor Swift and Willie Nelson.

Soul singers with pop and easy listening chart appeal included Ray Charles, Teddy Pendergrass, Natalie Cole, Marvin Gaye, The Fifth Dimension, The Commodores, George Benson, Lou Rawls, Diana Ross, Billy Preston, Bill Withers, Patti Labelle, Luther Vandross, Vanessa Williams, Jennifer Holliday, Peabo Bryson, Anita Baker, Billy Ocean and Smokey Robinson.

The Burt Bacharach Songbook

At the beginning of my career, I was a radio DJ. I started in 1958, a golden period for music. Because Payola was looming as an issue in our industry, we were required to keep logs of the songs that were played, containing the labels on which they appeared, the names of the composers and other information. In today's industry, that would be on spreadsheets. However, the manual writing of spreadsheets gave us the chance to digest and learn from the information, developing the skills to better program for our audience.

A bunch of records were in the Top 40 at that time: "Magic Moments" by Perry Como, "Story of My Life" by Marty Robbins, "The Blob" by the Five Blobs,

"Another Time Another Place" by Patti Page and "Hot Spell" by Margaret Whiting. I noted the music composer of these diverse hits was Burt Bacharach.

This was a talent to watch, as I was already familiar with established composers such as George Gershwin, Cole Porter, Irving Berlin and others. I sensed that Bacharach would belong in that upper echelon of icons.

Throughout the 1960s, the music of Burt Bacharach and lyricist Hal David was everywhere. In the rock era, there were still hits and radio airplay for easy listening music, ballads, movie title songs and the like. The playlists gave the public a full array of musical styles. One could spot a Bacharach tune because it had a definable style. Bacharach himself played piano on and conducted many of the important hits.

Through the 1960s and 1970s, Bacharach broadened and experimented in creative directions. There was a Broadway show, a TV musical revue, movie soundtracks and movie tie-in tunes. He hosted TV specials and performed concerts of his music.

In the 1980s, 1990s and 2000s, newer fans and younger generations kept discovering Burt Bacharach. His old songs spoke to them, were updated and re-recorded. He collaborated with other musical talents (Elvis Costello, Carole Bayer Sager and James Ingram). Every decade, he kept getting rediscovered and re-recorded. There were tribute concerts and retrospectives. The Body of Work stood the test of time and appealed to wider audiences.

With the popularity of CDs came the retrospectives of his early work. I acquired the compilations and fell in love with a whole new earlier Body of Work. There were songs that I had played on the radio but had not realized that they were by Burt Bacharach. These included "You're Following Me" by Perry Como, "Be True to Yourself" by Bobby Vee, "Keep Me in Mind" by Patti Page, "Heavenly" by Johnny Mathis, "Along Came Joe" by Merv Griffin, "Mexican Divorce" by The Drifters, "The Night That Heaven Fell" by Tony Bennett, "Blue on Blue" by Bobby Vinton and "Don't You Believe It" by Andy Williams.

I discovered songs from Bacharach's early work that I had never heard before. As a Bacharach fan since 1958, I found myself in the same company as the younger music fans who have discovered his work and found relevance to their contemporary lives. My favorites from these compilations included:

- "I Looked for You" by Charlie Gracie
- "Too Late to Worry" by Babs Tino and Richard Anthony
- "Long Day, Short Night" by The Shirelles, Dionne Warwick and Dawn Penn
- "With Open Arms" by Jane Morgan
- "Sitting in a Treehouse" by Marty Robbins
- "The Answer to Everything" by Sam Fletcher
- "Thirty Miles of Railroad Track" by the Hammond Brothers

These musical gems were magical. Many of those songs stood on their own merits, serving the needs of the performers at the time. They served as building blocks for what became the definitive Bacharach sound.

Chapter 14

FUN ROCK

Party Songs from the Wonder Years

The ultimate party song is "Louie Louie" by the Kingsmen. They formed as a garage band in Portland, OR, in 1957. The song was written by R&B singer Richard Berry in 1955. It was based on the tune "El Loco Cha Cha" by Rene Touzet. In 1963, the Kingsmen picked "Louie Louie" as their second record, following "Peter Gunn Rock." A mistake in the lead vocal was covered by drum fill. Due to microphone positioning, some lyrics in the rocking version were indecipherable, which lead to its mystique. "Louie Louie" became notorious and sounded like a rocking good time. It became a much-imitated classic.

The Beach Boys were the leading Beach Music band. They exemplified good times. Following their "Summer Days and Summer Nights" album, they were working on what became "Pet Sounds." Capitol Records requested another album for fall release. "Beach Boys Party" was recorded with their takes on golden oldies.

The hit song was "Barbara Ann," cover of the Regents' 1959 hit. Other covers on this live party album included the Beatles' "Tell Me Why," spoofs of two of their own hits and "Ruby Baby."

The Coasters were the "clown princes of rock." Their happy, energetic songs brought joy. Best known is "Charlie Brown," inspired by the character in the Peanuts comic strips. Other Coasters hits included "Yakety Yak," "Idol with the Golden Head," "Searching," "Young Blood," "Along Came Jones," "Little Egypt" and "Poison Ivy."

Jan Berry and Dean Torrence were friends with the Beach Boys. In addition to their beach songs, Jan & Dean recorded several fun-time hits, including "From All Over the World," "Popsicle," "Batman," "You Really Know How to Hurt a Guy" and "I Found a Girl."

Frankie Valli & the Four Seasons started as a doo-wop group, The Four Lovers. They borrowed their mainstream pop name from the marquee of a bowling alley in New Jersey. The Four Seasons were produced by Bob Crewe, with legendary arrangements by Charles Calello. The hits continued for years, including "Sherry," "Big Girls Don't Cry," "Walk Like a Man," "Candy Girl," "Dawn (Go Away)," "Ronnie," "Rag Doll," "Save It for Me," "Let's Hang On," "Bye, Bye Baby," "Who Loves You" and "December 1963 (Oh What a Night)." The group was immortalized in the Broadway show and movie "Jersey Boys."

The Cowsills were siblings from Rhode Island, who performed as a vocal group. Their first single on MGM Records was "The Rain, the Park and Other Things," which became a mega-hit. Others included "We Can Fly," "Indian Lake," "Poor Baby" and "Hair."

Inspired by The Cowsills, Columbia Screen Gems TV created "The Partridge Family," as they had done with The Monkees. The mother was played by Shirley Jones, a top singer, known for musicals like "Oklahoma" and "Carousel." Shirley won the Oscar as Best Supporting Actress in the 1960 film "Elmer Gantry." Lead singer was Shirley's stepson David Cassidy, himself an accomplished singer. Other family members were played by actors. The Partridge Family, like the Monkees, proved to be top hitmakers, including "I Think I Love You," "Doesn't Somebody Want to Be Wanted," "I'll Meet You Halfway," "I Woke Up in Love This Morning" and "It's One of Those Nights." Cassidy became a top teen idol. The TV series followed "Brady Bunch" as a most beloved series.

The Archies was a band created for the TV cartoon series "The Archie Show," based on the comic strip and books. The music was recorded by studio session musicians, with Ron Dante on lead and backup vocals by Toni Wine. Another member was Andy Kim, later known for his 1974 hit "Rock Me Gently." Background singers included songwriters Jeff Barry & Ellie Greenwich. Hit records by The Archies included "Sugar, Sugar," which hit #1 in 1969. Other hits included "Bang-Shang-a-Lang," "Feeling So Good," "Jingle Jangle," "Who's Your Baby" and "Sunshine."

Paul Revere & the Raiders were another garage band from Portland, OR. They moved to Los Angeles, CA, and recorded hit records, including "Stepping Out," "Just Like Me," "Kicks," "Hungry," "Good Thing," "Him or Me," "Too Much Talk," "Don't Take It So Hard," "Let Me," "We Gotta All Get Together" and "Indian Reservation." They hosted two TV series produced by Dick Clark, "Where the Action Is" and "Happening '68."

Other recording stars of Fun Rock included Jay & the Americans, Manfred Mann, Lou Christie, The Reflections, Sam the Sham, The McCoys, Sonny & Cher, Gary Lewis & the Playboys, Jay & the Techniques, the Grassroots, Turtles, 1910 Fruit Gum Company, Lemon Pipers, Foundations, Bee Gees, K.C. & the Sunshine Band and Barry White.

Lessons from The Monkees Apply to Success

It was the night of February 9, 1964. Davy Jones stood backstage at the Ed Sullivan Theatre in New York City. As a teenage actor and singer, he was in the cast of the Broadway hit "Oliver," starring British singer Georgia Brown. That was the night that The Beatles invaded America, starring on CBS-TV's "Ed Sullivan Show." There were other acts on the bill that night, including comedian Frank Gorshin, singer Tessie O'Shea, the comedy team of Charlie Brill & Mitzi McCall and the "Oliver" cast to perform scenes from the show for the TV audience.

Jones watched the Beatles perform in their American television debut and mused that he would like to get a gig like that one day. He in fact did two and a half years later, as a cast member in a TV sitcom that was inspired by The Beatles' movie "Hard Day's Night."

Hollywood responded to Beatlemania by putting together a group of actors to play a Beatles type teenage pop group. "The Monkees" was primarily a TV sitcom, and it was produced by Columbia-Screen Gems, whose other hits included "Bewitched," "I Dream of Jeannie," "Gidget" and "The Flying Nun." Stars Michael Nesmith and Davy Jones had music in their repertoire. Mickey Dolenz and Peter Tork were actors who portrayed pop musicians.

The songs were written by Tommy Boyce, Bobby Hart, Neil Diamond, Carole King, John Stewart and other top talents. The recordings featured studio musicians. The Monkees tended to the sitcom and lip-synced two songs per episode, one of them done in a new, original format: as a music video.

Once The Monkees debuted on NBC-TV, they were an instant hit. They primed the pre-teen market for such later luminaries as Herman's Hermits, Paul Revere & the Raiders, The Cowsills and The Partridge Family. The TV show spawned concert tours, and The Monkees had to learn to play instruments. There were guest shots, product tie-in's, merchandising and Monkees fan clubs. All this activity jelled with The Monkees, and it became the prototype for other pop acts packaged as big business.

Arguably, music videos were invented as theatrical shorts. Staging pop hits was popularized in the 1950s by NBC-TV's "Your Hit Parade." Variety shows such as Sullivan's brought the top recording acts to TV audiences. But it was The Monkees who set the prototype for music videos, which MTV later patterned its format.

Monkee Michael Nesmith not only was the creative juice behind music videos, but his mother was another trailblazer in the business world. As a secretary in Dallas, Texas, she invented the office product Liquid Paper.

Critics said that The Monkees were cute mop-tops. They were lambasted for not playing their own music. As the group took control of their instruments on stage, they began receiving respect as legitimate musicians. Their success helped to fund charitable causes.

The Monkees lasted only two seasons on NBC-TV. There was "Head," the Monkees movie. There were recordings and concert tours that outlasted the series. Monkee members Nesmith and Jones had solo careers. Periodically, The Monkees would reunite for nostalgia tours.

There are four basic kinds of companies:

1. Those who created the original concept. The people who created the widget then proceed to run the widget manufacturing and distribution enterprise.

The Monkees were a spoof of The Beatles, who created the widget. Yet, The Monkees created the music video component and the laughter-friendly audience acceptance of what was formerly mis-understood.

2. Companies who take someone else's concepts, perfect them and deliver them to new and different marketplaces than had the original widget firm. The Monkees went into living rooms. Parents saw them as "sons," when they were more suspicious of The Rolling Stones, The Animals, The Doors and other rock groups. The Monkees reached wider audiences, thus priming the pump for other comparable sitcoms.

3. Companies with a short life in the marketplace. They are nurtured as assets to be expanded in other directions, flipped to other sellers or taken to other levels. Though they only ran two seasons, "The Monkees" has been rerun ever since. They turned up on cable TV, VHS tapes and DVD box sets. Remarketed music sets continued to sell on records, tapes, CDs and Internet downloads. The Monkees' two-year stint in the original market has extended to 45 years in the after-market.

4. Companies that team with others, creating a synergy and diversified holding that individual players could not achieve on their own. This embodies the most important dynamic of modern business: Collaborations, Partnering and Joint Venturing. The Monkees led to "Michael Nesmith's Elephant Parts," which led to MTV music videos. Many TV shows have since incorporated music video inserts. Monkees money helped bankroll Woodstock and music videos by other artists.

The Monkees were that rare business enterprise that applied to all four categories of business. Then there is the dynamic of casting the right actors to play the right parts. Most musical groups came together by happenstance, many playing good music but not possessing charm and charisma.

Hank Moore's Top Party Songs Playlist:
- "Rock Around the Clock" by Bill Haley & his Comets, 1955
- "Bo Diddley" by Bo Diddley, 1955
- "Let the Good Times Roll" by Shirley & Lee, 1956
- "Long Tall Sally" and "Tutti Frutti" by Little Richard, 1956

- "Hound Dog," "Jailhouse Rock," "Teddy Bear" and "Don't Be Cruel" by Elvis Presley
- "Wake Up Little Susie" and "Bye Bye Love" by The Everly Brothers, 1957
- "Party Doll" by Buddy Knox, 1957
- "Tequila" by The Champs, 1958
- "At the Hop" and "Rock & Roll is Here to Stay" by Danny & the Juniors, 1958
- "Rocking Robin" by Bobby Day, 1958
- "Summertime Blues" and "C'mon Everybody" by Eddie Cochran, 1958
- "La Bamba" and "Come On Let's Go" by Ritchie Valens, 1958"
- "Splish Splash," "Dream Lover" and "Plain Jane" by Bobby Darin, 1958
- "Rave On" by Buddy Holly, 1958
- "Sweet Little 16" and "Johnny B. Goode" by Chuck Berry, 1958-59
- "Shout" by The Isley Brothers, 1959
- "The Twist" by Chubby Checker, 1961
- "The Wanderer" and "Donna Prima Donna" by Dion, 1963
- "Hey Baby" by Bruce Channel, 1962
- "The Monkey Time" by Major Lance, 1962
- "Hey Baby I'm Dancing" by Barry Mann, 1962
- "Party Lights" by Claudine Clark, 1962
- "Do You Love Me" by The Contours, 1962
- "Palisades Park" by Freddy Cannon, 1962
- "Twist and Shout" by The Isley Brothers, 1962
- "Don't Hang Up," "South Street" and "Crossfire" by The Orlons, 1962
- "Just One Look" by Doris Troy, 1962
- "It's My Party" by Lesley Gore, 1962
- "Locomotion" by Little Eva, 1962
- "Sherry," "Working My Way Back to You," "Opus 17" by Frankie Valli & Four Seasons
- "Baby Workout" by Jackie Wilson, 1962
- "Runaway," "Hats Off to Larry," "From Me to You" and "Stranger in Town" by Del Shannon
- "The Surfing Bird" by The Trashmen, 1963
- "Harlem Shuffle" by Bob & Earl, 1963

- "Heat Wave" by Martha & the Vandellas, 1963
- "Let's Lock the Door" by Jay & the Americans, 1964
- "Fun, Fun, Fun" and "Help Me Rhonda" by The Beach Boys, 1964
- "You Really Got Me" by The Kinks, 1964
- "She Loves You," "Hard Day's Night" and "I Saw Her Standing There" by The Beatles, 1964
- "Shoop Shoop Song" by Betty Everett, 1964
- "I Won't Tell" by Tracey Dey, 1964
- "Maybe I Know," "That's the Way Boys Are" and "The Look of Love" by Lesley Gore, 1964
- "Just Like Romeo & Juliet" and "Like Columbus Did" by The Reflections, 1964
- "Is It True" by Brenda Lee, with Jimmy Page, 1964
- "C'mon and Swim" by Bobby Freeman, 1964
- "This Diamond Ring" by Gary Lewis & the Playboys, 1965
- "In the Midnight Hour" by Wilson Pickett, 1965
- "One, Two, Three" by Len Barry, 1965
- "Satisfaction" by The Rolling Stones, 1965
- "Keep on Dancing" by The Gentrys
- "I Got You (I Feel Good)," "Papa's Got a Brand New Bag" by James Brown, 1965
- "Wooly Bully" and "Little Red Riding Hood" by Sam the Sham, 1965
- "I Want Candy" by The Strangeloves, 1965
- "Treat Her Right" by Roy Head, 1965
- "Love is Strange" and "It's the Little Things" by Sonny & Cher, 1966
- "Let Love Come Between Us" by The Rubber Band, 1966
- "Cool Jerk" by The Capitols, 1966
- "Lightning Strikes" by Lou Christie, 1966
- "Respect" by Aretha Franklin, 1966
- "Wild Thing" by The Troggs
- "You Baby" by The Turtles, 1966
- "Hold On I'm Coming" and "Soul Man" by Sam & Dave, 1967
- "The Pied Piper" and "You Were on My Mind" by Crispian St. Peter, 1966
- "But It's Alright" by J.J. Jackson, 1966

- "Brown Eyed Girl" by Van Morrison, 1967
- "Sweet Soul Music" by Arthur Conley, 1967
- "Cherry Cherry," "You Got to Me" and "Shilo" by Neil Diamond, 1967
- "Build Me Up Buttercup" by The Foundations, 1968
- "Mony Mony" by Tommy James & the Shondells, 1968
- "Everyday People" and "Dance to the Music" by Sly & the Family Stone, 1968
- "Suddenly You Love Me" by The Tremeloes, 1968
- "Midnight Confessions" by The Grass Roots, 1968
- "Nobody But You" by The Human Beinz, 1968
- "Hold Me Tight" and "I Can See Clearly Now" by Johnny Nash, 1968
- "Honky Tonk Women" by The Rolling Stones, 1969
- "Proud Mary" by Creedence Clearwater Revival, 1969
- "Sugar, Sugar" by The Archies, 1969
- "25 Miles" by Edwin Starr, 1969
- "Na Na Hey Hey, Kiss Him Goodbye" by Steam, 1969
- "Moondance" and "Blue Money" by Van Morrison, 1970
- "Venus" by The Shocking Blue, 1970
- "I Want You Back," "The Love You Save" and "ABC" by The Jackson Five
- "Express Yourself" by Charles Wright & the Watts 103rd Street Rhythm Band, 1970
- "Signed, Sealed, Delivered, I'm Yours" by Stevie Wonder, 1970
- "Tears of a Clown" by Smokey Robinson & the Miracles, 1970
- "Joy to the World" by Three Dog Night, 1971
- "Mr. Big Stuff" by Jean Knight, 1971
- "Burning Love" by Elvis Presley, 1972
- "Love Train" by The O'Jays, 1972
- "Superstition" by Stevie Wonder, 1973
- "Rock Me Gently" by Andy Kim, 1974
- "Everlasting Love" by Carl Carlton, 1974
- "Rock the Boat" by The Hues Corporation, 1974
- "Never Can Say Goodbye" by Gloria Gaynor, 1974
- "Rock Your Baby" by George McCrae, 1974
- "Rocking Chair" by Gwen McCrae, 1974

- "Kung Fu Fighting" by Carl Douglas, 1974
- "The Hustle" by Van McCoy, 1975
- "Get Down Tonight" by K.C. & the Sunshine Band, 1975
- "Lady Marmalade" by Labelle, 1975
- "Shame" by Evelyn Champaign King, 1977
- "Christine Sixteen" by Kiss, 1977
- "Staying Alive" by The Bee Gees, 1977
- "Brick House" by The Commodores, 1977
- "Rich Girl," "Out of Touch," "Private Eyes" and "You Make My Dreams Come True" by Hall & Oates, 1976
- "It's Ecstasy When You Lay Down Next to Me" by Barry White, 1977
- "Macho Man" and "Y.M.C.A." by The Village People, 1978
- "Le Freak" by Chic, 1978
- "Instant Replay" by Dan Hartman, 1978
- "My Sharona" by The Knack, 1979
- "Ring My Bell" by Anita Ward, 1979
- "Old Time Rock and Roll" by Bob Seger, 1979
- "We Are Family" by Sister Sledge, 1979
- "Knock on Wood" by Amii Stewart, 1979
- "Another Brick in the Wall" by Pink Floyd, 1980
- "Celebration" by Kool & the Gang, 1981
- "Tainted Love" by Soft Cell, 1981
- "I'm So Excited" by The Pointer Sisters, 1982
- "Mickey" by Toni Basil, 1982
- "Hurt So Good" by John Cougar Mellencamp, 1982
- "Centerfold" by the J. Geils Band, 1982
- "Break My Stride" by Matthew Wilder, 1982
- "Flashdance, What a Feeling" by Irene Cara, 1983
- "Beat It" and "Billie Jean" by Michael Jackson, 1983
- "Talking in Your Sleep" by The Romantics, 1983
- "It's Raining Men" by The Weather Girls, 1983
- "Footloose" by Kenny Loggins, 1984
- "Take on Me" by A-ha, 1984
- "Dancing in the Dark" by Bruce Springsteen, 1984

- "Material Girl" by Madonna, 1985
- "How Will I Know" by Whitney Houston, 1986
- "Don't Worry, Be Happy" by Bobby McFerrin, 1988
- "Unbelievable" by EMF, 1990
- "Jump Around" by House of Pain, 1992
- "Two Princes" by The Spin Doctors, 1993
- "I'm Gonna Be 500 Miles" by The Proclaimers, 1993
- "The Macarena" by Los Del Rio, 1993
- "Mambo No. 5, A Little Bit Of" by Lou Bega, 1999
- "Living La Vida Loca" by Ricky Martin, 1999
- "Who Let the Dogs Out?" by The Baha Men, 2000
- "Move Your Feet" by Junior Senior, 2002
- "Turn Me On" by Kevin Lyttle, 2003
- "The Reason" by Hoobastank, 2004
- "An Honest Mistake" by The Bravery, 2005
- "Listen to Your Heart" by D.H.T., 2005
- "Just the Girl" by The Click Five, 2005
- "Crazy" by Gnarls Barkley, 2006
- "What's Left of Me" by Nick Lachey, 2006
- "Billionaire" by Travie McCoy, 2010

Chapter 15
NON-HITS, BUBBLING UNDER THE CHARTS

Billboard is a music and entertainment trade magazine, published since 1894. It began covering coin-operated machines in 1899. It began covering the motion picture industry in 1907 and coalesced its focus on music in the 1920s. Its first hit parade music list was published in 1936. It introduced "Chart Line," which tracked best-selling records. Billboard had eight charts by 1987 and 28 charts by 1994.

In 1959, Billboard's weekly charts listed the Top 100 songs and records. New releases debuted near the bottom and progressed upward. Numbers of weeks on the charts and rankings determined which songs were hits, worthy of radio of airplay.

The expanded size of the charts reflected the volume of records being made and released in the 1950s and 1960s. Some artists had many releases, and it stood to reason that for all the hits, there might be some misses.

Songs that tracked below 100 were considered non-hits, thus the slogan "bubbling under the hot 100." These are the songs mentioned in this chapter.

Louis Armstrong was a cornerstone of jazz. He started recording in the 1920s, with many classics. In the late 1940s, Armstrong, known affectionately as Satchmo (a nickname bestowed by Bing Crosby), started recording pop vocals. His 1950s hits included "Mack the Knife," "A Kiss to Build a Dream On" and his "Now You Has Jazz" duet with Bing Crosby. In 1964, Armstrong hit gold by singing the title song from Broadway's "Hello Dolly." Seeking to repeat the gold, recording companies had Armstrong sing show tunes.

In 1967, Armstrong recorded the title song to Broadway's "Cabaret." The flip side was a wistful ballad, "What a Wonderful World." The record bombed, ranking 166 on the Billboard charts, missing the Top 100. The only other version of the song to chart at the time was the country version by Eddy Arnold. The song was resurrected in 1988, appearing in the movie "Good Morning, Vietnam." It was re-released as a single and hit gold. The song has been reprised many times in TV commercials and stands as a ballad for all time. Its second breath from the heap of non-charted records is a miracle success story.

There were reasons why songs fell short and failed to chart:

- Too many records were competing for radio airplay.
- Some followed artists' big hits and could not compare.
- Some were releases by artists just before their big breaks.
- Seasons in which records were released may have been wrong.
- Many failed to get the promotional support by record companies.
- Many sounded too much like other popular records.
- Not every title released as Number One material.
- Disc jockeys could not champion every record.
- Many records came from companies that were too small to market entire catalogs.
- Some came from companies that were too big to give promotion to every release.
- Many quality records simply fell by the wayside.
- Some records were later released and achieved chart status the second time around.

RCA Victor released "Get Together" by The Youngbloods in 1967, and it peaked at 52 on the charts. Two years later, RCA re-released "Get Together," and it rose all the way to #5.

Some great non-hits that failed to chart included:

- "Tell Me When" by The Applejacks, 1964
- "I Can't See Nobody" by The Bee Gees, 1967
- "Song From 'The Oscar'" by Tony Bennett, 1966
- "Four Strong Winds" by The Brothers Four, 1963
- *Saxophones" and "Pencil Thin Mustache" by Jimmy Buffett, 1974
- "Brand New Me" by Jerry Butler, 1969
- "He's a Rebel" by Vikki Carr, 1962
- "Am I Blue" by Cher, 1973
- "Splash I" by The Clique, 1967
- "Sweet Gingerbread Man" by The Mike Curb Congregation, 1971
- "Come September" by Bobby Darin, 1961
- *Baretta's Theme, Keep Your Eye on the Sparrow" by Sammy Davis Jr., 1976
- "Rita May" by Bob Dylan, 1977
- "Eleanor Rigby" by El Chicano, 1970
- "Brand New Heartache" by The Everly Brothers, 1960
- "Hello Dolly" by Ella Fitzgerald, 1964
- "Should I Tie a Yellow Ribbon 'Round the Old Oak Tree" by Connie Francis, 1973
- "Substitute" by Gloria Gaynor, 1978
- "Don't Envy Me" by George Hamilton, 1963
- "Something's Happening" by Herman's Hermits, 1969
- "Wanted: One Girl" by Jan and Dean, 1961
- "Plastic Fantastic Lover" by Jefferson Airplane, 1969
- "Dance With a Dolly" by Damita Jo, 1961
- "You Got Style" by Jon and Robin, 1968
- "My Hometown/Room Without Windows" by Steve Lawrence, 1964
- "Lu" and "Wear Your Love Like Heaven" by Peggy Lipton, 1970
- "I'm Coming Back to You" by Julie London, 1963
- "Little Miss USA." by Barry Mann, 1961
- "I Don't Want to Live Without Your Love" by Bobbi Martin, 1965
- "In the Summer of His Years" by Millicent Martin, 1963
- "Magic Town" by Jody Miller, 1965
- "Born Free" by Matt Monro, 1966

- "Ro Ro Rosey" by Van Morrison, 1967
- "Life" by Rick Nelson, 1973
- "Legend" by Poco, 1979
- "Grand Hotel" by Procol Harum, 1973
- "His Song Shall Be Sung" by Lou Rawls, 1972
- "Along Came Jones" by The Righteous Brothers, 1967
- "Take Life a Little Easier" by Rodney Allen Rippy, 1973
- "Searching/So Fine" by Johnny Rivers, 1973
- "What a Shame" by The Rolling Stones, 1965
- "Roll Away the Stone" by Leon Russell, 1970
- "Move It Over" by Del Shannon, 1965
- "Birds of a Feather" by Joe South, 1968
- "In the Middle of Nowhere" by Dusty Springfield, 1965
- "I Love My Dog" by Cat Stevens, 1966
- "Space Captain" by Barbra Streisand, 1971
- "The Cruel War" by Chad and Jill Stuart, 1966
- "Sweet Rhode Island Red" by Ike and Tina Turner, 1974
- "Some Velvet Morning" by Vanilla Fudge, 1969
- "Good Feeling" by War, 1979
- "I Won't Last a Day Without You" and "Inspiration" by Paul Williams, 1973
- "Sunlight" by The Youngbloods, 1969
- "Disco Boy" by Frank Zappa, 1977

Songs That Came Back for Successful Reboots

Then there are songs that failed to chart but which were recorded by other artists and released at later times, with chart success. The Beatles' first release of "From Me to You" failed to chart in 1963 and was covered by an American artist, Del Shannon. When The Beatles hit it big, "From Me to You" was included on one of their albums.

"I Left My Heart in San Francisco" was performed by contralto Claramae Turner, principal with the San Francisco Opera company. She regularly sang it in her stage shows but never got around to recording it. Ralph Sharon discovered the ten-year-old song and took it to Tony Bennett to record. Bennett's 1962 hit immortalized the song. In 1984, the City of San Francisco formalized it as their anthem.

The Isley Brothers were a prolific soul group, with hits including "Shout," "Twist and Shout," "It's Your Thing" and "Fight the Power." They wrote and recorded "Nobody but Me" in 1962 but it failed to chart. In 1968, The Human Beinz recorded the song, and it was a huge hit, their only hit.

Sam Cooke had an album cut called "Yeah Man," but it did not chart as a single. Arthur Conley recorded the song as "Sweet Soul Music," and it was a huge hit in 1967.

"Different Drum" was a song written in 1964 by Michael Nesmith and recorded in 1966 by The Greenbriar Boys, a bluegrass band. Nesmith was a regular on the Monkees TV series and offered the song to the producers of the show, which they turned down. Then, the song was recorded by Linda Ronstadt and the Stone Poneys, and it became a major hit in 1968.

"The Gambler" was written in 1976 by Don Schlitz and appeared on an album by Bobby Bare, though it did not chart. Other country artists were offered the song, but Kenny Rogers accepted it and made it a major hit in 1978.

"Honeycomb" was recorded by Georgie Shaw in 1954 as a big band song. It charted in 1957, with Jimmie Rodgers recording it as a folk-pop hit.

Scott English recorded a song called "Brandy" in 1972. It charted in the UK but not in the US In 1974, Barry Manilow revised the song as "Mandy," which became his first mega-hit records.

Marion Montgomery was a singer that was discovered by Peggy Lee, who recommended Marion to her label Capitol. Montgomery released a song called "That's Life," which did not chart. In 1966, Frank Sinatra recorded "That's Life," and it became a top hit.

"Wild Thing" was written by Chip Taylor and first recorded by The Wild Ones in 1965, failing to gain traction. In 1966, The Troggs recorded "Wild Thing" and hit gold.

Ginger Thompson recorded "Boy Watcher" in 1967, failing to hit the charts. It was retitled "Girl Watcher" and was a 1968 hit by The O'Kaysions.

"Venus in Blue Jeans" was recorded by Bruce Bruno in 1962, which could not chart. It was recorded by Jimmy Clanton and became a hit in the staple of teen pop records.

In 1979, Robert Hazard recorded "Girls Just Want to Have Fun." The song was recorded in 1983 by Cyndi Lauper, and it became one of the premier party records.

In 1974, Larry Weiss wrote and recorded "Rhinestone Cowboy." Its miss on the charts resulted in Glen Campbell recording it the next year, making it one of 1975's top hits.

Chapter 16
ONE-HIT WONDERS

W hen an artist has a hit record and cannot follow it up, that's called a one-hit wonder. Some of the most popular records came from artists who could not obtain further hits.

Not every artist is destined to sustain a long career. Some hits cannot be replicated or even sounded alike in sequels. Some artists only have one hit in them and, thus, a limited body of work. Most recording artists are victims of too much competition from other records, poor-timing and factors beyond their control.

Not every artist can score gold every time. There was a time when the volume of record releases far outweighed the demand. Therefore, many fine recordings fell by the wayside and went unnoticed. Many records never had follow-up releases. Some had second issues that did not hit big. Many one-hit wonders made attempts to come back that failed to materialize.

There are other factors to explain why some hits make it, while others cannot:

- Record companies do not always provide the promotion that is necessary.
- Radio stations cannot play every record and must carefully choose those releases that please the public the most.

- Trends come and go in the music industry. Some songs are hot at one time but may fall short in other seasons.
- While some records are big hits, the time frame for follow-up hits may have passed.
- Small independent record labels cannot compete with the larger companies. Sometimes, they lease out records to larger entities. Other times, artists' output is dependent upon contracts with labels.
- Delays in releases and recording production result in other records taking the chart positions.
- Artists who do follow-up recordings that are in different styles and unrecognizable formats are not accepted well by the public.
- The Billboard Top 100 charts had sub-categories: the Top 20, the Bottom 20 and lower on the charts.

Top Records that Were One-Hit Wonders
- "The Fool" by Sanford Clark, 1956
- "Happy Birthday Baby" by The Tune Weavers, 1956
- "To Know Him is to Love Him" by The Teddy Bears, 1958
- "Little Star" by The Elegants, 1958
- "Susie Darlin'" by Robin Luke, 1958
- "Rama Lama Ding Dong" by The Edsels, 1958
- "Oh Julie" by The Crescendos, 1958
- "One Summer Night" by The Danleers, 1958
- "Down the Aisle of Love" by The Quin-Tones, 1958
- "Tell Him No" by Travis & Bob, 1959
- "You Cheated" by The Shields, 1958
- "Buzz-Buzz-Buzz" by The Hollywood Flames, 1958
- "Endless Sleep" by Jody Reynolds, 1958
- "Money" by Barrett Strong, 1959
- "The Walk" by Jimmy McCracklin, 1959
- "Three Stars" by Tommy Dee, 1959
- "Sandy" by Larry Hall, 1959
- "Angela Jones" by Johnny Ferguson, 1960
- "Mountain of Love" by Harold Dorman, 1960

- "Chills and Fever" by Ronnie Love, 1960
- "Those Oldies but Goodies Remind Me of You" by Little Caesar & Romans, 1960
- "Love You So" by Ron Holden, 1960
- "Please Love Me Forever" by Cathy Jean & the Romantics, 1960
- "Angel Baby" by Rosie & the Originals, 1960
- "I Wish That We Were Married" by Ronnie & the Hi-Lites, 1960
- "There's a Moon Out Tonight" by The Capris, 1961
- "Smoky Places" by The Corsairs, 1961
- "Shout, Shout, Knock Yourself Out" by Ernie Maresca, 1962
- "Soothe Me" by The Simms Brothers (Sam Cooke & Lou Rawls), 1962
- "Dear One" by Larry Finnegan, 1962
- "Let the Little Girl Dance" by Billy Bland, 1962
- "Remember Then" by The Earls, 1962
- "Midnight Mary" by Joey Powers, 1962
- "If You Want to Be Happy" by Jimmy Soul, 1963
- "Hippy, Hippy Shake" by The Swinging Bluejeans, 1964
- "Last Kiss" by J. Frank Wilson & the Cavaliers, 1964
- "Everlasting Love" by Robert Knight, 1967
- "Gimme Good Lovin'" by Crazy Elephant, 1967
- "Cinnamon" by Derek, 1968
- "Rocking Chair" by Gwen McCrae, 1974
- "Life is a Rock but the Radio Rolled Me" by Reunion, 1974
- "Seasons in the Sun" by Terry Jacks, 1974
- "Hooked on a Feeling" by Blue Swede, 1974
- "Disco Duck" by Rick Dees, 1975
- "Wham Bam" by Silver, 1975
- "Don't Give Up on Us" by David Soul, 1976
- "Play That Funky Music" by Wild Cherry, 1976
- "The Boys Are Back in Town" by Thin Lizzie, 1976
- "Afternoon Delight" by Starland Vocal Band, 1976
- "Float On" by The Floaters, 1977
- "Jeans On" by David Dundas, 1977
- "Driver's Seat" by Sniff N' the Tears, 1979

- "Don't Let Me Down" by Santa Esmerelda, 1979
- "Video Killed the Radio Star" by The Buggles, 1979
- "Pop Muzik" by M, 1979
- "Funkytown" by Lipps, Inc., 1979
- "Turning Japanese" by The Vapors, 1980
- "867-5309, Jenny" by Tommy Tutone, 1981
- "Mickey" by Toni Basil, 1982
- "Pass the Dutchie" by Musical Youth, 1982
- "I Melt with You" by Modern English, 1982
- "It's Raining Men" by The Weather Girls, 1982
- "Come On Eileen" by Dexys Midnight Runners, 1982
- "The Safety Dance" by Men Without Hats, 1983
- "Too Shy" by Kajagoogoo, 1983
- "Somebody's Watching Me" by Rockwell, 1984
- "Walking on Sunshine" by Katrina & the Waves, 1985
- "Rock Me Amadeus" by Falco, 1985
- "The Future's So Bright, I Got to Wear Shades" by Timbuk 3, 1987
- "Died in Your Arms" by Cutting Crew, 1987
- "Unbelievable" by EMF, 1990
- "Ice Baby" by Vanilla Ice, 1990
- "There She Goes" by The Las, 1990
- "I Touch Myself" by The Divinyls, 1991
- "Walking in Memphis" by Marc Cohn, 1991
- "Jump Around" by House of Pain, 1992
- "Stay" by Shakespeare's Sister, 1992
- "Would I Lie to You?" by Charles & Eddie, 1992
- "No Rain" by Blind Melon, 1992
- "What is Love" by Haddaway, 1993
- "Two Princes" by The Spin Doctors, 1993
- "I'm Gonna Be 500 Miles" by The Proclaimers, 1993
- "What's Up" by Four Non-Blondes, 1993
- "A Girl Like You" by Edwyn Collins, 1994
- "Send Me on My Way" by Rusted Root, 1994
- "Saturday Night" by Whitfield, 1995

- "Wake Up Boo" by The Boo Radleys, 1995
- "Breakfast at Tiffany's" by Deep Blue Something, 1995
- "How Bizarre" by OMC, 1996
- "In the Meantime" by Spacehog, 1996
- "Your Woman" by White Town, 1997
- "MMM Bop" by Hanson, 1997
- "You're Not Alone" by Olive, 1997
- "Bitter Sweet Symphony" by The Verve, 1997
- "Torn" by Natalie Imbruglia, 1997
- "You Get What You Give" by The New Radicals, 1998
- "Closing Time" by Semisonic, 1998
- "Mambo No. 5, A Little Bit Of" by Lou Bega, 1999
- "Steal My Sunshine" by Len, 1999
- "She's So High" by Tal Bachman, 1999
- "Groovejet, If This Ain't Love" by Spiller, 2000
- "It Feels So Good" by Sonique, 2000
- "Absolutely, Story of a Girl" by Nine Days, 2000
- "Because I Got High" by Afroman, 2001
- "The Ketchup Song" by Las Ketchup, 2002
- "Move Your Feet" by Junior Senior, 2002
- "Stacy's Mom" by Fountains of Wayne, 2003
- "Turn Me On" by Kevin Lyttle, 2003
- "The Reason" by Hoobastank, 2004
- "An Honest Mistake" by The Bravery, 2005
- "Listen to Your Heart" by D.H.T., 2005
- "Just the Girl" by The Click Five, 2005
- "Crazy" by Gnarls Barkley, 2006
- "What's Left of Me" by Nick Lachey, 2006
- "Billionaire" by Travie McCoy, 2010

These Were Too Big and Hard to Follow
- "Sunny" by Bobby Hebb, 1966
- "Elusive Butterfly" by Bob Lind, 1966
- "Expressway to Your Heart" by The Soul Survivors, 1967

- "Angel of the Morning" by Merilee Rush, 1968
- "Na Na Hey Hey, Kiss Him Goodbye" by Steam, 1969
- "Love Can Make You Happy" by Mercy, 1969
- "Morning Girl" by The Neon Philharmonic Orchestra, 1969
- "Kung Fu Fighting" by Carl Douglas, 1974
- "Feelings" by Morris Albert, 1975
- "You Light Up My Life" by Debbie Boone, 1977
- "Ring My Bell" by Anita Ward, 1979
- "Tainted Love" by Soft Cell, 1981
- "Take on Me" by A-ha, 1984
- "Don't Worry, Be Happy" by Bobby McFerrin, 1988
- "Living La Vida Loca" by Ricky Martin, 1999
- "Who Let the Dogs Out?" by The Baha Men, 2000

Instrumental One-Hit Wonders
- "Nut Rocker" by B. Bumble and the Stingers, 1961
- "Popcorn" by Hot Butter, 1972
- "Let's Go" by The Routers, 1962
- "Stick Shift" by The Duals, 1961
- "Percolator Twist" by Billy Joe & the Checkmates, 1962
- "Woo-Hoo" by The Rockateens, 1959
- "Kokomo" by Asia Minor, 1961
- "Axel F" by Harold Faltermeyer, 1983

Novelty Song One-Hit Wonders
- "Alley Oop" by The Hollywood Argyles, 1959
- "Mister Custer" by Larry Verne, 1960
- "Take Me to Your Ladder" by Buddy Clinton, 1960
- "The All American Boy" by Bill Parsons (Bobby Bare), 1959
- "Purple People Eater" by Sheb Wooley, 1958
- "Ding Dong the Witch is Dead" by The Fifth Estate, 1967

Foreign Hits to Make the US Charts Once

"Nel Blu Dipinto Di Blu" by Domenico Modugno was released in 1958. It was Italy's entry into the Eurovision contest and even won the first Grammy Award as Song of the Year. It was subsequently covered by Dean Martin and Bobby Rydell as "Volare."

"Sukiyaki" by Kyu Sakamoto, 1963. It was popular in Japan under the title "Ue o Muite Arukō," which translates as "I Look up as I Walk." The name "Sukiyaki" was chosen for the English version. Sung by Kyu Sakamoto, "Sukiyaki" was number one for three weeks in 1963. An English cover version by A Taste of Honey was released in 1980.

"Dominique" was sung in 1963 by Jeannine Deckers, a French-speaking nun from Belgium, the song is about Saint Dominic, who founded the Dominican Order, of which she was a member.

Other international one hit wonders included:

- "Sailor" by Lolita, 1960
- "Eres Tu" by Mocecades, 1973
- "Dime (Feelings)" by Morris Albert, 1975
- "Der Kommissar" by Falco, 1982
- "99 Red Balloons" by Nena, 1984
- "Rock Me Amadeus" by Falco, 1986
- "La Bamba" by Los Lobos, 1987
- "Macarena" by Los Del Rio, 1996
- "Despacito" by Luis Fonsi and Daddy Yankee, featuring Justin Bieber, 2017

Chapter 17
MUSIC JARGON, GLOSSARY OF TERMS

S heet music includes the notes and words to songs, utilized for playing piano and singing along. Choirs utilize sheet music, with different parts charted. Orchestras and bands utilize sheet music created by arrangers and composers.

Song-sheets were prominent in the early twentieth century. They were inventories of tunes, their authors, their publishers and copyright information. They set categories of music, including cake walks, hesitations, intermezzos, show tunes, piano roll compositions, dances, folk music, instrumentals, marches, the blues, ballads, apparel songs, Dixie songs, tunes about foreign lands, mother songs, name songs, lullabies, war songs and dance crazes.

Public domain material comes from eras before copyrights, notably classical music and folk songs handed down over the years. It includes songs that were not copyrighted or whose coverage expired. This explains why vintage material is often updated with new lyrics.

Woodcuts and engravings are artistic renderings of music icons, including instruments, composers, performers and music being enjoyed by audiences. Designs of the nineteenth century gave way to "clip art" in the twentieth century.

When one gets "images" today from the internet, they are getting what used to be called woodcuts and engravings.

Music coaches work with artists in perfecting their techniques at performance of music. These include vocal coaches, piano teachers, music clinics and "artist in residence" retreats. Similarly, coaches work with composers, arrangers, orchestrators, conductors and management of arts organizations.

The Record Industry

Artists and repertoire executives for each record label set the tone for what is recorded. They identify styles and trends in music, encouraging their recording artists to make the most of the opportunities. One of the most influential was Mitch Miller at Columbia Records in the 1950s. Miller anchored the label to pop music with lilting melodies, musical hooks, novelty songs and commercialized pop versions of country and R&B songs. Miller was succeeded in the rock era by Clive Davis, who nurtured Janis Joplin, Chicago and Blood, Sweat & Tears at the label.

Producers of records oversee the sessions, including the arrangers, conductors, artists, background singers and technical personnel who will record the sessions. Some of the great producers included George Martin, Phil Spector, Nick Venet, Snuff Garrett, Hugo Peretti & Luigi Creatore, Lou Adler, Owen Bradley, Mickie Most, Andrew Loog Oldham, Mitch Miller, Berry Gordy, Don Law, James William Guercio, Tony Hatch, Herman Diaz, Billy Sherrill, John Barry, Norman Petty and Jimmy Bowen.

Many performers became successful producers of their own records, plus those of other artists. This royal roster includes Paul Simon, Chet Atkins, Peter Asher, Smokey Robinson, Herb Alpert, Pharrell Williams, Roy Acuff, Jennifer Lopez, Quincy Jones, Van McCoy, Gordon Jenkins, Shorty Rogers, Nicholas Ashford & Valerie Simpson, Mitch Miller, Jennifer Hudson and Sam Cooke.

Composers write the songs. Most composers work as teams, one doing the music and the other penning the lyrics. Some of the greater composer teams included Richard Rodgers & Lorenz Hart, Richard Rodgers & Oscar Hammerstein, Sammy Cahn & James Vanheusen, George & Ira Gershwin, Burt Bacharach & Hal David, Gerry Goffin & Carole King, John Lennon & Paul McCartney, Doc Pomus & Mort Shuman, Elton John & Bernie Taupin, Barry Mann & Cynthia Weil, Neil Sedaka & Howard Greenfield, Norman Whitfield & Barrett Strong, Jerry Lieber &

Mike Stoller, Mick Jagger & Keith Richards and Eddie Holland, Lamont Dozier & Brian Holland.

Other legendary composers included Cole Porter, George M. Cohan, Johnny Mercer, Marvin Hamlisch, Otis Blackwell, Smokey Robinson, Duke Ellington, Bert Berns, Jimmy Webb, Irving Berlin, Andrew Lloyd Webber, Jerome Kern, Stephen Sondheim, E.Y. Harburg and Allen Toussaint.

Arrangers are hired by record producers to take songs and score them for the sessions. Top arrangers come with knowledge of classical music, jazz and pop music. Many arrangers cut their teeth by working with big bands in the 1940s and 1950s. Some of the great arrangers included Stan Applebaum, whose "Stand By Me" by Ben E. King is still performed decades later. Others included Perry Botkin Jr., Artie Butler, Leon Russell, Marty Paich, Charles Calello, Ray Ellis, Ernie Freeman, Buddy Bregman, Peter Matz, Gene De Paul, Ralph Burns, Robert Russell Bennett, Al Delory, Marty Manning and Jimmie Haskell.

Conductors lead the orchestras and bands on the recording sessions. Some of the great conductors included Percy Faith, Nelson Riddle, Gordon Jenkins, Don Costa, Barry White, Ray Conniff, Leroy Holmes, Billy May, Dave Barbour, Paul Weston, Jimmy Carroll, Victor Young, John Scott Trotter, Garry Sherman, Henri Rene, Hugo Winterhalter, Johnny Mann, Archie Bleyer, H.B. Barnum, Billy Vaughn, Pete King, Claus Ogerman, Russ Case, Mitchell Ayres, Dave Cavanaugh, Bernie Lowe, Hal Mooney, Jack Nitzsche, Don Costa, Nick Perito, Burt Bacharach, Axel Stordahl, Jack Rael, Buddy Cole, Glenn Osser, Frank Hunter, David Carroll, Robert Mersey, Bill Walker, Jack Pleis, Sammy Lowe and Frank Devol. Most of these also had hit instrumental records under their own names.

Record deals are made with labels, overseen by artists and repertoire executives. Most record deals cover several releases. The goal is to develop talent for the record label and nurture the performers in order to achieve best results.

Cut some sides refers to recordings made in the 1920–1950 era. A typical studio session resulting in three "sides" being recorded: both sides of one 78RPM disc and a side for a future release.

Studio musicians worked for hire on various recordings for different producers and artists. Some musicians were freelancers, and others were moonlighting from their regular band or orchestra gigs. Some came from symphony orchestras and played on pop music sessions to broaden their musical expressions. One of the most prolific studio session players was saxophonist King Curtis, who performed on recordings for The Coasters, Lloyd Price, Ruth Brown and Aretha Franklin. King Curtis & the Kingpins had records under their own name. An important studio musician was guitarist Glen Campbell, who subsequently had his own solo singing career.

Background singers worked on most recordings, adding harmony, "call and response," rhythmic support and extra melodies. Many such singers appeared on records, commercials, radio jingles and soundtracks for films. Sometimes, established stars appeared as background singers on their friends' recordings, such as Mick Jagger appearing with Carly Simon on 1973's recording of "You're So Vain." Sometimes, composers such as Carole King, Ellie Greenwich and Laura Nyro did background tracks on recordings of their songs.

Overdubbing was the process of adding to previously recorded tracks. The original version of "Sounds of Silence" by Simon & Garfunkel was an acoustical folk version. Instrumentation was overdubbed to give the recording more of a folk-rock sound. Often strings and other instruments were overdubbed, as were additional voices, to amplify the power of existing recordings. Artists like Les Paul and Eddie Cochran overdubbed themselves playing all the parts. Singers like Patti Page, Andy Williams and Georgia Gibbs overdubbed their own voices as four-part harmony on certain recordings.

Multi-tracking came into common usage in the 1960s. Originally, it was two tracks on the tape, then four and finally up to 16. This allowed for instrumental tracks to be layered over each other, with vocals added later, followed by other touches to create finished products.

House bands appeared on recordings, notable the Wall of Sound on the Phil Spector recordings, with regular musicians and studio musicians added. House bands on radio and TV shows backed the headlining stars and the guest stars. Ray Bloch led the house band on CBS-TV's "Ed Sullivan Show" for twenty-four years. Leaders of NBC-TV's "Tonight Show" house band have included Skitch Henderson, Jose Melis, Milton Delugg, Doc Severinsen, Branford Marsalis, Kevin Eubanks and The Roots.

Music hooks and hangers are instrumental passages that appear at the beginning of recordings and recur throughout them, assuring a memorable performance.

Recordings of the 1960s and 1970s relied upon hooks and hangers as mainstays of commercial hit appeal.

Listening booths were part of retail record stores in the 1940s and 1950s. These were alcoves and enclosed rooms where people could "audition" the latest releases. For teens in the '50s, listening booths created mini-parties, where they could buy records, dance and visit with their friends. The emergence of discount stores and the mass distribution of record sales beyond record shops caused the listening booths to go away.

Record clubs created the path to online record sales. In the 1950s, record companies pushed LP releases with record clubs, offering albums mailed to homes. Customers could audition certain records and keep what they wanted. They collected loyalty points, usually getting two extra records for every ten bought.

Music Distribution

Piano rolls carried eighty-eight notes and were engraved to launch songs on player pianos. Piano rolls were introduced in 1896, with 45,000 titles introduced. The first works by Scott Joplin and George Gershwin were available as piano rolls. The recording industry replaced piano rolls with waxed performances of songs by prominent performers.

Cylinders were invented by Thomas Edison in 1877. His first words spoken into a cylinder recording machine: "Mary had a little lamb." The cylinder recording machine was first developed as office equipment, later known as the Dictaphone. First musical recordings were made on cylinders, which the Edison company continued to market until 1929.

Record players were developed to play discs. The first machines were gramophones, with the speaker looking like a large horn. Thus, the RCA Victor mascot dog Little Nipper was seen listening to the horn, with the slogan "his master's voice."

78RPM was the original speed that records played. It was the first record speed developed in 1888 and was known by recording engineers as "the mother speed," meaning that it produced the best possible sound due to the fast speed. 78RPM recordings featured wide grooves. The first discs were 12" in diameter, with a blank B side. Then B sides were added. The disc size standardized to 10" in 1906. 78RPM recordings continued to be marketed until 1960, though 33-1/3RPM recordings were introduced in 1948 and 45RPM records in 1949.

Albums were introduced in the 1940s. Cardboard covers were accompanied by envelopes featuring 78RPM records. Albums had library binding and included three, four or five discs in sleeves. The term "album" remains to this day, signifying recordings with multiple songs.

45RPM records were light and portable. They were the industry standard for singles, replacing 78RPM breakable discs. They were generally released on non-breakable vinyl. They had large holes, and spindles were on record players to accommodate stacks of 45s.

A variation of the 45RPM single was the Extended Play record. It had two songs on each side, plus a cardboard picture sleeve. EPs often were collections of two singles by an artist, as well as collections of various hits. Some EPs featured songs by multiple artists. Other EPs were abbreviations of LP albums in numbered volumes. EP box sets included all the songs from LPs, in numbered discs.

Records playing at the speed of 33-1/3RPM, also known as LPs, were first introduced in 1948. Pressed on vinyl, the first LPs were in 10" discs, in cardboard picture sleeves. The early LPs featured four songs on each side. LPs then went to 12" discs, with microgroove recording, allowing up to eight songs per side. Expansions to LPs included foldout panels, lyric sheets, two-disc albums and box sets.

Quadraphonic sound was developed in the early 1970s as the next stage past dual stereophonic sound. It was a failure due to technical incompatibilities. The quadraphonic units were much more expensive to produce than two-channel stereo. Very few record releases were made in the quadraphonic format. The process is the equivalent to what is known as 4.0 surround sound.

Solid-state was the music equipment technology of the late-1960s, 1970s and 1980s. Tube receivers were replaced with solid-state technology, notably transistors, microprocessor chips and RAM. This paved the way for the later digital equipment technology.

Reel-to-reel tapes have been the music recording standard since the 1950s. Also known as open-reel recording tape, the process was developed in Germany in the 1930s and perfected by the US military during World War II. Bing Crosby imported reel-to-reel tape from Germany to the US in 1946, so that he could prerecord his radio show. This move signaled the end of live radio shows on networks. In the 1960s, reel-to-reel versions of record albums began releases to the public.

Cassette tapes were smaller and handier. Cassettes were first released in 1962. They came in plastic cases and accommodated up to 120 minutes of recorded material. Record albums were released on cassette. Spoken word recordings, also known as "books on tape," proliferated in the 1970s and 1980s. Cassette decks had the ability to play and record. People often taped off the radio and taped borrowed record albums. Many of us made customized tapes of songs, music genres and favorite artists.

Eight-track tapes were known as Stereo 8 and 8-track cartridges. They utilized reel-to-reel tape, which had a bandwidth double that of cassette tapes. Stereo songs played on four stages in the tape. The format was created in 1964 and was popular through the 1970s, being upstaged by the more popular cassette tapes. One of the problems with 8-tracks was that songs would be interrupted when the tape switched to the next track. 8-tracks were more breakable and did not have the portable convenience of cassettes. After the fad of 8-tracks waned, cassette tape remained the dominant format.

Walkman audio cassette players were introduced in the late 1970s. They were small cassette tape players, with earpieces. Walkman players were used by people "on the go" and were seen in parks, cars and on the jogging trail. Some portable recorders were used for dictating thoughts and ideas (as was the original concept behind Edison's cylinder recording).

Music icons

Chapter 18

CLASSICAL MUSIC
ADAPTED TO POP SONGS

M usic of the masters was adapted for pop tunes. Source melodies came from symphonies, chamber music pieces, operas, ballets and suites. Classical music was known for romantic, melodic works. Great composers wrote memorable compositions that are still performed by orchestras. The piano was a lead instrument, and string charts assured classic status.

With the dawning of pop music in the twentieth century, the classics were often updated as instrumentals for big bands, jazz groups and rock ensembles. Often, pop lyrics were added to create memorable songs that charted well and enjoyed longevity in the public psyche. Most of the classics were in the public domain, and their familiarity with the public assured that pop tunesmiths went back to the well of classical music regularly.

Great composers such as Beethoven, Rachmaninoff, Bach, Chopin, Schubert, Liszt, Brahms, Wagner, Mahler, Verdi, Debussy, Tchaikovsky, Strauss, Rimsky-Korsakov, Ravel and others provided great melodies for pop standards. The popular operas influenced stage musicals, which influenced pop vocals in grandiose ballads.

Eric Carmen's 1976 hit "Never Gonna Fall in Love Again" was based upon Rachmaninoff's "Second Symphony."

Eric Carmen's "All By Myself" was based on the second movement (Adagio sostenuto) of Sergei Rachmaninoff's Piano Concerto No. 2 in C minor, Opus 18, used to underscore the 1945 British film "Brief Encounter." The chorus was taken from the song "Let's Pretend," which Carmen wrote and recorded with The Raspberries in 1972.

Allen Sherman's 1962 satirical song "Hello Muddah, Hello Fadduh, A Letter from Camp Granada" was set to the tune of "Dance of the Hours," the 19th century ballet by Amilcare Ponchiello.

John Denver pulled the tune of the second movement of Tchaikovsky's "Fifth Symphony" for his 1974 love ballad to his wife, "Annie's Song." Lyrics: "You fill up my senses like a night in a forest. Like the mountains in springtime. Like a walk in the rain."

"Candy" by The Astors 1966 had its melody based upon "On the Trail" from "Grand Canyon Suite" by Ferde Grofe. That same classical piece provided music for several of the Phillip Morris cigarette commercials on radio and TV.

Procol Harum's 1967 hit, "Whiter Shade of Pale was inspired by Johann Sebastian Bach's "Sleepers, Wake." It uses the melody of Bach's "Air On a G-String" from his Orchestral Suite #3.

Two Elvis Presley hits had roots in the classics. "I Can't Help Falling in Love with You" was based upon "Plaisir D'Amour," a French love song written in 1784 by Jean-Paul-Egide Martini. "It's Now Or Never" was inspired by the operatic "O Sole Mio" by Eduardo di Capua, also known as the Cornetto song.

The Elegants, doo-wop group from New York had a 1959 hit with "Little Star," based upon Mozart's first composition at age 5, "Twinkle Twinkle Little Star."

"Mr. Paganini" by Ella Fitzgerald in 1960 was a tribute to Niccolo Paganini, celebrated Italian violinist and composer of the early 19th century, one of the most influential on modern violin technique.

"Pavanne" from "Symphonette No. 2" was written by Morton Gould in 1938. Glenn Miller had the hit in 1939 with a swinging big band version of "Pavanne." Miller had "Pavanne" on the flip side of "Little Brown Jug," which was based upon a children's song.

Rock group Queen styled its 1984 hit "It's A Hard Life" after the melody from Ruggero Leoncavallo's "Vesti La Giubba,'" from his opera "Pagliacci." The original operatic version was recorded in 1904 by Enrico Caruso.

Tommy Dorsey's 1937 big band hit "Song of India" came from the aria "Pesniā Indiĭskogo Gostiā" from Nikolai Rimsky-Korsakov's 1896 opera "Sadko." Singer Lesley Gore added lyrics in 1963, and it became her hit recording "Just Let Me Cry."

"I'm Always Chasing Rainbows" from 1941 took its melody from Frederic Chopin's 1834 "Fantaisie-Impromptu."

R&B superstar Jackie Wilson was suited to hyper-emotional pop versions of classical music. Writers turned "Vesti La Giubba" from the opera "I Pagliacci" into "My Empty Arm." Tchaikovsky's First Piano Concerto was turned into "Alone At Last." Jackie Wilson also recorded "Night," an adaptation of the aria in which Delilah bewitches Samson in Saint-Saens' opera "Samson Et Dalilah."

The Toys had a number-one hit in 1965 with "A Lover's Concerto," with lyrics added to Johann Sebastian Bach's, "Minuet in G."

The Beethoven-meets-hip-hop anthem "I Can" was recorded in 2003 by rapper and artist Nas. The song encourages youth to pursue their dreams and stay drug-free, to the tune of Ludwig van Beethoven's "Fur Elise."

The hit songs "Stranger in Paradise" and "Baubles, Bangles, and Beads" are from the Broadway and movie musical "Kismet." Music in the show was taken from Alexander Borodin's "Prince Igor."

Simon & Garfunkel's 1970 hit "El Condor Pasa (If I Could)" featured lyrics by Paul Simon, written to the tune of an 18th century folk melody from Peru.

"Musetta's Waltz" from Giacomo Puccini's opera "La Boheme" spawned two hits. It was given two sets of pop lyrics, "You" by Sammy Kaye in 1952 and "Don't You Know" in 1959 by Della Reese.

"Greensleeves" is a traditional English folk song, dating back to 1580. Holiday songs with the same tune began circulating in 1686. The most popular adaptation was "What Child is This," written in 1865.

Sting's 1986 hit "Russians" was based on Sergei Prokofiev's "Romance Melody" in his "Lieutenant Kije Suite."

The Beach Boys recorded "Lady Lynda" in 1979 for their "L.A. Light" album. The song was put in baroque to the tune of Johann Sebastian Bach's 1720 composition "Jesu, Joy of Man's Desiring." Apollo 100's 1972 instrumental "Joy" was based on the same tune.

"Nut Rocker" was an instrumental based on Tchaikovsky's 1892 composition "Nutcracker Suite." The 1962 version was by B. Bumble & the Stingers. The 1972 version was by Emerson, Lake & Palmer.

The 1961 instrumental "Asia Minor" by Kokomo (pianist Jimmy Wisner) was based upon Edvard Grieg's "Piano Concerto in A Minor."

Walter Murphy studied classical and jazz piano at the Manhattan School of Music. He was an arranger for Doc Severinsen and the "Tonight Show" orchestra. He led a band of studio musicians. They record library music cues for the Major/Valentino label. One of the library tracks was released as a commercial recording. It was "A Fifth of Beethoven" in 1976, based on Ludwig van Beethoven's "Fifth Symphony," written 1804-1808.

In 1956, rock n' roll star Chuck Berry scored with a rocking hit, "Roll Over Beethoven," In 1974, Jeff Lynne and The Electric Light Orchestra re-recorded the song, interspersed with melodies from Ludwig van Beethoven's "Fifth Symphony."

The Mindbenders' 1966 hit "A Groovy Kind of Love" uses the main theme from Muzio Clementi's "Sonatina No. 5, Third Movement."

Barry Manilow's 1975 hit "Could it be Magic" is from Frederic Chopin's 1839 "Prelude in C Minor, Opus 28, Number 20."

"Go West" was recorded in 1992 by The Village People and in 1993 by The Pet Shop Boys. It is set to the tune of Pachelbel's "Canon in D."

The band Yes recorded "Cans and Brahms" on their 1971 album "Fragile," based on the third movement of Johannes Brahms' "Third Symphony."

In 1874, "Piano Concerto No. 1 in B-Flat Minor, Opus 23" was composed by Pyotr Ilyich Tchaikovsky. In 1938, the tune was used as theme song for Orson Welles' "Mercury Theatre on the Air" radio show. 1941, Freddy Martin added lyrics, making it "Tonight We Love," his band's theme song.

In 1938, Larry Clinton recorded "My Reverie," based on Achille-Claude Debussy's 1890 composition "Reverie."

Lou Christie's 1966 hit "Rhapsody in the Rain" had music based upon Tchaikovsky's "Romeo And Juliet."

Lou Christie's other 1966 hit "Painter" had music based upon Wagner's 'Ride of the Valkyries," from "Die Walküre," which is part of the composer's famous "Ring Cycle."

Classical Music Influences

Neil Sedaka was one of pop music's hottest stars. He studied classical piano at the Julliard School of Music, learning to perform the classics. He played the chimes on a rock n' roll recording in 1956, "Church Bells May Ring" by The Five Willows. Then came his singing career and a string of hits on RCA Victor, including "Oh Carol," "Breaking Up Is Hard To Do," "Calendar Girl," "Happy Birthday, Sweet Sixteen" and "Next Door to An Angel." He wrote songs for other artists, including "Where the Boys Are" for Connie Francis, "Working on a Groovy Thing" for Patti Drew and "Puppet Man" for The Fifth Dimension. In 1996, Neil Sedaka got back to his classical music roots. His album "Classically Sedaka" had his own new lyrics added to classical music. He toured the world, presenting concerts of those songs with symphony orchestras.

Many pivotal figures popularized classical music for the wider audiences, opening the doors for musical appreciation and pop music adaptations. These included Arthur Fiedler, Andre Previn, Van Cliburn, Beverly Sills, Placido Domingo, Jan Peerce, Luciano Pavarotti, Itzak Perlman, Enrico Caruso, Mario Lanza, Leontyne Price and Robert Merrill.

Several notable figures in pop music were trained in classical music. These included Mitch Miller, John Williams, The Piano Guys, Ferrante & Teicher, Liberace, Frankie Carle, Roger Williams, Skitch Henderson, Ray Bloch and Percy Faith. They are discussed in in the "Musical Directors" chapter.

Some pop stars got their names from the classical music realm. Engelbert Humperdinck was born Arnold George Dorsey. His name was chosen to honor the nineteenth century German composer of operas such as "Hansel and Gretel," "The Christmas Dream" and "Sleeping Beauty."

P.D.Q. Bach is the creation of musician Peter Schickele. These compositions by Schickele are attributed to the forgotten son of Bach. While paying tribute to the genre of Bach, this material is comical in nature and represents fun pop listening. P.D.Q. Bach recordings were made from 1965–1998 and the group toured over five decades.

The Swingle Singers formed in Paris, France, in 1962, directed by Ward Swingle. Eight singers performed a cappella, with rhythmic renditions of classical and pop tunes. Several of their tunes have been used in TV shows, including "Sex in the City," "The Two Ronnies," "The West Wing," "Miami Vice" and Glee." Their music appeared in movies such as "Wedding Crashers" and "Thank You for Smoking." The group created the London A Cappella Festival and won five Grammy awards.

Classics Everywhere in Pop Music

One of the great sources of pop hits, Motown, had strong classical influences. Musicians in the house band, The Funk Brothers, had classical and jazz experience. Gordon Staples led the Motown string section on recordings requiring full orchestration. Staples also served as the concertmaster of the Detroit Symphony Orchestra. This explains classical riffs in many Motown arrangements.

Motown hits with classical riffs included "My Girl" and "Just My Imagination" by The Temptations, "Ain't No Mountain High Enough" by Marvin Gaye & Tammi Terrell and "What Becomes of the Broken Hearted" by Jimmy Ruffin. These included Four Tops recordings "Reach Out I'll Be There," "Bernadette," "Standing in the Shadows of Love" and "Still Water of Love."

Diana Ross & the Supremes songs with classical string flourishes by Gordon Staples included "I Hear a Symphony," "Stop in the Name of Love," "Love Child" and "Someday We'll Be Together." Martha & the Vandellas songs with classical string flourishes included "Live Wire," "In My Lonely Room" and "Love Makes Me Do Foolish Things."

Classical music with pop arrangements served as themes for movies, radio and television programs. In 1938, the radio show "The Lone Ranger" chose the finale of Gioachino Rossini's 1829 composition "William Tell Overture" (the last of his 39 overtures) as its signature theme. The piece was also used as theme for the 1956 TV series "The Adventures of William Tell," with lyrics added.

The theme for radio's "The Green Hornet" was "Flight of the Bumble Bee" by Rimsky-Korsakov. Big band recordings were made by Harry James and Ralph Marterie. "Bumble Boogie" was the rock instrumental in 1961 by B. Bumble & the Stingers. The disco instrumental was "Flight '76" by Walter Murphy and the Big Apple Band. "The Green Hornet" (Britt Reid) was the cousin of "The Lone Ranger" (John Reid).

The hit movie, *10,* starred Bo Derek. The love scenes were to the tune of Ravel's "Bolero." The popularity of that film caused an avalanche of customers to classical music sections of record stores, requesting recordings of "Bolero."

Chapter 19
1970s MUSIC, THE WORLD'S CULTURE

Music of the 1970s was diverse and dynamic. Soul was everywhere. Rock got progressive. Singer-songwriters influenced the world with quality compositions. Disco raised the dancing fever pitch. Pop ballads were influential. Record albums came of age. Country music matured. Pop singers stretched their expanse with new material. Novelty tunes were plentiful. And 1950s nostalgia swept the country.

By the 1970s, the quantity of music started shrinking. There was almost half the amount of music that was released in the 1960s. Radio stations began playing fewer songs every hour because records had gotten longer. Long album tracks were played on the radio, along with singles.

Radio stations started tightened the music playlists. The Top 100 of the 1950s shrank to the Top 40 in the 1960s, then to the Top 20 in the 1970s. The amount of time where there were no repeats got shorter. FM stations started playing continuous music, which reduced the appeal of personality radio. Some stations began simulcasting others. There were fewer radio stations running recorded music because many switched to news and talk formats.

Stars to come out of 1960s groups became major headliners in the 1970s. They included Linda Ronstadt, Rod Stewart, Frankie Valli, Lou Rawls, Michael Jackson, Eric Clapton, Diana Ross, David Bowie, Mac Davis, Billy Preston, Joe Cocker, Elton John, Paul Simon, Kenny Rogers and Bob Seger.

When rock and roll got progressive, it lost the roll. It merged with pop. In the 1970s, A new generation joined the youth movement. The decade saw experimentation, and rock matured. Terms apply to the music that merged: hard rock, folk rock, acid rock, jazz rock, soul rock, blues rock and the inevitable commercial copies of the trailblazers.

The Beatles broke up in 1970, after helping to revolutionize music in the 1960s. There were Beatle spinoffs. Paul McCartney, John Lennon, George Harrison and Ringo Starr all enjoyed hit recordings on the Beatles' Apple label. Other Beatles friends to record for Apple included Badfinger, Mary Hopkin, James Taylor and Billy Preston.

The World's Music

In the 1960s, international music started entering the American pop charts. It really took hold in the 1970s.

Nederpop, also known as Dutch pop music, took hold in the late 1960s and throughout the 1970s. They sang phonetically in English, with strong pop melodies, musical hooks and quality production for the world market. The Shocking Blue's biggest hits were "Venus" and "Mighty Joe" in 1970. Mouth & MacNeil hit the charts in 1972 with "How Do You Do." Focus climbed the charts in 1971 with "Hocus Pocus." Golden Earring had "Radar Love" in 1973 and "Twilight Zone" in 1982. Kayak called their presentation "art rock," with 1974 hits "Wintertime" and "We Are Not Amused." In 1970, The Tee Set hit big with "Ma Belle Amie" and "If You Believe in Love." The George Baker Selection hit the states in 1970 with "Little Green Bag," and its other huge hit was 1975's "Paloma Blanca."

Jeanne-Paule Marie Deckers was known as Sœur Sourire (French for "Sister Smile") and often called The Singing Nun in English-speaking countries. She was a Belgian singer-songwriter and a member of the Dominican Order in Belgium. Her 1963 hit "Dominique" topped record charts. Her appearance on CBS-TV's "Ed Sullivan Show" resulted in a 1966 MGM movie made about her.

Sister Janet Mead was an Australian Catholic nun. For her 1974 pop-rock version of "The Lord's Prayer," she received a Grammy nomination and Golden Gospel Award.

Jose Feliciano, from Puerto Rico, sang Latin folk ballads in New York City clubs. He recorded several English language hits on RCA Victor in the late 1960s. His biggest hit was the Christmas classic "Feliz Navidad," sung in English and Spanish.

Morris Albert, from Sao Paulo, Brazil, became an international singing star in 1975 with "Feelings." There was a South American version called "Dime."

Julio Iglesias, from Madrid, Spain, won a 1968 international song festival. He recorded albums throughout the 1970s. He moved to Miami, FL, in 1979 and recorded in multiple languages ever since. He recorded duets with major US stars, the biggest being 1984's "To All the Girls I've Loved Before" with Willie Nelson.

Mocedades represented Spain in the 1973 Eurovision Song Contest. Their winning number, "Eres Tu," became an international sensation.

The biggest international recording artist was ABBA. They won the Eurovision Song Contest in 1974 with "Waterloo." They recorded primarily in English, with certain songs in other languages. The ABBA hits are a pop soundtrack to the 1970s, including "Fernando," "SOS," "Dancing Queen," "Knowing Me, Knowing You," "Take a Chance on Me," "The Name of the Game" and "The Winner Takes It All." The group disbanded after ten years, but their music lived on. "Mamma Mia" was an ABBA tribute musical on Broadway and in two movies.

Singer-Songwriters of the 1970s

In the Tin Pan Alley era of music, there were songwriters, and there were those who performed the songs. In the 1950s, there were a few who wrote their own songs, including Buddy Holly, Patsy Cline, Chuck Berry, Paul Anka, John Lee Hooker and Hank Williams. The 1960s British Invasion brought groups like The Beatles, who were adept at writing songs, crafting the arrangements and performing them on records, TV and in concerts. Other 1960s singer-songwriters included Paul Simon, Bob Dylan, Donovan, Harry Nilsson, Laura Nyro, Roger Miller, Smokey Robinson and Crosby, Stills, Nash & Young.

The 1970s was the era of the singer-songwriters. Elton John was the biggest rock-pop star of the decade. His hits included "Your Song," "Friends," "Levon,"

"Tiny Dancer," "Rocket Man," "Honky Cat," "Crocodile Rock," "Daniel," "Goodbye Yellow Brick Road," "Bennie & the Jets," "Philadelphia Freedom," "Someone Saved My Life Tonight," "Island Girl," "Don't Let the Sun Go Down on Me," "Sorry Seems to Be the Hardest Word" and "Don't Go Breaking My Heart." His career and music were dramatized in the movie "Rocketman."

Carole King was a songwriter in the 1960s. She wrote hits for Bobby Vee, Aretha Franklin, Steve Lawrence, The Monkees, The Drifters, Herman's Hermits, Little Eva, The Cookies and many more. In 1971, she released "Tapestry," which stands as one of the top albums of all-time. Her 1970s hits were plentiful and a staple of radio programming. Her 1970s hits included "It's Too Late," "So Far Away," "Sweet Seasons," "Been to Canaan," "Believe in Humanity," "Corazon," "Jazzman," "Nightingale" and "Only Love is Real." Her career was tributed in the Broadway musical "Beautiful."

Paul Simon wrote the songs that he and Art Garfunkel performed in the 1960s. After Simon & Garfunkel ended in 1971, Paul pursued a solo career. His string of 1970s hits included "Mother and Child Reunion," "Kodachrome," "Loves Me Like a Rock," "Gone at Last," "50 Ways to Leave Your Lover," "Still Crazy After All These Years" and "American Tune."

Neil Diamond wrote pop hits for other singers, including Jay & the Americans, Ronnie Dove and The Monkees. He launched his solo singing career in 1966 with "Solitary Man," "Cherry Cherry" and "You Got to Me." In the '70s came "Crackling Rosie," "I Am, I Said," "Stones," "Song Sung Blue," "Be," "Skybird," "If You Know What I Mean," "Desiree," "You Don't Bring Me Flowers" and "Forever in Blue Jeans."

Cat Stevens, from London, England, had two albums to be certified platinum, 1970's "Tea for the Tillerman" and 1971's "Teaser and the Firecat." His 1972 album "Catch Bull at Four" went to #1 on Billboard in 1972. His song "First Cut is the Deepest" has been a hit for four other artists. His hits include "Wild World," "Moon Shadow," "Peace Train," "Morning Has Broken," "Sitting," "The Hurt," "Oh Very Young," "Another Saturday Night," "Ready," "Two Fine People" and "Remember the Days of the Old Schoolyard."

James Taylor is one of the best-selling artists of all time, more than 100 million records. He was born in Boston, MA, where his father was a physician. He learned the guitar, inspired by the folk music of Woody Guthrie. His first recording was for Apple Records, produced by Peter Asher. He moved to California, keeping Asher as his manager and record producer on the Warner Bros. label. His first LP "Sweet Baby James" won Album of the Year. The hits included "Fire and Rain," "Country Road," "You've Got a Friend," "Long Ago and Far Away," "Don't Let Me Be Lonely Tonight," "Mockingbird," "How Sweet It Is," "Mexico," "Handy Man," "Your Smiling Face" and "Up on the Roof."

Carly Simon was one of the most popular singer-songwriters of the 1970s. She started singing with her sister Lucy in a folk group. Her 70s hits included "That's the Way I've Always Heard It Should Be," "Anticipation," "Legend in Your Own Time," "You're So Vein," "The Right Thing to Do," "Mockingbird," "Haven't Got Time for the Pain," "Attitude Dancing," "Waterfall," "Nobody Does It Better" (from the James Bond film "The Spy Who Loved Me"), "You Belong to Me" and "Vengeance."

John Denver began as a folk singer, a member of the Chad Mitchell Trio. He wrote "Leaving on a Jet Plane" for Peter, Paul & Mary. He recorded and released 300 songs, 200 of which he wrote. He had 33 albums and singles which were certified as Gold and Platinum. His biggest hits were "Take Me Home, Country Roads," "Friends with You," "Everyday," "Goodbye Again," "Rocky Mountain High," "I'd Rather Be a Cowboy," "Sunshine on My Shoulders," "Annie's Song," "Back Home Again," "Sweet Surrender," "Thank God I'm a Country Boy," "I'm Sorry," "Calypso," "Fly Away," "Looking for Space" and "My Sweet Lady."

Don McLean was a child on Feb. 3, 1959, when he heard of Buddy Holly's plane crash. As a pop-folk singer, he told the story of that day and chronicled the growth of pop culture in 1971's "American Pie," which became a generational anthem. McLean's other hits have included "Vincent," "Dreidel," "Castles in the Air," "If We Try," "Wonderful Baby" and "Crying." McLean was tributed in the Roberta Flack hit "Killing Me Softly with His Song."

Jim Croce, from Philadelphia, PA, was a pop-folk singer whose hits included "You Don't Mess Around with Jim," "Operator," "Bad Leroy Brown," "I Got a Name," "Time in a Bottle," It Doesn't Have to Be that Way" (Christmas song) and "I'll Have to Say I Love You in a Song." As his career was rising, Croce was killed in a plane crash on Sept. 20, 1973.

Billy Joel is a major recording artist and concert draw. His 1970s hits include "Piano Man," "Just the Way You Are," "Moving Out," "Only the Good Die Young,"

"She's Always a Woman," "My Life," "Big Shot" and "Honesty." His greatest hits albums are among the industry's best-selling compilations.

Jackson Browne's signature album was 1977's "Running on Empty." He co-wrote "Take It Easy" for The Eagles. His hits included "Doctor My Eyes," "Rock Me on the Water," "Redneck Friend," "Here Come Those Tears Again," "The Pretender," "Stay" and "The Load-Out."

Other singer-songwriters of the 1970s included Van Morrison, Kenny Loggins, Gordon Lightfoot, Al Stewart, Boz Scaggs, Joni Mitchell, Barry Manilow, Judy Collins, Dave Mason, Arlo Guthrie, Todd Rundgren, Dan Fogelberg, Stevie Wonder and Lionel Richie.

Led Zeppelin is considered one of the most influential bands in rock history. They formed in London, with members from the 1960s group The Yardbirds. Most of the songs were written by Jimmy Page. Their hits included "Whole Lotta Love," "Immigrant Song," "Black Dog," "Rock and Roll," "Over the Hills and Far Away," "Stairway to Heaven," "Trampled Under Foot" and "Fool in the Rain."

Queen was dramatized in the 2018 movie "Bohemian Rhapsody," meaning the life of artists. Queen formed in London in 1970. Their hit streak began in 1975 with "Killer Queen." Then followed "Bohemian Rhapsody," "You're My Best Friend," "Somebody to Love," "We Are the Champions," "Crazy Little Thing Called Love," "Play the Game" and "Another One Bites the Dust." Queen wrote music for the soundtrack of "Flash Gordon."

Fleetwood Mac was formed as a British blues band in 1967. Following band changes, they moved to California to record. Lindsey Buckingham joined as lead guitarist and Stevie Nicks as lead singer, giving the band more of a pop-rock sound. Their LP "Fleetwood Mac" hit #1, with 1977's "Rumors" winning the Grammy Award as Album of the Year. Their biggest hits included "Go Your Own Way," "Dreams," "Don't Stop," "Over My Head," "Say You Love Me," "Rhiannon," "You Make Loving Fun," "Tusk" and "Sara." They are one of the best-selling bands, with 120 million records worldwide.

Groups who wrote their own songs included Electric Light Orchestra, The Eagles, Steely Dan, Seals & Crofts, The Moody Blues, America, The Bee Gees, Fleetwood Mac and Crosby, Stills, Nash & Young.

Hank Moore's Top 1970s Rock Songs Playlist

- "Black Magic Woman" and "Oye Como Va" by Santana, 1970
- "Green Eyes Lady" by Sugarloaf, 1970
- "Mississippi Queen" by Mountain, 1970
- "The Rapper" by The Jaggerz, 1970
- "Vehicle" by the Ides of March, 1970
- "All Right Now" by Free, 1970
- "The Letter" and "Cry Me a River" by Joe Cocker, 1970
- "Up on Cripple Creek" and "Rag Mama Rag" by The Band, 1970
- "Closer to Home" and "Feeling Alright" by Grand Funk Railroad, 1971
- "Games" by Redeye, 1971
- "Get It On" by Chase, 1971
- "I Hear You Knocking" by Dave Edmunds, 1971
- "Them Changes" by Buddy Miles, 1971
- "Do You Know What I Mean" by Lee Michaels, 1971
- "Cry Baby," "Me & Bobby McKee," "Get It While You Can" by Janis Joplin, 1971
- "Maggie Mae" by Rod Stewart, 1971
- "Layla" by Derek & the Dominos, 1971
- "I'd Love to Change the World" by Ten Years After, 1971
- "Brown Sugar" and "Wild Horses" by The Rolling Stones, 1971
- "Signs" by Fire Man Electrical Band, 1971
- "Eighteen" and "School's Out" by Alice Cooper, 1971-72
- "Hot n' Nasty" by Humble Pie, 1972
- "Tumbling Dice," "Happy" and "Angie" by The Rolling Stones, 1973
- "Looking for a Love," "Give it to Me" and "Must of Got Lost" by the J. Geils Band
- "Smoke on the Water by Deep Purple," 1973
- "China Grove" and "Long Train Running" by The Doobie Brothers, 1973
- "The Joker" by the Steve Miller Band, 1973
- "Right Place, Wrong Time" by Dr. John, 1973
- "Free Ride" by Edgar Winter, 1973
- "Smoking in the Boys' Room" by Brownsville Station, 1973

- "We're an American Band" and "Walk Like a Man" by Grand Funk Railroad, 1973
- "Rambling Man" by The Allman Brothers, 1973
- "Little Willy," "Ballroom Blitz," "Fox on the Run" and "Love is Like Oxygen" by The Sweet
- "Rock and Roll Hootchie Coo" by Rick Derringer, 1974
- "Hooked on a Feeling" by Blue Swede, 1974
- "Sweet Home Alabama" and "Freebird" by Lynard Skynard, 1974
- "I Shot the Sheriff" by Eric Clapton, 1974
- "Can't Get Enough" by Bad Company, 1974
- "Taking Care of Business" and "You Ain't Seen Nothing Yet" by Bachman-Turner Overdrive
- "Rock On" by David Essex, 1974
- "Born to Run" by Bruce Springsteen, 1975
- "You Are So Beautiful" by Joe Cocker, 1975
- "I'm on Fire" by Dwight Twilley, 1975
- "That's the Way I Like It" and "Get Down Tonight" by K.C. & the Sunshine Band, 1975
- "Love Hurts" by Nazareth, 1975
- "Slow Ride" by Foghat, 1976
- "Don't Fear the Reaper" by Blue Oyster Cult, 1976
- "Saturday Night" by the Bay City Rollers, 1976
- "Dream Weaver" and "Love is Alive" by Gary Wright, 1976
- "Show Me the Way," "Baby I Love Your Way" and "Do You Feel Like We Do" by Peter Frampton, 1976
- "More Than a Feeling" and "Don't Look Back" by Boston, 1977
- "Magic Man," "Barracuda," "Crazy on You" and "Heartless" by Heart
- "Cat Scratch Fever" by Ted Nugent, 1977
- "Jet Airliner" by Steve Miller Band, 1977
- "Who Are You" and "Squeeze Box" by The Who
- "Feels Like the First time," "Cold as Ice," "Hot Blooded, and "Double Vision" by Foreigner
- "Give a Little Bit," "The Logical Song" and "Take the Long Way Home" by Supertramp

- "Help is On the Way," "Reminiscing," "Lonesome Loser," "Lady" by Little River Band
- "Werewolves of London" by Warren Zevon, 1978
- "Baby Hold On" and "Two Tickets to Paradise" by Eddie Money, 1978
- "Miss You," "Beast of Burden" and "Shattered" by The Rolling Stones, 1978
- "Life's Been Good" by Joe Walsh, 1978
- "Lay Down Sally," "Wonderful Tonight" and "Promises" by Eric Clapton, 1978
- "Hold the Line" by Toto, 1978
- "Hollywood Nights" by Bob Seger, 1978
- "Instant Replay" and "I Can Dream About You" by Dan Hartman, 1978
- "Just What I Needed," "Good Times Roll" and "Let's Go" by The Cars
- "Every Kind of People" and "Bad Case of Loving You" by Robert Palmer
- "I Want You to Want Me" and "Dream Police" by Cheap Trick, 1979
- "Sultans of Swing" by Dire Straits, 1979
- "Heart of Glass," "Dreaming" and "One Way or Another" by Blondie, 1979
- "My Sharona" and "Good Girls Don't" by The Knack, 1979

Soul

Major soul stars of the 1970s included Aretha Franklin, the Isley Brothers, Al Green, Barry White and Earth, Wind & Fire. Northern soul was a dance movement, with recordings made in Detroit, Chicago and Philadelphia. Its record labels included Veejay, Chess, Brunswick, Mirwood, Golden World, Motown, Ric-Tic, Shout and Okeh.

Southern soul records were recorded in Memphis, TN, Muscle Shoals, AL, Atlanta, GA, and New Orleans, LA. Its record labels included Stax, Atlantic, Murco and Jewel.

Motown continued in the 1970s to produce hit records for the changing market. Marvin Gaye's releases took more of a message focus to contemporary issues. Stevie Wonder's material was mature, rich and creative. Diana Ross left The Supremes in 1970 to become a solo singer, while the group kept recording. The newcomers to the label were The Jackson Five, with bubblegum youth appeal.

The Philadelphia sound emerged as a 1970s rival to Motown. It was a producers' genre, thanks to Kenny Gamble, Leon Huff and Bunny Sigler. The Philadelphia International house band was called MFSB, and they also recorded the theme to TV's "Soul Train." Its stable of artists included The O'Jays, Intruders, Three Degrees, Harold Melvin & the Blue Notes, Billy Paul, Patti Labelle, People's Choice, MFSB, Lou Rawls, Deedee Sharp, Jones Girls and Teddy Pendergrass.

Disco was a form of soul that generated dances, fashions and a happy lifestyle in the second half of the decade. Its primary stars included Gloria Gaynor, Donna Summer and The Village People.

Hank Moore's Top 1970s Soul Songs Playlist

- "Love or Let Me Be Lonely" by the Friends of Distinction, 1970
- "Good Guys Only Win in the Movies" by Mel & Tim, 1970
- "Band of Gold" by Freda Payne, 1970
- "Montego Bay" by Bobby Bloom, 1970
- "Viva Tirado," "Brown Eyed Girl" and "Tell Her She's Lovely" by El Chicano
- "West Bound #9" by The Flaming Ember, 1971
- "Whatcha See is What You Get" by The Dramatics, 1971
- "I Love You for All Seasons" by The Fuzz, 1971
- "Groove Me" and "Baby Let Me Kiss You" by King Floyd, 1971
- "The First Time Ever I Saw Your Face" and "Killing Me Softly" by Roberta Flack, 1971
- "You Are Everything," "Betcha by Golly Wow," "Stone in Love with You" by Stylistics
- "Ain't No Sunshine," "Grandma's Hands," "Lean on Me" and "Use Me" by Bill Withers
- "Me and Mrs. Jones" by Billy Paul, 1972
- "Jungle Fever" by The Chakachas, 1972
- "Have You Seen Her" and "Ooh Girl" by The Chi-Lites, 1972
- "I Can See Clearly Now" by Johnny Nash, 1972
- "Everybody Plays the Fool" by The Main Ingredient, 1972

- "If You Don't Love Me by Now," "The Love I Lost," "Bad Luck" and "Wake Up Everybody" by Harold Melvin & the Blue Notes
- "I'm Doing Fine Now" by New York City, 1973
- "Pillow Talk" by Sylvia, 1973
- "Midnight Train to Georgia" and "I've Got to Use My Imagination" by Gladys Knight & the Pips, 1973
- "Natural High" by Bloodstone, 1973
- "Sweet Charlie Babe" by Jackie Moore, 1973
- "Show & Tell" and "Touch & Go" by Al Wilson, 1973
- "Rock the Boat" by The Hues Corporation, 1974
- "Jungle Boogie" and "Hollywood Swinging" by Kool & the Gang, 1974
- "Best Thing That Ever Happened to Me," "On and On" by Gladys Knight & the Pips
- "Everlasting Love" by Carl Carlton, 1974
- "It Only Takes a Minute" by Tavares, 1975
- "Once You Get Started" by Rufus, 1975
- "Walking in Rhythm" by The Blackbyrds, 1975
- "You Sexy Thing" by Hot Chocolate, 1975
- "The Hustle" by Van McCoy, 1975
- "Get Up and Boogie" by Silver Convention, 1976
- "Kiss & Say Goodbye" by The Manhattans, 1976
- "Car Wash" by Rose Royce, 1976
- "Disco Inferno" by The Trammps, 1976
- "Trying to Love Two" by William Bell, 1976
- "Right Back Where We Started From" by Maxine Nightingale, 1976
- "I'll Be Good to You" and "Strawberry Letter #23" by the Brothers Johnson, 1977
- "Dancing Man" by Q, 1977
- "Brick House" by The Commodores, 1977
- "Dance, Dance, Dance" by Chic, 1977
- "So into You" by the Atlanta Rhythm Section, 1977
- "Best of My Love" by The Emotions, 1977
- "Native New Yorker" by Odyssey, 1977

- "Hotline" by The Sylvers, 1977
- "Don't Leave Me This Way" by Thelma Houston, 1977
- "Gonna Fly Now" (theme from "Rocky") by Bill Conti, Rhythm Heritage and Maynard Ferguson, 1977
- "Whatcha Gonna Do" by Pablo Cruise, 1977
- "Boogie Nights," "Always & Forever" and "The Groove Line" by Heatwave
- "On Broadway" by George Benson, 1978
- "I Love the Nightlife" by Alicia Bridges, 1978
- "Shame" by Evelyn Champaign King, 1978
- "Close the Door" by Teddy Pendergrass, 1978
- "Shake Your Groove Thing" and "Reunited" by Peaches & Herb, 1979
- "Ladies Night" by Kool & the Gang, 1979
- "Lead Me On" by Maxine Nightingale, 1979
- "Ain't No Stopping Us Now" by McFadden & Whitehead, 1979

Hank Moore's Top 1970s Pop Songs Playlist

- "Dancing in the Moonlight" by King Harvest, 1972
- "I Am Woman" by Helen Reddy, 1972
- "Summer Breeze," "Hummingbird," "Diamond Girl," "We May Never Pass This Way Again," "I'll Play for You" and "Get Closer" by Seals & Crofts
- "The Way We Were" by Barbra Streisand, 1973
- "Come and Get Your Love" by Redbone, 1974
- "Billy Don't Be a Hero" by Bo Donaldson & the Heywoods, 1974
- "The Night Chicago Died" by Paper Lace, 1974
- "My Eyes Adored You" by Frankie Valli, 1975
- "Sky High" by Jigsaw, 1975
- "Afternoon Delight" by the Starland Vocal Band, 1976
- "Devil Woman" by Cliff Richard, 1976
- "I'd Really Love to See You Tonight," "Nights Are Forever Without You," "It's Sad to Belong," "We'll Never Have to Say Goodbye Again" and "Love Is the Answer" by England Dan & John Ford Coley
- "Margaritaville" by Jimmy Buffett, 1977

- "Follow You, Follow Me" by Genesis, 1978
- "She Believes in Me" and "You Decorated My Life" by Kenny Rogers

Chapter 20
NOTABLE SONGS WITH MESSAGES

"Lean on Me" by Bill Withers is ranked #208 on Rolling Stone's list of "The 500 Greatest Songs of All Time." Numerous versions have been recorded. It is one of only nine songs to have reached No. 1 with versions by two different artists, Withers in 1972 and Club Nouveau in 1986. Withers was inducted into the Songwriters Hall of Fame in 2005 and the Rock and Roll Hall of Fame in 2015. "Lean on Me" has been frequently performed on virtual TV specials and at graduations.

"Stand By Me," anthem for modern times. In 1961, my friend Stan Applebaum took a gospel song called "Lord, Stand By Me" and turned it into Ben E. King's hit song "Stand By Me." His arrangement is still performed today. "Stand By Me" became a popular 1986 movie. Lyrics: "When the night has come, and the land is dark. And the moon is the only light we'll see. No, I won't be afraid. Just as long as you stand by me. Whenever you're in trouble, won't you stand by me? When all of our friends are gone."

"I Love New York" is a slogan, a logo and a song that were the basis of a 1977 campaign. The logo was designed by Milton Glaser in 1976 in the back of a taxi and was drawn with red crayon on scrap paper. The original drawing is held in the

Museum of Modern Art in Manhattan. The song "I Love New York," written by Steve Karmen, was adopted in 1980 as the state song of New York. The campaign became especially prominent following the Sept. 11, 2001, attacks on the city, which created a sense of unity among the populace and worldwide.

"If I Can Dream" was Elvis Presley's 1968 mega-hit. To Elvis, this was one of his favorite records because of the message. Lyrics: "If I can dream of a better land, where all my brothers walk hand in hand. While I can dream, please let my dream come true right now." Song written by Walter Earl Brown, notable for quotations of Dr. Martin Luther King, Jr., whom Elvis respected. When Presley heard the demo, he proclaimed: "I'm never going to sing another song I don't believe in. I'm never going to make another movie I don't believe in."

On Feb. 29, 1972: John Lennon's immigration visa expired, and he began a four-year struggle to obtain a resident's permit. Neil Sedaka wrote and recorded a song about Lennon's plight, "The Immigrant." Lyrics: "It was a time when strangers were welcome here. Music would play, they tell me the days were sweet and clear. It was a sweeter tune and there was so much room that people could come from everywhere."

The song "Happy Birthday" by Stevie Wonder was a 1981 tribute to Dr. Martin Luther King, Jr. It called for MLK's birthday to become a national holiday, which transpired in 1986. Wonder used the song to popularize the campaign for the holiday, holding the Rally for Peace Press Conference in 1981. President Ronald Reagan approved the creation of the holiday, signing it into existence on Nov. 2, 1983. The first official Martin Luther King, Jr. Day was held Jan. 20, 1986, and was commemorated with a concert, where Stevie Wonder was the headlining performer.

Song for the times by Major Lance: "Walking through the park, it wasn't quite dark. There was a man sitting on a bench. I asked this man what he meant. Sometimes everyone must sing this song. Um, um, um, um, um, um." This 1963 hit was performed by Major Lance when he opened for The Beatles in their 1964 US concert tour. His daughter is Keisha Lance Bottoms, Mayor of Atlanta. When Major Lance performed in England, his backup band was Bluesology, whose piano player was Reggie Dwight, soon to become Elton John.

Finding humor in life. Lyrics from the first rap record to be certified gold, "The Breaks" by Kurtis Blow (1980): "If your woman steps out with another man, and she runs off with him to Japan. Ma Bell sends you a whopping bill with eighteen phone calls to Brazil. And you borrowed money from the mob, and yesterday you lost your job. Well, these are the breaks. Break it up, break down." Kurtis Blow was the first commercially successful rapper and became an ordained minister in 2009. His Hip Hop Church is in Harlem, NY. Kurtis took the idea for this song to his producers, J.B. Moore and Robert Ford. J.B. had the concept of other implied meanings for "breaks." Says Kurtis: "He referred back to this old song, a philosophy song from 1920, where a guy said your girlfriend left you, and you lost your job and your car got towed away. Good breaks and bad breaks can happen in life, but don't worry because there's always another tomorrow."

Graduation memories come in the song "Graduation Day." Lyrics: "Though we leave in sorrow. All the joys we've known. We can face tomorrow knowing we'll never walk alone. We'll remember always." The Beach Boys recorded the song in 1965 as a tribute to their role model vocal group, The Four Freshmen, who first recorded it in 1956. I emceed The Beach Boys in concert in 1974 and 1981, plus The Four Freshmen in 1980.

"Home of the Brave" was recorded by Jody Miller, 1965, with Billy Strange orchestra. It was written by Barry Mann and Cynthia Weill, of Brill Building fame. The premise was that we all have a right to be different. The song was from the perspective of a mom, wishing that her son could "be what he wants to be. He's just a little bit different."

The city of Ft. Lauderdale, FL, began a swim forum in 1938. By 1960, students came in great numbers, and local businesses took advantage of this influx. MGM filmed the movie "Where the Boys Are," released in early 1961. The movie made crowds soar, making Ft. Lauderdale the primary destination for students partying during spring break. I met two of the movie's stars, Yvette Mimieux and George Hamilton. Connie Francis sang the title song, written by Neil Sedaka and orchestrated by Stan Applebaum. The next three most popular spring break destinations are Panama City, FL, South Padre Island, TX, and Cancun, Mexico. Students on spring break spend $1 billion yearly, boosting local economies.

Chapter 21
SONGS USED IN COMMERCIALS

Advertising jingles exist in our psyche. We recall them at a moment's notice. We quote them to our kids. We use them in memos and meetings. They are the brain waves for our lives. Thus, they were effective in creating recall value.

Advertising jingles are more than cute lyrics and catchy tunes. They are designed to market the worth of the sponsoring organization and its products. By hearing a jingle at least seven times, we have a familiarity of the product. Through repetition, we increase loyalty to the point that buying patterns commence.

"To look sharp every time you shave. To feel sharp and be on the ball. Just be sharp. Use Gillette Blue Blades for the quickest slickest shaves of all." This jingle was written in 1953 by Mahlon Merrick, who was Jack Benny's television conductor.

Composers of advertising jingles are a rare breed. Pop music superstar Barry Manilow cut his teeth on ad jingles for State Farm Insurance, Band-Aid and McDonald's in the early 1970s. Manilow ably learned the secrets of commercial hit records as having comparable traits as commercial jingles, including clever slogans, sense of humor, pertinence to the product, musical hooks, sing-a-long potential, memorability and mass-market appeal.

These are some of the best jingles of the twentieth century included:

- "A little dab will do you. Use more, only if you dare. The girls will all pursue you. They love to get their fingers in your hair." Brylcreem
- "You deserve a break today." McDonald's
- "50 million times a day, at home, at work or on the way, there's nothing like a Coca-Cola."
- "If you've got the time, we've got the beer." Miller High Life
- "See the USA in your Chevrolet. America is asking you to call. Drive the USA in your Chevrolet. America is the greatest land of all."
- "Better things for better living through chemistry." Dupont
- "You'll wonder where the yellow went when you brush your teeth with Pepsodent."
- "Like a good neighbor, State Farm is there." State Farm Insurance Co.
- "Now it's Pepsi, for those who think young." Pepsi-Cola
- "Wet and wild. Seven Up is first against thirst. So crisp, so smooth."
- "When you say Bud, you've said it all. The King of Beers." Budweiser
- "Come alive. You're in the Pepsi generation." Pepsi-Cola
- "The best to you each morning." Kellogg's cereals
- "The cereal that's shot from guns." Quaker Puffed Wheat

Ad Jingles That Became Hit Records

Advertising jingles were subsequently remade as hit records. The New Seekers had a Coca-Cola jingle "I'd Like to Buy the World a Coke" in 1970. A year later, "I'd Like to Teach the World to Sing" was a hit, and it became an anthem for global peace. Another Coke jingle, "Country Sunshine," was a country hit for Dottie West in 1973.

Coca-Cola had another jingle, "It's the Real Thing." They had name recording artists of the 1960s to perform their takes on the jingle, in the style of their hottest hits. Stars doing the radio jingles included The Bee Gees, The Box Tops, Ray Charles, Aretha Franklin, Petula Clark, Neil Diamond, The Fifth Dimension, Lesley Gore, Roy Orbison, Jan and Dean, Lulu, The Moody Blues, Nancy Sinatra, Diana Ross and the Supremes, The Tremeloes and Vanilla Fudge.

Cigarette commercials were on radio in the 1930s and 1940s. Ferde Grofe's "Grand Canyon Suite, On the Trail" was adapted for Philip Morris spots. Elmer Bernstein's "Magnificent Seven" theme was adapted for Marlboro commercials. Benson & Hedges highlight "The Disadvantages of You" (1966) Brass Ring. Vaughn Monroe's hit song "Sound Off" was used as jingles for Chesterfield Cigarettes.

Kent Cigarettes had two of its jingles adapted into hit records, including "The Duke of Kent" by Pat Suzuki, 1958, and "That's What Happiness Is" by the Ray Conniff Singers, 1964. The Broadway song "Hey Big Spender" was used in commercials for Muriel Cigars.

Pepsi Cola used "Music to Watch Girls By" as its jingle in the 1960s.The song became a hit for Bob Crewe Generation and Andy Williams.

Loewenbrau Beer had a 1970s jingle, "Here's To Good Friends." It was recorded in 1978 by Arthur Prysock. "When You Say Bud, You've Said It All" was a 1970s jingle for Budweiser Beer. It was re-recorded in 1972 as "When You Say Love," the country version by Bob Luman and the pop version by Sonny & Cher.

Maxwell House Coffee had an advertising slogan "Good to the Last Drop." Its commercials featured happy coffee cups. A hit song based on it was 1961's "The Percolator" by Billy Joe & the Checkmates.

Alka Seltzer had ads in the 1960s, "No Matter What Shape Your Stomach Is In." The T-Bones had a hit record with it, "No Matter What Shape," in 1966. Another Alka Seltzer jingle was "Plop Plop Fizz Fizz. Oh What a Relief It Is," which was later recorded by Sammy Davis Jr.

Schlitz Beer's jingle "The Joy of Living" was re-recorded by Nelson Riddle in 1958. Fresca's jingle, "The Blizzard Song" was hits for Trini Lopez and Mitch Miller in 1967. The John F. Kennedy Presidential campaign used "Walking Down to Washington," based upon Mitch Miller's 1959 recording.

Gillette Safety Razors sponsored the Friday Night Fights on TV in the 1950s. Its jingle, "Look Sharp, Be Sharp," was a classical and pop hit for Arthur Fielder and the Boston Pops Orchestra.

In 1973, an adorable little boy named Rodney Allen Rippy talked about loving Jack-in-the-Box hamburgers. The jingle urged viewers to "Take Life a Little Easier." Rippy scored a hit recording with a song of the same title.

"The Time of Your Life" was a song by Paul Anka in 1976. At the time, it was for Kodak film commercials. Four decades later, the song is used to advertise Downy April Fresh Softener.

Hit Recordings Used in Advertising

Name recordings have been used in many commercials. They are picked for recognition value, the appeal of golden oldies to multiple generations and hit recordings that connote happy times.

Using name songs is practical, in that agencies pay the same royalties as they would to commission original music. Original recordings offer great production value. Those songs spark public interest, as shown by downloads and CD sales. The public gets introduced to great music as a result of advertising.

Among those that have graced the airwaves in commercials included:

- Honey Nut Cheerios, "Yummy Yummy Yummy" by the Ohio Express, 1968
- Anoro, "Go Your Own Way" by Fleetwood Mac, 1978
- AT&T, "I Just Called to Say I Love You" by Stevie Wonder, 1984
- Purina Cat Chow, "Calendar Girl" by Neil Sedaka, 1961
- Lincoln Continental, "Whatever Lola Wants" by Sarah Vaughan, 1955
- Lincoln Aviator "It's a Most Unusual Day" by Jane Powell, 1948
- Jardiance, "Apache" by The Incredible Bongo Band, 1973
- Ozempic, "Magic" by Pilot, 1975
- TD Ameritrade, "Cat's in the Cradle" by Harry Chapin, 1974
- Heineiken Beer, "It's Your Thing" by The Isley Brothers, 1969
- Volkswagen Atlas, "America" by Simon & Garfunkel, 1964
- Toujeo, "Let's Groove Tonight" by Earth, Wind & Fire, 1981
- Carnival Cruise Lines, "You're My Best Friend" by Queen, 1976
- Mercedes Benz, "Born to Be Wild" by Steppenwolf, 1968
- Nutrish Big Life dog food, "We're Not Going to Take It" by Twisted Sister, 1984
- Applebee's, "Can't Get Enough of Your Love," by Barry White, 1974
- Heinz Ketchup, "Anticipation" by Carly Simon, 1971

- Target, "Me and My Shadow" by Frank Sinatra and Sammy Davis Jr., 1963
- Maxwell House Coffee, "Our House" by Fine Madness, 1983
- Visa Card, "A Kiss to Build a Dream On" by Louis Armstrong, 1951
- K-Mart, "Vacation" by Connie Francis, 1962
- Capital One, "I've Had the Time of My Life" by Bill Medley & Jennifer Warnes, 1988
- Beechnut Gum, "Mexican Shuffle" by Herb Alpert & the Tijuana Brass, 1964
- Tide Detergent, "Anything You Can Do" by Ethel Merman & Ray Middleton, 1946
- Chevrolet, "Over Under Sideways Down" by The Yardbirds, 1966
- Fidelity Investments, "Mr. Big Stuff" by Jean Knight, 1971
- One-A-Day Vitamins, "Heather" by The Carpenters, 1972
- TIAA Cref Financial Services, "Somewhere" by Dionne Warwick, 1967
- Best Western Hotels, "The Best is Yet to Come" by Tony Bennett, 1962
- Crest Strips, "When You're Smiling" by Steve Allen, 1958
- Papa John's Pizza, "Mambo Italiano" by Dean Martin, 1955
- Cialis, "Be My Baby" by The Ronettes, 1963
- Dannon Yogurt, "Groove Me" by King Floyd, 1971
- Wal-Mart, "Help is On the Way" by the Little River Band, 1977
- Wal-Mart, "Working in the Coal Mine" by Pure Prairie League, 1988
- Wal-Mart, "I Got You Babe" by Etta James, 1968 cover of Sonny & Cher's 1965 hit
- GEICO, "Sometimes When We Touch" by Dan Hill, 1978
- E-Harmony.com, "This Will Be" by Natalie Cole, 1975
- Vasolene, "Take Good Care of My Baby" by Bobby Vee, 1961
- Fancy Feast cat food, "At Last" by Etta James, 1961
- Buick, "Paperback Writer" by The Beatles, 1966
- Nissan, "Comin' Home Baby" by Mel Torme, 1962
- Google, "It's Alright" by The Impressions, 1963
- T.J. Maxx, Marshall's, Home Goods, "Make My Dreams Come True" by Hall & Oates, 1981

- Kohl's, "From Me to You" by The Beatles, 1964
- HEB, "Love Will Keep Us Together" by The Captain & Tennille, 1975
- Alexa, Amazon, "I Only Have Eyes for You" by The Flamingos, 1961
- Skechers Shoes, "On the Road Again" by Willie Nelson, 1980
- Michelob Ultra, "Showdown" by Electric Light Orchestra, 1976
- NFL, "Rip It Up" by Little Richard, 1956
- Kia, "Total Eclipse of the Heart" by Bonnie Tyler, 1985
- Applebee's, "Where Everybody Knows Your Name," theme from "Cheers," 1982
- Applebee's, "Chicken Fried" by Zac Brown Band, 2005
- Applebee's, "Gonna Make You Sweat (Everybody Dance Now)" by C+C Music Factory, 1990
- Applebee's, "No Particular Place To Go" by Chuck Berry, 1964
- Nordic Track and US Postal Service, "I've Been Everywhere" by Hank Snow, 1962
- Fragrances by Dior at Macy's, "Cry Baby" by Janis Joplin, 1970
- Chime Credit Builder, "In the Hall of the Mountain King," classical piece
- GMC Sierra, "We Will Rock You" by Queen, 1980
- The Farmer's Dog, "What You See is What You Get" by The Dramatics, 1971
- Peacock Streaming Service, "Somebody to Love" by Jefferson Airplane, 1967
- Nutella, "Upside Down" by Diana Ross, 1980
- T-Mobile 5G Internet, "I Feel Pretty," from "West Side Story"
- Virgin Cruises, "Like a Virgin" by Madonna, 1984
- Target, "Best of My Love" by The Emotions, 1977
- Heinz Catsup, "This Magic Moment" by The Drifters, 1959
- Comcast, "Put a Little Love in Your Heart" by Jackie DeShannon, 1969
- Campbell's Soup, "Together Forever" by Rick Astley, 1988
- Campbell's Soup, "It's So Easy" by Buddy Holly, 1958
- Hershey's Chocolate Candy, "C'mon Everybody" by Eddie Cochran, 1958
- Dick's Sporting Goods, "There She Is, Miss America" by Johnny Desmond
- Dick's Sporting Goods, "Come Together" by The Beatles, 1969
- Claritin, "The Most Wonderful Time of the Year" by Andy Williams

- Tropicana Orange Juice, "It's a Lovely Day Today" by Ella Fitzgerald
- VRBO, "Right Where I Belong" by Kermit the Frog, 1984
- Modelo Beer, "The Ecstasy of Gold" by Ennio Morricone, from "The Good, The Bad and the Ugly," 1967

The song most covered in commercials is "Feeling Good," written by Anthony Newley for the 1960s Broadway musical "The Roar of the Greasepaint, The Smell of the Crowd." Products using the song in their spots include Trelegy, Coors Beer, T-Mobile, Vista Print and Peloton.

The next most covered in commercials is "What a Wonderful World" by Louis Armstrong. When Armstrong's record was introduced in 1967, it failed to chart. The song was resurrected in 1988, appearing in the movie "Good Morning, Vietnam." The song has been reprised many times in TV commercials and stands as a ballad for all time.

Modern technology companies brought back the oldies. Samsung used "Rocket Man" by Elton John, 1972. General Electric featured "Catch the Wind" by Donovan, 1965. Google adapted "It's Alright" by The Impressions, 1963. SBC Yahoo DSL played "Wonderful Tonight" by Eric Clapton, 1978.

Amazon Prime commercials used the song "Little Man" by Sonny & Cher, from 1966. It featured a miniature pony purchased by an enthusiastic customer. Other songs in Amazon commercials include "It Wasn't Me" by Chuck Berry, "Driver's Seat" by Sniff n' the Tears, "Trouble Ahead" by Nat King Cole and "Rapunzel" by Nicki Minaj.

Two moms surviving their young partying past appeared in T-Mobile TV commercial. Two friends discuss changing phone carrier service. They lament another past decision, getting matching Spring Break 1999 tattoos during their college days. Ends with Burt Bacharach and Hal David's song "Always Something There to Remind Me" by Naked Eyes, 1983 rock remake of Sandie Shaw's 1964 pop hit.

The Rybelsus commercial features the song "You Are My Sunshine." The song was written and recorded in 1943 by Jimmie Davis. On the strength of his popularity as a country singer, Davis was elected Governor of Louisiana. The Rybelsus ad features a contemporary version of "You Are My Sunshine" by The Next Great American Novelist.

"I've Gotta Be Me" is used in Volkswagen TV commercials. It inspires resolve for life. Hit recording by Sammy Davis Jr. It appeared in the Broadway musical "Golden Rainbow," starring Steve Lawrence and Eydie Gormé. Lyrics: "I want to live, not merely survive. And I won't give up this dream of life that keeps me alive. The dream that I see makes me what I am. Daring to try, to do it or die. I've gotta be me."

A Target TV commercial used the song "Round and Round" by Perry Como, which hit #1 on the charts in Feb. 1957. It was covered by Sia Furler (Australian singer) in the Target holiday commercial and on her CD, retaining much of the Joe Reisman arrangement on Como's 1957 record. "Find a wheel and it goes round, round, round. As it skims along with a happy sound. As it goes along the ground, ground, ground. Till it leads you to the one you love. Find a ring and put it round, round, round. And with ties so strong that two hearts are bound. Put it on the one you've found, found, found. For you know that this is really love."

The Fage Total Yogurt commercials used Richard Wagner's 'Ride of the Valkyries," from "Die Walküre," which is part of the composer's four-part "Ring Cycle."

Cute TV commercial for Xfinity satirized teen movie comedies. "You Must Be Steven" features a teenager scaling the house to visit a girlfriend late at night. While entering the window, the girl's father surprises them, having intercepted a network connection from "Steven's phone." The song used in the ad was "Go Where Baby Lives," a 1957 record by The Strollers, R&B group from Chicago. Put in 1957 jargon, Steven was caught joining the party line.

Allstate Insurance has utilized hit records for its commercials, including "Grazing in the Grass" by Hugh Masekela, 1968, "Non, Je Ne Regrette Bien" by Edith Piaf, 1953 and "Our House" by Fine Madness, 1983.

Other songs featured in radio and TV commercials included:

- "Mambo Italiano" by Rosemary Clooney, 1955
- "My Eyes Adored You" by Frankie Valli, 1975
- "Mr. Roboto" by Styx, 1986
- "Got to Give It Up" by Marvin Gaye, 1976
- "She's a Rainbow" by The Rolling Stones, 1968
- "Happy Together" by The Turtles, 1967

- "The Boys Are Back in Town" by Thin Lizzie, 1974
- "Woo Hoo" by The Rockateens, 1959
- "Tonight is the Night" by Rod Stewart, 1976
- "Rock You Like a Hurricane" by The Scorpions, 1984

Chapter 22
NICK NAMES FOR MUSIC STARS

Endearing things, they were called:
The Singing Rage, Miss Patti Page

Her Nibs, Miss Georgia Gibbs

Little Miss Dynamite, Brenda Lee

Sentimental Gentleman of Swing, Tommy Dorsey

Ace Drummer Man, Gene Krupa

That Honey in the Horn Sound, Al Hirt

The Sing-along Gang, Mitch Miller

Lady Day, Billie Holiday

Father of Rock n' Roll, Chuck Berry

The Kings included:
King of Rock n' Roll, Elvis Presley

King of Pop, Michael Jackson

King of Jazz, Paul Whiteman

King of Swing, Benny Goodman

Kings of Country Music, Roy Acuff, Johnny Cash, George Jones and George Strait

King of Calypso, Harry Belafonte

King of Rap, Kurtis Blow

King of Rock n' Soul, Solomon Burke

King of Christmas, Bing Crosby

King of the Blues, John Lee Hooker

King of the Surf Guitar, Dick Dale

King of Cool, Dean Martin

King of Skiffle, Lonnie Donegan

King of Rockabilly, Carl Perkins

King of Mambo, Perez Prado

King of Parody, Weird Al Yankovic

King of the Jukebox, Louis Jordan

King of the High C's, Luciano Pavarotti

King of the Clarinet, Artie Shaw

King of Mambo, Perez Prado

King of Parody, Weird Al Yankovic

King of the Jukebox, Louis Jordan

King of the High C's, Luciano Pavarotti

King of the Clarinet, Artie Shaw

The Queens included:

Queen of Latin Pop, Gloria Estefan

Queen of Jazz, First Lady of Song, Ella Fitzgerald

Queen of R&B, Ruth Brown

Queen of Soul, Aretha Franklin

Queen of Rock, Tina Turner

Queen of Rockabilly, Wanda Jackson

Queen of Disco, Gloria Gaynor

Queen of Folk, Joan Baez

Queen of Christian Pop, Amy Grant

Queen of Rock and Roll, Janis Joplin

Queens of Country, Kitty Wells, Tammy Wynette and Reba McEntire

Queen of Gospel, Mahalia Jackson
Queen of Funk, Chaka Khan
Soul Queen of New Orleans, Irma Thomas
Caribbean Queen, Rihanna
Teen Queen, Miley Cyrus

Nick Names for Music Stars included:

First Lady of Country, Tammy Wynette
First Tycoon of Teen, Phil Spector
Godfather of Soul, Mr. Dynamite, Soul Brother No. 1, James Brown
Godfather of Britpop, Ray Davies
Godfather of Rhythm and Blues, Johnny Otis
Godfather of Punk, Lou Reed
Godmother of Soul, Patti Labelle
Godfather of Shock Rock, Alice Cooper
Grandfather of Rock and Roll, Robert Johnson
High Priestess of Pop, Madonna
Diva of Divas, Barbra Streisand
Mister Show Business, Sammy Davis Jr.
Mama Africa, Miriam Makeba
Princess of Pop, Ariana Grande
Dr. Winston O'Boogie, John Lennon
Macca, Paul McCartney
Magpie, The Quiet One, George Harrison
Ringo Starr, Real name Richard Starkey
Architect of Rock and Roll, Les Paul
The Boss, Bruce Springsteen
Rocket Man, Pinball Wizard, Elton John
The Ghostess with the Mostess, Marni Nixon
The Purple One, Prince
America's Oldest Teenager, Dick Clark
Empress of the Blues, Bessie Smith
Empress of Soul, Gladys Knight
Stringbean JT, James Taylor

Eunice, Doris Day

David Seville & the Chipmunks, Ross Bagdasarian

The Tijuana Brass, Herb Alpert

Ol' Blue Eyes, Chairman of the Board, Frank Sinatra

The Killer, Jerry Lee Lewis

The Possum, George Jones

Bocephus, Hank Williams Jr.

Mr. Excitement, Jackie Wilson

Mr. Showmanship, Liberace

Mr. Radio, Casey Kasem

Forces Sweetheart, Vera Lynn

The Man in Black, Johnny Cash

Mr. C., Perry Como

Mr. Country Music, Red Foley

Mr. & Mrs. Talent, Steve Lawrence and Eydie Gorme

The Gambler, Kenny Rogers

Toad, Blake Shelton

Baby, Judy Garland

Slowhand, Eric Clapton

Major, Glenn Miller

World's Greatest Entertainer, Al Jolson

Prince of Darkness, Ozzy Osbourne

Bonzo, Led Zeppelin's John Bonham

Thin White Duke, Master of Reinvention, David Bowie

The White Witch, Stevie Nicks

The Pope of Mope, Morrissey

Satchmo, Satchel Mouth, Dipper Mouth, Louis Armstrong

The Voice, Whitney Houston

Mr. Guitar, Chet Atkins

Yardbird, Bird, Charlie Parker

Lennie, Leonard Bernstein

Pops, John Williams

The Wall of Sound, Phil Spector house band

The Voice of Protest, Bob Dylan

Piano Man, Billy Joel

Chapter 23
RADIO MEMORIES AND FORMATS

The History of Radio and Evolution of Music Presentations

S amuel F.B. Morse was an artist and opened a studio in Boston, MA, in 1815. While on a voyage to Europe for art studies in 1832, a conversation on discoveries in electromagnetism inspired in him an invention for the transmission of information. While still onboard the ship, he drafted sketches for a telegraph. By 1838, Morse had a working model for translating letters into dots and dashes. In 1843, Congress appropriated funds to build the first telegraph line. In 1844, Morse tapped the first message, "What hath God wrought."

In 1877, at age thirty, Thomas Edison invented the phonograph unintentionally. At the time, Edison was trying to devise a high-speed telegraph machine as a counterpart to the telephone that Alexander Graham Bell had invented a year before.

In the 1880s, Heinrich R. Hertz discovered of electromagnetic waves, including radio waves. In the 1890s, Guglielmo Marconi developed the first apparatus for long distance radio transmissions. In 1900, the first audio was sent, covering one mile. By 1910, these wireless systems were called radio.

John Wanamaker started working as a delivery boy and entered the clothing business at 18. In 1861, with Nathan Brown, he founded Brown and Wanamaker, which became the leading men's clothier in the US within ten years. In 1875, he opened a dry goods and clothing business, inviting other merchants to sublet from him. In 1896, he purchased A.T. Stewart in New York and broadened the department store chain. In 1918, Wanamaker's stores piped music to each other, this innovation giving birth to commercial radio.

David Sarnoff studied engineering and began work in 1906 on wireless communications services. In 1913, he joined the Marconi Radio Company as chief inspector and rose through the ranks to management. Marconi was merged with Radio Corporation of America in 1919. Sarnoff was elected general manager of RCA in 1921, executive vice president in 1929, president in 1930 and chairman of the board in 1947. RCA was the leading manufacturer of radio sets in the 1920s, and Sarnoff championed the founding of the National Broadcasting Company to provide programming. Then came television, and RCA pioneered in the manufacture of color TV sets.

William S. Paley took a chain of sixteen radio stations and grew it into the Columbia Broadcasting System in 1927. Paley grasped the potential of radio, with great programming essential to advertising sales and revenue. He created a major news division that coincided with World War II. CBS was known as the "tiffany network" for its quality in every programming real. CBS excelled in phonograph records with its Columbia label, developing the LP in 1948. CBS expanded into television. In 1976, Paley founded the Museum of Broadcasting.

Lee De Forest was an electrical engineer and inventor. His first patent was for an electrolytic detector that made possible the use of headphones with wireless receivers. In 1906, he invented the triode electron tube, with potential for relaying radio signals. His sound process evolved into radio. In 1919, De Forest developed a sound system for motion pictures. He made important contributions to the electric phonograph, television, radar and diathermy. He made and lost four fortunes in his life and remained committed to the educational potential for radio and TV.

Radio Programming

In the 1920s, local radio stations broadcast a variety of programming. The "service radio" format had stations offering different shows throughout the day, including music performed by local bands, concert remotes, news and interviews.

With the dawning of network radio, there were programs of all types, drawing millions of listeners.Radio's Golden Age of the 1930s and 1940s provided comedies, drama, quiz shows, soap operas, talent contests, news, sports and special events.

Music filled variety shows on network radio. Stars catapulting their careers via regular radio appearances included Bing Crosby, Frank Sinatra, Rudy Vallee, Rosemary Clooney, Ben Bernie, Kate Smith, Eddie Cantor, Perry Como, Patti Page, Frances Langford, Dinah Shore, Arthur Godfrey, Kay Kyser, Glenn Miller, Jimmy Durante, Judy Garland, Burl Ives, Al Jolson and Gracie Fields.

Many of the radio shows moved to television in the 1950s. Network radio shows continued up until 1962, after which network broadcasts were mostly news.

Local stations grew dramatically in the 1920s and 1930s. Some carried network broadcasts from NBC, CBS and Mutual. Most carried programs with phonograph records supplying the music. This increased outlet for showcasing music caused record labels to produce infinitely more releases, and star rosters expanded to enlarge the pool of popular music.

By the late 1940s, radio was king. The ABC Radio Network spun off from NBC. Local station programming became essential to communities. Radio grew internationally, only to be joined by television in the 1950s.

In the 1960s, radio formats expanded even further. Service radio grew into niche formats playing Top 40, middle-of-the road pop, country, soul, hard rock, jazz, religious music and classical.

Local Radio, My Memories

I got into radio in 1958, as a disc jockey. My role model was Dick Clark, whose "American Bandstand" on ABC-TV was the kingpin of music shows. I had a lot of mentors at that station, who gave me advice that served me well for decades.

That station had a "service radio" format. The daily schedule included a morning music and news block called "Sound Service."At 8:00 a.m., it carried "The Cactus Pryor Show." Then, they joined the CBS Radio Network, carrying "The Arthur Godfrey Show."That was followed by 15-minute soap operas: "Romance of Helen

Trent," "Second Mrs. Burton," "Guiding Light" and "Brighter Day." At noon was more "Sound Service," followed by a half-hour of country music at 12:30. Back to CBS at 1:00 to carry the radio version of "Perry Mason," followed by a charming music show co-hosted by Bing Crosby and Rosemary Clooney. At 3:00 was "On the Town," hosted by local DJ Bob Presley, featuring current Top 40 hits, followed by "CBS World News Tonight." It was back to Top 40 for "On the Town," with DJ Ricci Ware, who later achieved stellar fame at KTSA in San Antonio. The late-night show, "On the Drag," carried jazz and mellow music.

Saturdays and Sundays on KTBC Radio were a steady diet of Top 40 music. There were two blocks of CBS weekend shows. We taped "The Metropolitan Opera" on Saturday afternoons and played it late Sunday nights, logging it as public affairs programming. The two-hour Sunday afternoon CBS block included "Gunsmoke," "Have Gun Will Travel," "Suspense" and "Yours Truly, Johnny Dollar."

Elvis Presley was the King of Rock n' Roll. I met Elvis in 1958. He came to visit me at KTBC Radio in Austin, TX, when he was a private in the US Army. The next time was in 1962 at the Seattle World's Fair, where he was making a movie. The last time was backstage at his 1975 concert at Hofheinz Pavilion in Houston. First question I asked Elvis was his favorite food. Answer: burnt bacon, because that's what they served to him in Army basic training at Fort Hood. He kept the affinity for burnt bacon the rest of his life. Second question was about the staying power of rock n' roll, then known as kids' music. Answer: "They won't always be kids."

Lyndon B. Johnson taught me: "You always start at the top." Frank Sinatra told me: "Nobody is Number One forever." Sonny Bono told me: "There's nothing more permanent than change. History repeats itself. The beat goes on."

Remembering Cactus Pryor

One never forgets their first mentor. I have had several great ones, who in turn taught me the value of passing it on to others. That's why I advise businesses, write books, speak at conferences and more.

That first great mentor sticks with you always. Mine was legendary humorist and media figure Cactus Pryor. I started working for him in 1958, at KTBC Radio in Austin, TX. A new show had premiered on TV entitled "American Bandstand." I was ten years old and wanted to be the Dick Clark of local media. Cactus was the program director and morning radio personality. His show, filled with humor and music, was the natural lead-in to "Arthur Godfrey Time," which we carried from the CBS Radio Network.

Cactus was thirty-four at the time that he began mentoring me. He had grown up around show business. His father, Skinny Pryor, owned a movie theatre and entertained audiences with comedy routines during intermissions. Cactus was inspired by all that he saw. He joined KTBC as a disc jockey in 1945, becoming program director. When the station signed on its TV station on Thanksgiving Day, 1952, Cactus was the first personality on the screen. He welcomed viewers and introduced the first two programs, the University of Texas vs. Texas A&M football game, followed by the "Howdy Doody Show" from the NBC-TV Network.

Cactus had been doing his morning show from his home, with his kids as regulars, with the repartee comparable to Art Linkletter interviewing children. Early in 1958, he was doing his morning show back in the studio. I started as his regular on Saturday mornings, and he gave me segments to do.

From him, I learned several early valuable lessons:

- You cannot be a carbon copy of everyone else. He wanted me to like and respect Dick Clark but not become a clone of him.
- Being one of a kind is a long quest. He wanted me to set my own tone and not be labeled by others.
- Cactus Pryor said to me: "Nobody cares about you unless you're behind the microphone."

From Cactus Pryor and a twenty-four-year-old newscaster named Bill Moyers, I learned that if you take the dirtiest job and do it better than everyone else, you will be a solid expert. In the good old days of regulated broadcasting, stations had to keep logs of the music, to avoid the hint of Payola, a growing controversy at the time. I kept the logs and learned about the music, the record companies, the composers and much more.

Stations also had to perform Community Ascertainment by going into the community, inquiring about issues, and assuring that broadcasting addressed those issues. That's where I learned to file license renewals. That's where I learned the value of public service announcements and public affairs program, which deregulation precluded broadcasting from doing. From that mentoring, I fell in love with the non-profit culture, the organizations and the client bases affected by them. That early Community Ascertainment inspired me to the lifelong championing of not-for-profit groups and their fine works. From that experience, I wrote my book "Non-Profit Legends."

The early days of television were creative. Cactus hosted a local variety show on KTBC-TV. He interviewed interesting locals, showcased local talent and performed comedy material. One of his advertisers was an appliance store and, while showing the latest TV sets, Cactus kicked their screens to demonstrate their rugged qualities. When the station left its first temporary home at the transmitter atop Mount Larson, Cactus was carried out in the chair in which he was sitting, a symbol that the variety show would move to the new studio at the corner of 6th and Brazos.

Cactus began developing special characters, with unique personas. That first year in which I worked with him, he created a puppet, Theopolous P. Duck. It was inspired by Edgar Bergen's characters. Mr. Duck delivered jokes with a cultured accent. He appeared in comedy spoof segments on local KTBC-TV shows, such as "Now Dig This" (hosted by Ricci Ware), "Woman's World" (hosted by Jean Covert Boone) and the "Uncle Jay Show" (hosted by Jay Hodgson).

Cactus loved to play on words, giving twists to keep the listeners alert. He used phrases such as "capital entertainment for the capitol city" and "that solid sound in Austin town." In talking breaks for our sister station (KRGV), he said "that solid sound in the valley round."

He taught me how to deliver live commercials and to ad-lib. In those days, we would do live remotes for advertisers, inviting people to come out, get prizes and meet us at the external location. Doing such remotes got us appearance fees, and they really drew for the advertisers.

Through the remotes, I learned how to feed lines and develop the talent to speak in sound bites, as I do for business media interviews to this day. I was with Cactus at a remote for Armstrong-Johnson Ford. The outcue was to describe the 1959 Ford model. Cactus said, "It's sleek and dazzling, from its car-front to its car-rear." That was a cue for the studio DJ to play a commercial for the Career Shop, a clothing retailer. Today, when I use nouns as verbs and place business terms out of context to make people think creatively, I'm thinking back to Cactus Pryor.

One remote on which I joined Cactus was for the fourth KFC franchise in the United States. We got to interview Colonel Harlan Sanders on his new business venture. Little did I know that twenty years later, KFC would be a corporate client of mine, and I would be advising them how to vision forward, following the Colonel's death.

Music programming was important to Cactus Pryor and, thus, to me. Mentees of his understood and advocated broad musical playlists, with the variety to appeal broadly. Under a "service radio" format, different dayparts showcased different musical genres. He believed that virtually any record could be played, within context. One of the programming tricks that I taught him was to commemorate Bing Crosby's birthday each May by playing "White Christmas" and other holiday hits out of season, which got the listeners fascinated.

In those days, you could play rock n' roll hits from the KTBC Pop Poll, a list that was circulated to local record stars as a cross-promotion. There were also positions in the "clock" devoted to easy listening artists, instrumentals, country crossovers and what Cactus called "another KTBC golden disc, time tested for your pleasure." Cactus liked rock n' roll but wanted to see that easy listening records got proper attention.

Humor was the beacon over everything that he did. Cactus began recording comedy records, such as "Point of Order" on the Four Star Label and still others for Austin-based Trinity Records. He began writing a humorous newspaper column, "Cacti's Comments."

Besides his radio work, Cactus Pryor got bookings as an after-dinner speaker. In the early years, he gave comedy monologues and historical narratives. Always entertaining, he inspired audiences to think the bigger ideas and look beyond the obvious. I follow his tenets in delivering business keynotes and facilitating think tanks and corporate retreats.

His gigs got more humorous. Cactus created different personas, replete with costume and makeup. His first was a European diplomat who had the same voice and inflection as Theopolous P. Duck. He would deliver funny zingers, often touching upon political sacred cows. Then, he would peel off the mustache and ask, "Ain't it tacky?" He would then divulge that he actually was humorist Cactus Pryor. The act was well accepted and perfected during the era when our boss, Lyndon B. Johnson, was President of the United States.

Cactus did national TV variety shows. He was the "other Richard Pryor." He continued developing characters and entertaining audiences up through the 1990's, when his son Paul had begun doing the circuit as well. Paul is a funny satirist as well, something that I had known back when he was a school buddy of my sister Julie.

John Wayne called Cactus "one of the funniest guys around" and invited him to appear in two classic Wayne movies. I recall visiting Cactus on the set of "The Green Berets" in Benning, Georgia, and seeing him keep stars John Wayne, David Janssen, Jim Hutton and Bruce Cabot in stitches in between shots and poker games.

Though national fame beckoned, he kept his roots in Austin, claiming, "There is no way to follow laughs onstage but with pancakes at City Park." He stayed in his beloved Centex community. He wrote books on Texas history. There were contributions to the news-talk stations. Those of us who have known and worked with Cactus Pryor will never forget his humor, his sense of fairness, his encouraging ways, the twinkle in his eyes and the lasting impacts made on our later successes.

Hank Moore in his years as a radio DJ

Hank Moore pioneered the radio "golden oldies"
format and emceed nostalgia dances.

Chapter 24
AMBIANCE MOOD MUSIC

From Elevator Music to Stimulus Progression

Piped-in music creates atmosphere and stimulates activity. The first usage occurred in 1918 when the Wanamaker department store played recorded music simultaneously in its Philadelphia and New York stores. That paved the way for radio. Recorded music is piped into retail stores via continuous-loop recordings, microwave transmissions, tapes, CDs and the playing of radio stations on the loudspeaker system.

Muzak was a company that custom designed music for retail establishments, in such a way as to maximize urges to shop, buy and trade with stores who subscribed to their service. Muzak referred to its scientifically designed music as "stimulus progression." The Muzak recordings were played on LP discs, piped over store sound systems. Then, they went to tape and still later to digital formats.

Elevator music is a variation of the Muzak concept. Its recorded music concept focused on soothing sounds, designed to relieve the tensions caused by putting large groups of people into small spaces. Elevator music was instrumental in nature and was piped in via recordings on elevator sound systems. Elevator music was often confused with FM radio stations who broadcast similar music, but they fulfilled distinctively different purposes.

Natural ambient sounds were recorded in the 1940s and 1950s as sound effects. One of the first uses of ambient sounds in pop music was Martin Denny's 1959 hit "Quiet Village." The Mystic Moods Orchestra recorded several albums of easy listening music, with ambient sounds added, these records being romantic standards. This paved the way for the Windham Hill sound of New Age music, prominently featuring ambient sounds. Businesses such as massage parlors rely on soft music to create relaxing ambience.

Recorded messages are used on telephones, including music tracks. There are companies that recorded customized messages, often with artwork for video display on websites and fan pages. Ringtones feature hit songs and are utilized on landlines, cell phones and websites greeting visitors. When callers are kept on hold, the music is often from libraries of techno-pop tunes, designed for interruptions and repetition.

Ambiance music was adopted by other commercial establishments. Wired connections piped music to stores, including departments and offices. This music was designed to create calming moods and make relaxing conditions. Music in retail settings was designed to stimulate buying and commerce.

Ambiance music in office buildings and elevators developed into a lucrative business. Beginning in 1922, such recorded ambiance became known as "elevator music" and "lift music." Elevators were new at the time, and the music tended to calm fearful passengers.

Calm, relaxing music was piped into shopping centers, airports and transportation carriers. Recorded music for business telephone systems was developed, serving to calm people kept on hold. Background music was designed for offices, with the aim to improve worker output and productivity.

Some Muzak tunes were popular hits recorded by orchestras. Many were original compositions.

Muzak developed the concept of Stimulus Progression, with points affecting behaviors and moods. Blocks of music went in cycles, hoping that listeners would pick up the pace at shopping and work. Vocal and choral music was added to the mix in the 1950s. By the 1970s, the pace of the music was more contemporary, paralleling the disco trend. Background music added soft-rock melodies. By the 1980s, elevator music no longer sounded like its old stereotype.

Delivery of background music advanced as technology was developed. In the 1940s and 1950s, stores played ambiance music via vinyl records. Services entered the market to mix name hits onto reel-to-reel tape, later conveying continuously mixed backgrounds on cassette tape. The CD era saw multi-disc changers installed in stores. In the 2000s, ambiance music was distributed via digital downloads.

With the advent of satellite radio, more than 100 formats transmitted niche music tracks, everything from traditional elevator music to golden oldies to rock hits to mellow jazz to mixed bags of music genres.

Recorded Backgrounds for Life

An emerging form of mellow music developed in the 1960s. New Age music created ambiances in homes and cars. Tony Scott's "Music for Zen Meditation" in 1964 was considered the first New Age album. Then came the Mystic Moods Orchestra albums of the late-1960s and 1970s. Also in that genre was Irv Teibel's "Environments" series. In the 1980s, that space was broadened by soft-jazz records by Kenny G, The Rippingtons and others. Labels such as Wyndham Hill marketed records and CDs to general audiences.

Ambiance categories and genres include:

- Incidental music.
- Elevator music.
- Retail and commerce music.
- Business environment music.
- Furniture music.
- Baseball-park crowd stimulation.
- Tracks balanced for running and jogging.
- Fitness workout music.
- Children's play songs.
- Dinner music.
- Concert intermission music.
- Christmas season soundtracks.
- Sports events music.

- Arts and crafts inspiration music.
- Golden oldies of various eras.
- Music for telephone systems.
- Tracks for corporate work environments, best sounds for getting things done.
- Music to study by.
- Healthcare institution background music.
- Neurological enhancement music.
- Activity venues, including skating rinks, miniature golf and bowling alleys.
- Ringtones.
- Video game and blog music.

Ambiance music is recorded on custom CDs for restaurants, to deliver guest experiences. Music at Olive Garden is a blend of pop music great singers, show tunes, jazzy rhythms and selections from the great songbooks. Music at Outback is a blend of contemporary pop, dance rhythms, country and happy melodies. Theme restaurants use tracks with Spanish music, soul, mellow jazz and golden oldies.

Many restaurants play satellite channels. There are all formats available on the internet, from traditional elevator music to mellow jazz to rock to country.

There are companies that lease the sound equipment and the soundtracks to retail establishments. Systems are set up to pipe music to multiple locations. They control the content and pacing. Royalties are covered in subscription fees. Modern systems allow guests to request songs from their phones.

Chapter 25
1980s MUSIC, HYBRID POP

This was the era where Hybrid Pop was the theme. Rock, soul and country music all came of age. All crossed into the other. People hummed familiar tunes, under the Adult Contemporary banner. Consumers still bought records and cassette tapes, were introduced to CDs, became captivated by music videos and shared musical expressions under the banner Pop.

In the 1980s, the quantity of music continued shrinking. There was 30 pervent less music than was released in the 1970s. Radio stations continued tightened the music playlists. The amount of time where there were no repeats got shorter. There were fewer radio stations running recorded music because many switched to news and talk formats.

Movies starring John Travolta institutionalized music of the era. Disco was typified by 1977's "Saturday Night Fever." Then came 1978's "Grease," revisiting music of the late 1950s and early 1960s. 1980-81 was the heyday of "Urban Cowboy," which took country music uptown, replete with line dances.

Major recording artists of the 1980s and 1990s included some from the 1960s and 1970s that remained trailblazers included Elton John, Stevie Wonder, Paul

McCartney, Billy Joel, Tina Turner, Dolly Parton, Daryl Hall & John Oates, ZZ Top and Natalie Cole.

The 1980s saw teen pop and dance pop dominate, including post-disco and European disco music. The decade saw the rise of New Wave. More recording went digital, and the decade saw use of synthesizers. Electronic genres developed included electro, techno, house, freestyle and Eurodance.

Pop Superstars Influencing the Era

Six music superstars exemplify the 1980s and 1990s: Michael Jackson, Bruce Springsteen, Madonna, Kenny Rogers, Whitney Houston and Lionel Richie. Four of the superstars came together for the music event of the era. The American Music Awards were held in Los Angeles, CA, on Jan. 28, 1985. Michael Jackson, Bruce Springsteen, Kenny Rogers and Lionel Richie were all winners that night. Other winners included Cyndi Lauper, Willie Nelson, Tina Turner, Huey Lewis & The News and The Pointer Sisters.

Ken Kragen had organized USA for Africa, raising awareness and funds to address hunger famine. Kragen asked Jackson, Rogers and Richie to spearhead an all-star recording session after the awards ceremony, held at Lion Share Studio on Beverly Blvd. They invited all those winners and many others to participate.

On Jan. 28, 1985, forty-seven top stars recorded the song "We Are the World," conducted by Quincy Jones. Among those also on the record were Diana Ross, Harry Belafonte, Ray Charles, Bob Dylan, Smokey Robinson, Stevie Wonder, Dionne Warwick, Bob Geldof, Daryl Hall, John Oates, Jeffrey Osborne, Kim Carnes, Billy Joel, Kenny Loggins, Paul Simon, James Ingram, Steve Perry, Al Jarreau, Bette Midler, Sheila E., Dan Aykroyd, Lindsey Buckingham and Jackson family members.

Michael Jackson

Joe Jackson had performed with The Falcons, whose lead singer was Wilson Pickett. Joe and wife Katherine had nine children, destined to be a musical group. Joe arranged for the group to play at a 1969 fundraiser for Gary, IN, Mayor Richard Hatcher, who asked Diana Ross to come and hear the group. She was so impressed that she called Motown boss Berry Gordy, insisting that he sign her new discoveries.

The Jacksons ranged in age from ten to sixteen on their first album. With lead singer Michael Jackson on "I Want You Back," the first single, millions of preteens (white and black) had one of their own to identify with. Hits like "The Love You Save," "ABC" and "Mama's Pearl" followed. Ballads like "I'll Be There" and "Never Can Say Goodbye" appealed to broader age groups.

The world watched The Jackson Five mature before its eyes. The Jacksons graced the covers of music magazines and headlined TV shows. Their 1971 British tour was likened to what The Beatles had done in America in 1964. In 1971, some of the Jackson brothers recorded solo records.

The Jacksons shined onstage. They enjoyed being singers, as father Joe had prepared them to be. They moved to Epic Records in 1976. At the dawn of the 1980s, Michael was acknowledged as one of the most popular recording stars. His mature material spanned the gamut, including his 1982 duet with Paul McCartney. Michael hit the pinnacle in 1983 with "Billie Jean" and "Beat It." Michael's energy, singing appeal and dance moves made him the king of music videos and concerts.

The Michael Jackson hits of the 1980s and 1990s continued with "Wanna Be Starting Something," "Pretty Young Thing," "Human Nature," "Thriller," "I Just Can't Stop Loving You," "Bad," "The Way You Make Me Feel," "Man in the Mirror," "Dirty Diana," "Smooth Criminal," "Black or White," "Remember the Time," "In the Closet," "Jam," "Heal the World," "Who Is It" and "Will You Be There."

Bruce Springsteen

He is fondly known as the boss of rock and roll. Bruce Springsteen is known for long concerts filled with energy. From Freehold, NJ, his hits started with 1975's "Born to Run." He wrote Manfred Mann's 1977 hit "Blinded by the Light."

Springsteen dominated the music charts for thirty years. His 1980s hits included "Hungry Heart," "Fade Away," "Dancing in the Dark," "Cover Me," "Born in the USA.," "I'm on Fire," "Glory Days," "I'm Going Down," "My Hometown," "War," "Fire," "Brilliant Disguise," "Tunnel of Love" and "One Step Up." His 1990s hits included "Human Touch," "Better Days," "57 Channels," "Leap of Faith," "Lucky Town," "Streets of Philadelphia," "Secret Garden" and "Sad Eyes." His 2000s hits included "The Rising," "Waiting on a Sunny Day," "Devils and Dust," "Radio Nowhere," "Girls in Their Summer Clothes," "My Lucky Day," "The Wrestler,"

"We Take Care of Our Own," "Death to My Hometown," "High Hopes," "Hello Sunshine," "Letter to You," "Tucson Train" and "Ghosts."

Bruce Springsteen won twenty Grammy Awards, two Golden Globes, an Oscar and a special Tony Award for "Springsteen on Broadway." In 2016, he was awarded the Presidential Medal of Freedom by Barack Obama. He is ranked twenty-third on Rolling Stone Magazine's list of the greatest rock and roll acts of all-time.

Madonna

In her first TV appearance in 1983, Madonna appeared on "American Bandstand." She performed her first hit, "Holiday." Host Dick Clark asked what her goals were. Madonna replied: "To rule the world." She pretty much did in pop-rock music.

Madonna Louise Ciccone was the biggest pop-rock star of the 1980s and 1990s. She hailed from Michigan. In 1978, she moved to New York City to pursue a career in modern dance. As a singer, she rose to fame in 1983, with her debut album.

The hits kept coming, including "Borderline," "Lucky Star," "Like a Virgin," "Material Girl," "Crazy for You," "Angel," "Dress You Up," "Live to Tell," "Papa Don't Preach," "True Blue," "Open Your Hearty," "La Isla Bonita," "Who's that Girl," "Causing a Commotion," "Like a Prayer," "Express Yourself," "Cherish," "Keep It Together," "Vogue," "Hanky Panky," "Justify My Love," "Rescue Me," "This Used to Be My Playground," "Erotica," "Deeper and Deeper," "Bad Girl," "Rain." "Take a Bow," "Hung Up," "Frozen," "4 Minutes," "Rain," "Power of Goodbye," "You'll See," "Beautiful Stranger," "Hey You" and "Nothing Really Matters."

Madonna appeared in the movies "Desperately Seeking Susan," "Dick Tracy," "A League of Their Own" and "Evita." The Queen of Pop, she is the most successful solo artist in the history of the Billboard Hot 100 Charts. VH1 ranked her as the greatest music video artist of all time.

Kenny Rogers

He personified the love balladeer and was equally big on the pop and country charts. The edges of his voice spoke realism. He sang of the wants and needs of the common man.

I met him in 1960 and introduced him in concert in 1976 and 1986. During his six-decade career, Kenny Rogers released sixty-five albums and sold more than 165 million records, one of the most successful recording artists of all time. He won three Grammy Awards, thirteen American Music Awards, six Country Music Assn. Awards, CMA Lifetime Achievement Award, CMT Artist of a Lifetime Award.

Kenny Rogers was a 1956 graduate of Jeff Davis High School. He began his musical career in 1958 as a member of The Scholars. In 1960, he became the bass player with the Bobby Doyle Trio, performing at the Tidelands Club. His first recorded as Kenneth Rogers, later becoming a member of such groups as the Kirby Stone Four and the New Christy Minstrels. Kenny expanded his singing skills to include pop, folk and country. In 1967, he formed Kenny Rogers & the First Edition, composed of former Minstrels members. He left the group in 1973 and became a major solo entertainer. His autobiography book was called "Making It with Music."

Whitney Houston

Whitney Houston was one of the biggest selling recording artists of all time. She was the daughter of Cissy Houston and cousin of Dionne Warwick. Her hits included "Hold Me," "You Give Good Love," "Saving All My Love for You," "How Will I Know," "Greatest Love of All," "I Wanna Dance with Somebody," "Didn't We Almost Have it All," "So Emotional," "Where the Broken Hearts Go," "Love Will Save thew Day," "One Moment in Time," "I'm Your Baby Tonight," "All the Man that I Need," "Miracle," "I Will Always Love You," "I'm Every Woman," "I Have Nothing," "I Know Him So Well," "Exhale," "Count on Me," "Step by Step," "I Believe in You and Me" and "My Love is Your Love."

She won two Emmy Awards, eight Grammy Awards, fourteen World Music Awards, sixteen Billboard Music Awards and twenty-two American Music Awards. She was the only artist to have seven consecutive #1 singles on Billboard's Hot 100 charts.

Lionel Richie

From Tuskegee, AL, Lionel Richie was the leader singer with the Funk band The Commodores. The group's hits on Motown included "Machine Gun," "Slippery When Wet," "I Feel Sanctified," "Sweet Love," "Just to Be Close to You," "Fancy

Dancer," "Easy," "Brick House," "Too Hot to Trot," "Three Times a Lady," "Flying High," "Sail On," "Still," "Lady, You Bring Me Up," "Old-Fashion Love," "Oh No" and "Nightshift."

In 1981, Richie had a duet with Diana Ross, "Endless Love." Thereafter he had hit records as a single artist, with hits including "Truly," "You Are," "My Love," "All Night Long," "Running with the Night," "Hello," "Stuck on You," "Penny Lover," "Say You, Say Me," "Dancing on the Ceiling," "Love Will Conquer All," "Ballerina Girl" and "Se La." "Say You, Say Me" won both the Academy Award and the Golden Globe for Best Song of 1985. He received the Songwriter's Hall of Fames highest honor, the Johnny Mercer Award. Richie has been the popular judge on ABC-TV's "American Idol."

When Country Music Became Cool

For years, it was called Hillbilly Music. The Grand Ole Opry fashioned country and western music for hometown American audiences. In the 1950s, country music crossed over to pop radio and drew legions of fans. By the 1960s, it had lost the "and western" moniker. Country music refined in the 1970s and grew its appeal. By the 1980s, it was cool and uptown. The "Urban Cowboy" trend brought country music to the mainstream of world music.

Stars and groups shined in the 1980s, appealing to pop and rock fans. These included Eddie Rabbitt, Alabama, George Jones, Tammy Wynette, Conway Twitty, Dottie Werst, Kenny Rogers, the Bellamy Brothers, Rosanne Cash, Crystal Gayle, Juice Newton, Garth Brooks, George Strait, Waylon Jennings, Willie Nelson, Barbara Mandrell, David Frizzell, Loretta Lynn, Johnny Lee and Mickey Gilley.

Don Williams was the king of mellow in country music. I met him in 1966 in Austin, TX, at suggestion of our mutual friend, Farrah Fawcett. She and I were eighteen-year-old freshmen at UT. Don led a folk group, Pozo-Seco Singers, from Corpus Christi, TX. They had a 1965 hit "Time," a Peter, Paul & Mary sound-alike. Don played me a demo of their next record, "I Can Make It with You Baby," an up-tempo rocker. I told Don and Farrah that his future was in mellow ballads, not folk rock. She became a star in 1976 with "Charlie's Angels."

In 1981, I emceed Don Williams in concert at Gilley's and asked him to perform that 1966 off-hit as a favor to me and Farrah, seeing how far he had come.

His record "I Believe in You" was #1 at the time. Williams was the 2010 inductee to the Country Music Hall of Fame, amassing seventeen #1 country hits.

Music of the 1980s

Other recording and concert stars of the 1980s included Prince, Cyndi Lauper, Phil Collins, George Michael, The Eurythmics, Belinda Carlisle, Janet Jackson, Billy Ocean, The Pet Shop Boys, Pat Benatar, Laura Branigan, Richard Marx, Paula Abdul, Culture Club, Depeche Mode, Peter Gabriel, Gloria Estefan and REO Speedwagon.

Classics of the decade included:

- "Love Come Down" by Evelyn "Champagne" King
- "Caribbean Queen" by Billy Ocean
- "Jump For My Love" by The Pointer Sisters
- "Sweet Dreams Are Made of This" by The Eurythmics
- "We Built This City" by Starship
- "Centerfold" by The J. Geils Band
- "Mickey" by Toni Basil
- "Jessie's Girl" by Rick Springfield
- "Talking in Your Sleep" and What I Like About You" by The Romantics
- "She Blinded Me with Science" by Thomas Dolby
- "Broken Wings" by Mister Mister
- "Too Shy" by Kajagoogoo
- "Ghostbusters" by Ray Parker, Jr.
- "Don't Rush Me" by Taylor Dayne
- "I Ran So Far Away" by A Flock of Seagulls
- "Wake Me up Before You Go-Go" by Wham!
- "Keep on Loving You" by REO Speedwagon
- "Girls Just Want to Have Fun" and "Time After Time" by Cyndi Lauper
- "Total Eclipse of the Heart" by Bonnie Tyler
- "Walk Like an Egyptian" by The Bangles
- "The Power of Love" by Huey Lewis & the News
- "Let's Hear It For the Boy" by Deniece Williams
- "Rosanna" and "Africa" by Toto

- "Who Can It Be Now?" by Men at Work
- "Every Time You Go Away" by Paul Young
- "867-5309 (Jenny)" by Tommy Tutone
- "99 Red Balloons" by Nena
- "Almost Paradise" by Mike Reno and Ann Wilson
- "Major Tom (Coming Home)" by Peter Schilling
- "Come On Eileen" by Dexys Midnight Runners
- "Take on Me" by A-ha
- "Living on a Prayer" by Bon Jovi
- "Super Freak" by Rick James
- "Call Me," "The Tide is High" and "Rapture" by Blondie
- "Jump" by Van Halen
- "What's Love Got to Do with It" by Tina Turner
- "Don't Stop Believing" by Journey
- "Sweet Child of Mine" by Guns & Roses
- "Love Shack" by The B-52s
- "Walk This Way" by Run DMC
- "Never Gonna Give You Up" by Rick Astley
- "Under Pressure" by Queen
- "Just Like Heaven" by The Cure
- "Don't You Forget About Me" by Simple Minds
- "With or Without You" by U2
- "Sledgehammer" by Peter Gabriel
- "Walking on Sunshine" by Katrina and the Waves
- "Hungry Like the Wolf" by Duran Duran
- "Nasty" and "What Have You Done for Me Lately" by Janet Jackson
- "We Got the Beat" by The Go-Go's
- "Whip It" by Devo
- "Free Falling" by Tom Petty
- "The Sweetest Taboo" by Sade
- "I Love Rock and Roll" by Joan Jett
- "Kiss on My List," "You Make My Dreams," "Private Eyes" by Daryl Hall & John Oates
- "Hold Me," "Gypsy," "Big Love" and "Little Lies" by Fleetwood Mac

- "Give Me the Night" and Turn Your Love Around" by George Benson
- "Silent Running" and "All I Need is a Miracle" by Mike & the Mechanics
- "What's New," "How Do I Make You," "Somewhere Out There" and "Don't Know Much" by Linda Ronstadt

Chapter 26

1990s MUSIC, A BEACON
FOR WHAT CAME NEXT

Throughout the decade of the 1990s, R&B, hip hop and urban genres became commonplace. Fusion genres popular included new-jack swing, neo-soul, hip hop soul and gangster-funk. The 1990s saw resurgences of older styles with new contexts, including third-wave ska, nu-metal, funk-jazz and fusion.

In the 1990s, the quantity of music continued shrinking. There was 25 percent of music on the market that was released in the 1960s. Radio stations continued tightened the music playlists. The amount of time where there were no repeats got shorter. There were fewer radio stations running recorded music because many switched to news and talk formats.

The third generation of rock and roll music fans championed the music of this era. Those in the Silent Generation embraced rock and roll in the 1950s. The Baby Boomers were the fans of pop music in the 1960s and 1970s. Generation X embraced the 1980s and 1990s recordings and stars. Fans of 2000s music are the Generation Y/Millennials, who also listen to the classic sounds from previous years.

Major Stars of the 1990s

Mariah Carey has a five-octave vocal range and is known as "Songbird Supreme" and the "Queen of Christmas." Her musical influences were Billie Holiday, Sarah Vaughan, Stevie Wonder, Al Green and Aretha Franklin.

Carey hit the market in 1990 with her first record. Her first five singles all reached #1 on Billboard's Hot 100 charts. 1994's "All I Want for Christmas is You" is one of the most popular seasonal hits. She authored two books, "The Meaning of Mariah Carey" and "The Christmas Princess."

Beyoncé Giselle Knowles is one of the world's current superstars. She was born in 1981 in Houston and performed in singing and dancing competitions as a child. She rose to fame in the 1990s as lead singer of R&B girl-group Destiny's Child. Managed by her father, Mathew Knowles, the group became one of the world's best-selling girl groups of all time.

Beyoncé released her debut solo album in 2003, selling eleven million copies, earning five Grammy Awards and featuring two number-one singles, "Crazy in Love" and "Baby Boy." After disbanding Destiny's Child in 2005, she released her second solo album, including the hits "Irreplaceable" and "Beautiful Liar." She ventured into acting, with a Golden Globe-nominated performance in "Dreamgirls" (2006), and starring roles in "The Pink Panther" (2006) and "Obsessed" (2009). Beyoncé's portrayal of Etta James in "Cadillac Records" (2008) influenced her third album, which included "At Last," Etta's 1961 cover of Glenn Miller's 1942 hit. She remains an all-time crowd pleaser in concert.

Michael Bolton, from New Haven, CT, sang in church and rock bands. He mellowed as a singer-songwriter known for ballads His top hits included "How Am I Supposed to Live Without You," "How Can We Be Lovers," "To Love Somebody," "Said I Loved You," "Missing You Now," "Lean on Me," "Love is a Wonderful Thing" and "Time, Love & Tenderness." His book was titled "The Soul of It All: My Music, My Life."

Celine Dion is a highly skilled vocalist. From Quebec, Canada, she wrote her first song, "It Was Only a Dream," at age twelve. Her father mortgaged the family home to fund her first record, which became a hit and made her an instant star. At age eighteen, she saw Michael Jackson in concert and vowed to be a performer like him. At age twenty, she won the Eurovision Song Contest. She learned English and made her global debut in 1990.

Her 1990s record hits included "Any Other Way," "Unison," "Where Does My Heart Beat Now," "The Last to Know," "Beauty and the Beast" (with Peabo Bryson), "Have a Heart," "If You Asked Me To," "Nothing But My Heart," "Love Can Move Mountains," "Water from the Moon," "When I Fall in Love" (with Clive Griffin), "Misled," "Think Twice," "The Last to Know," "Have a Heart," "Only One Road," "To Love You More," "Because You Loved Me," "It's All Coming Back to Me Now," "All By Myself," "Tell Him" (with Barbra Streisand), "My Heart Will Go On," "Immortality" (with The Bee Gees), "I'm Your Angel" (with R. Kelly) and "That's the Way It Is." In 1991, she was a featured soloist on the charity record, "Voices that Care."

Celine Dion has sold more than 200 million records worldwide, plus Las Vegas residence engagements. In 1999, she received a star on Canada's Walk of Fame. In 2013, she was awarded Canada's highest rank, the Companion of the Order of Canada.

U2 formed in Dublin, Ireland, in 1975. With Bono's expressive vocals, they had singles in the 1980s that included "Fire," "Gloria," "A Celebration," "Desire," "Where the Streets Have No Name," "Pride in the Name of Love," "Angel of Harlem," "All I Want is You" and "With or Without You." They performed at Live Aid in 1985.

Their 1990s hits included "The Fly," "Mysterious Ways," "One," "Even Better than the Real Thing," "Ride Your Wild Horses," "If God Will Send His Angels," "Stay (Faraway So Close)," "Sweetest Thing," "Last Night on Earth," "Miss Sarajevo," "Discotheque," "Staring at the Sun" and "Hold Me, Thrill Me, Kiss Me, Kill Me."

U2 is one of the greatest pop-rock acts of all-time. They won six MTV Awards, eleven Q Awards, two Juno Awards, two Golden Globe Awards, five NME Awards and fourteen Meteor Awards in Ireland.

Pearl Jam broke into the mainstream of their album "Ten" in 1991. "Ten" stayed on Billboard's Top 200 album charts for almost five years. Their second album, "Vs," sold almost one million copies in its first week of release. 1994's "Vitalogy," their third album, became the second fastest-selling CD at the time.

Pearl Jam's biggest hits of the 1990s included "Spin the Black Circle," "Jeremy," "Who Are You," "Given to Fly," "Nothing As It Seems," "I Am Mine," "Last Kiss," "Watchlist," "Go" and "Daughter." They were one of the key bands in the grunge movement and ranked as one of the Top 10 Live Acts of All-time in a reader poll in *Rolling Stone Magazine*.

Music of the 1990s

Boy bands of the 1990s included the Backstreet Boys, New Kids on the Block, Boyz II Men, Bell Biv DeVoe, 98 Degrees, Dream Street, Hanson, Take That and INSYNC.

The 1990s saw a revival of the singer-songwriter genre of the 1970s, with top stars including Alanis Morissette, Sheryl Crow, Tori Amos, Natalie Merchant, Sarah MacLachlan, Lisa Loeb, Jewel, Natalie Imbruglia, Fiona Apple and Liz Phair.

Other recording and concert stars of the 1990s included Nelson, Hootie & the Blowfish, Nirvana, Guns N' Roses, The Beastie Boys, Dr. Dre, Radiohead, the Red Hot Chillipeppers, Green Day, Snoop Dogg, Seal, Barenaked Ladies, Mary J. Blige, Blind Melon, The Black Crowes, The Roots, Lenny Kravitz, Creed and Arrested Development.

Classic Hits of the 1990s

- "I Swear" by All-4-One
- "Must Have Been Love" and "Dangerous" by Roxette
- "Nothing Compares to You" by Sinead O'Connor
- "Sacrifice" and "The One" by Elton John
- "Swing the Mood" by Jive Bunny
- "Black or White," "Remember the Time" and "Heal the World" by Michael Jackson
- "Alive" by Pearl Jam
- "Hold On" and "Release Me" by Wilson Phillips
- "All I Wanna Do" and "If It Makes You Happy" by Sheryl Crow
- "Pump Up the Jam" by Technotronic
- "All the Small Things" by Blink-182
- "Losing My Religion" and "Night Swimming" by R.E.M.
- "November Rain" by Guns N' Roses
- "Love and Affection" by Nelson
- "Baby Got Back" by Sir Mix-a-Lot
- "Rhythm Nation," "Come Back to Me" and "Alright" by Janet Jackson

- "Waterfalls" by TLC
- "Here We Are" by Gloria Estefan
- "The Sign" by Ace of Base
- "I'll Be" by Foxy Brown with Jay Z
- "Love Shack" and "Roam" by The B-52s
- "Smells Like Teen Spirit" by Nirvana
- "All Around the World" by Lisa Stansfield
- "You Ought to Know" by Alanis Morissette
- "End of the Road," "Motown Philly" and "I'll Make Love to You" by Boyz II Men
- "Doo Wop" by Lauryn Hill
- "Another Day in Paradise" by Phil Collins
- "Un-Break My Heart" by Toni Braxton
- "Downtown Train" by Rod Stewart
- "The Boy is Mine" by Monica
- "I Want It That Way" and "Everybody" by The Backstreet Boys
- "Torn" by Natalie Imbruglia
- "Black Velvet" by Alannah Myles
- "Can't Touch This" by M.C. Hammer
- "Linger" by The Cranberries
- "Wonderwall" by Oasis
- "Genie in a Bottle" by Christina Aguilera
- "You Get What You Give" by the New Radicals
- "Semi-Charmed Life" by Third Blind Eye
- "Close to You" by Maxi Priest
- "Back to Life" by Soul II Soul
- "Sometimes" by Britney Spears
- "Don't Let Go" by En Vogue
- "The River of Dreams," "I Go to Extremes," "That's Not Her Style" by Billy Joel
- "Crash Into Me" by the Dave Matthews Band
- "Kiss Me" by Sixpence None the Richer
- "Vision of Love" and "Always Be My Baby" by Mariah Carey
- "Blaze of Glory" by Jon Bon Jovi

- "Mr. Jones" by Counting Crows
- "Ready or Not" by After 7
- "Gonna Make You Sweat" by C+C Music Factory
- "Closing Time" by Semisonic
- "Poison" by Bell Biv DeVoe
- "Man! I Feel Like a Woman!" and "You're Still the One" by Shania Twain
- "Truly Madly Deeply" by Savage Garden
- "I Wanna Be Rich" by Calloway
- "I Don't Want to Miss a Thing" by Aerosmith
- "Say My Name" by Destiny's Child
- "Wannabe" by The Spice Girls
- "Umbrella" by Rihanna

Chapter 27

B-SIDES, FLIP SIDES
AND DOUBLE-SIDED HITS

W hen 45RPM singles went away in the early 1990s, so did B-sides. Young music fans in the digital download era do not know about the unusual and creative gems that were put on the back of hit records.

During the eras of vinyl singles, they all had B-sides. The earliest Victrola singles by RCA Victor (classical and operatic) had one side. In 1904, the record industry made 2-sided records the standard. In the 1920s and 1930s, the records were recorded as double potential hits. In the big band years of the 1940s, swing tunes on A-sides were backed by ballads. Throughout the twentieth century, records were double-sided.

In the early rock era, artists put out double-sided hits, including Elvis Presley, The Beach Boys, The Beatles and The Rolling Stones. The goal was to get both sides played on the radio and maximize coverage. When A sides hit the top of the charts, so did their B-sides.

Some multi-talented singers put out hit A-sides for the teen record buyers and mellow pop as B-sides for older fans. Those included Rosemary Clooney, Steve Lawrence, Eydie Gorme, Pat Boone, Perry Como and Frank Sinatra.

Steve Lawrence's 1962 hit "Go Away Little Girl" (written by Carole King and Gerry Goffin) had as its B-side his self-penned "If You Love Her, Tell Her So." Eydie Gorme's 1964 hit "I Want to Meet My Baby" (written by Barry Mann and Cynthia Weil) had as its flip side "Can't Get Over the Bossa Nova," written by herself and husband Steve Lawrence.

Sam Cooke had pop-soul singles, and his flip sides included glitzy show music and ballads. His 1959 hit "Wonderful World" had as its B-side "Along the Navajo Trail," cover of Roy Rogers' 1945 hit. 1963's "Frankie and Johnny" had "Cool Train" as the backside. 1958's "For Sentimental Reasons" had "Desire Me" as the flip. 1964's "Good News" was backed by "Basin Street Blues." 1957's "You Send Me" was backed by the Gershwin classic "Summertime."

Known for Great B-Sides

Nat King Cole had many great albums, but his B-sides to singles were original songs, rather than album tracks. Notable Cole B-sides included:

- "In the Cool of Evening," backing 1946's "The Christmas Song"
- "Summer Time's A-Coming," flip to 1952's "Easter Sunday Morning"
- "If I May," B-side to 1953's "A Blossom Fell"
- "Don't Let Your Eyes Go Shopping," backing 1954's "Pretend"
- "Back in My Arms," back of 1954's "Angel Smile"
- "Do I Like It," backing 1958's "Looking Back"
- "The Good Times," flip to 1962's "Rambling Rose"
- "Who's Next in Time," B-side to 1962's "Dear Lonely Hearts"
- "In the Cool of the Day," flip of 1963's "Lazy-Hazy-Crazy Days of Summer"
- "I Don't Want to See Tomorrow," backing 1964's "L-O-V-E"

Notable Elvis Presley B-sides included:

- "Any Way You Want Me," flip to 1956's "Love Me Tender"
- "I Was the One," B-side to 1956's "Heartbreak Hotel"

- "All That I Am," backed with 1966's "Spinout"
- "Help Me," flipside to 1974's "If You Talk in Your Sleep"
- "High Heel Sneakers," backing side to 1968's "Guitar Man"
- "It Hurts Me," flip to 1963's "Kissing Cousins"
- "Where Do You Come From," B-side to 1962's "Return to Sender"
- "Patch It Up," flipside to 1969's "You Don't Have to Say You Love Me"
- "I Got Stung," backing up 1959's "One Night"
- "Anything That's Part of You," backside to 1962's "Good Luck Charm"

Notable Beatles B-sides included:

- "Old Brown Show," backing 1969's "The Ballad of John and Yoko."
- "There's a Place," B-side to 1964's "Twist and Shout"
- "I'm Down," flipside to 1965's "Help"
- "You Can't Do That," the back of 1964's "Can't Buy Me Love"
- "Thank You Girl," B-side to 1964's "Do You Want to Know a Secret"
- "I Don't Want to Spoil the Party," backup to 1965's "Eight Days a Week"
- "I'll Cry Instead," flip to "I'm Happy Just to Dance with You"
- "Slow Down," the B-side of 1964's "Matchbox"
- "Yes It Is," B-side to 1965's "Ticket to Ride"

Notable Rolling Stones B-sides included:

- "Ruby Tuesday," flip to 1967's "Let's Spend the Night Together"
- "2000 Light Years from Home," flip to 1968's "She's a Rainbow"
- "Gotta Get Away," B-side to 1966's "As Tears Go By"
- "Child of the Moon," backing 1968's "Jumping Jack Flash"
- "Down in the Hole," backside to 1980's "Emotional Rescue"
- "The Under Assistant West Coast Promotion Man," flip to 1965's "Satisfaction"
- "You Can't Always Get What You Want," B-side to 1969's "Honky Tonk Women"

Notable Monkees B-sides included:

- "A Man without a Dream," flip to 1969's "Tear Drop City"
- "Tapioca Tundra," B-side to 1968's "Valleri"
- "Going Down," backed up 1967's "Daydream Believer"
- "Someday Man," flip of 1969's "Listen to the Band"
- "It's Nice to Be with You," backing 1968's "D.W. Washburn"
- "The Girl I Knew Somewhere," B-side to 1967's "A Little Bit Me, A Little Bit You"
- "Take a Giant Step," flipside to 1966's "Last Train to Clarksville"

Notable Beach Boys B-sides included:

- "She Knows Me Too Well," flip to 1964's "When I Grow Up"
- "You're So Good to Me," backing 1965's "Sloop John B"
- "Let Him Run Wild," other side of 1965's "California Girls"
- "You're Welcome," B-side to 1967's "Heroes and Villains"
- "There's No Other," backed with 1966's "The Little Girl I Once Knew"
- "Let's Go Away for Awhile," backing up 1966's "Good Vibrations"
- "Wake the World," backup to 1968's "Do It Again"
- "Please Let Me Wonder," B-side to 1965's "Do You Wanna Dance"
- "The TM Song," flip to 1976's "Rock and Roll Music"
- "The Warmth of the Sun," backing 1964's "Dance, Dance, Dance"

The Who's memorable flip sides:

- "Whiskey Man" backed their 1967 hit "Happy Jack."
- "Out in the Street" backed the hit "My Generation."
- "Bald Headed Woman" was the flip of their first hit, "I Can't Explain."
- "Doctor, Doctor" was the back of 1967's "Pictures of Lily."
- 1968's "Call Me Lightning" was backed with "Dr. Jekyll & Mr. Hyde."
- The Who released "My Wife" as the backside to two of their singles, 1971's "Behind Blue Eyes" and 1979's "Long Live Rock."

Paul McCartney had his share of B-sides with The Beatles. When he formed Wings in the 1970s, his records had catchy creative flip sides. "Helen Wheels" was backed with "Country Dreamer." "I Lie Around" backed "Live and Let Die." "Sally G" was the B-side of "Junior's Farm." "With a Little Luck" had two songs on its backside, "Backwards Traveler" and "Cuff Link." "Nineteen Hundred and Eighty-Five" was the flip of "Band on the Run." "Silly Love Songs" was backed with "Cook of the House."

"Listen the Snow is Falling" was the B-side of John Lennon's "Happy Xmas" (the War is Over). The back of "Instant Karma" was "Who Has Seen the Wind?" "Touch Me" was the flip of "Power to the People." "Beef Jerky" was the other side of "Whatever Gets You Through the Night."

"Early 1970" was the flip of Ringo Star's "It Don't Come Easy." "Snookeroo" was the back of "The No Song." Ringo's "Back Off Boogaloo" was backed by "Blindman." The B-side of "Only You" was "Call Me." The back of "Goodnight Vienna" was "Oo-Wee."

George Harrison's hit "Crackerbox Palace" was backed with "Learning How to Love You." "Isn't It a Pity" was the B-side of "My Sweet Lord." "Writings on the Wall" was the flip of "All Those Years Ago." The other side of "Blow Away" was "Soft-Hearted Hana."

Elton John's 1975 mega-hit "Philadelphia Freedom" had as its B-side "I Saw Her Standing There," his duet with John Lennon. Other memorable Elton John flip sides include "Elderberry Wine," the flip of "Crocodile Rock." There was "Young Man's Blues," backing "Goodbye Yellow Brick Road." Elton sang "Harmony" as the back of "Bennie and the Jets." "Slave" was the B-side of "Honky Cat." "Saturday Night's Alright for Fighting" had two songs on its backside, "Jack Rabbit" and "Whenever You're Ready." "House of Cards" backed up "Someone Saved My Life Tonight."

Frank Sinatra had some excellent B-sides. 1966's "Strangers in the Night" was backed with "Oh, You Crazy Moon." 1954's "Young at Heart" had as its B-side "Take a Chance." 1955's "Learning the Blues" was backed with "If I Had Three Wishes." 1957's "Witchcraft" has "Tell Her You Love Her" on the flipside. His 1963 single "Call Me Irresponsible" had as its flip side "Tina," a tribute to his daughter. "You Are There" was the back of 1967's "The World We Knew." "Then

Suddenly Love" was the B-side of 1964's "Softly, As I Leave You." His signature hit "My Way" had "Blue Lace" as its backside.

Two of Bruce Springsteen's biggest hits had Christmas songs as B-sides. "Santa Claus is Coming to Town" was the backside of "My Hometown" in 1985. "Merry Christmas Baby" was the flip side of "War" in 1986.

Record producer Phil Spector had major hits with energetic vocal talents like The Crystals and The Ronettes. For most of the B-sides, Spector released instrumentals by studio session players, members of the Wall of Sound band.

B-sides were also known as flipsides, as radio DJs liked to sample both sides of the platters. "Happy Happy Birthday" by The Tune Weavers, 1957, was originally released as the B-side of "Old Man River." A radio DJ accidentally played it, and the flip became the hit.

In 1968, Cliff Nobles recorded "Love Is All Right." The B-side was the instrumental track, titled "The Horse." The instrumental side became a huge hit and sparked a trend in records releasing non-vocal tracks as flip sides. Subsequent releases by Cliff Nobles had the instrumentals as A-sides and vocals as B-sides.

Hank Moore's Top B-Songs Playlist
- "Unchained Melody" by Les Baxter, 1954
- "Gloria" by The Cadillacs, 1954
- "Thirteen Women" by Bill Haley & his Comets, 1955
- "You Don't Have to Be a Baby to Cry" by Tennessee Ernie Ford, 1955
- "Everybody's Got a Home but Me" by Eddie Fisher, 1955
- "I'll Be Home" by Pat Boone, 1956
- "99 Ways" by Charlie Gracie, 1957
- "Cool Shake" by the Del-Vikings, 1957
- "The Midnite Man" by Bill Justis, featuring The Spinners, 1958
- "Over and Over" by Bobby Day, 1958
- "Was There a Call for Me" by Bobby Darin, 1959
- "I Can't Begin to Tell You" by Jane Morgan, 1959
- "Oh, Cindy" and "San Miguel" by The Kingston Trio, 1959
- "Nobody But Me" by The Drifters, 1960
- "Don't Gild the Lily" by Del Shannon, 1961

- "Jailer Bring Me Water" by Bobby Darin, 1962
- "He Hit Me and It Felt Like a Kiss" by The Crystals, 1962
- "Haunted House" by The Kingsmen, 1962
- "Unchain My Heart" by Trini Lopez, 1963
- "Silence is Golden" by The Four Seasons, 1964
- "It's Alright" by Gerry & the Pacemakers, 1964
- "I Like It Like That" by The Nashville Teens, 1964
- "Gates of Eden" by Bob Dylan, 1965
- "Once Upon a Time" by Tom Jones, 1965
- "Try Me Baby" by Bob Kuban & the In-Men, 1966
- "Bacon Fat" by The Sir Douglas Quintet, 1966
- "Dancing in the Street" by the Mamas & the Papas, 1967
- "This Town," "Coasting" and "Leave My Dog Alone" by Nancy Sinatra, 1967
- "The Great Mandella" (Wheel of Life) by Peter, Paul & Mary, 1967
- "The Ambushers" by Tommy Boyce & Bobby Hart, 1968
- "Conquistador" by Gene Pitney, 1968
- "Laughing" by The Guess Who, 1969
- "Samba Pa Ti," "Waiting" and "Taboo" by Santana, 1970
- "Pay My Dues" by Blues Image, 1970
- "The Steeler" by Free, 1970
- "He's the Light of the World" by The Osmonds, 1972
- "Photographs & Memories" by Jim Croce, 1972
- "This Masquerade" by The Carpenters, 1974
- "Boogie Shoes" by K.C. & the Sunshine Band, 1975
- "Rufusized" by Rufus, featuring Chaka Khan, 1975
- "Slip Away" by The Four Seasons, 1976
- "It's Alright with Me" by Crystal Gayle, 1977
- "Babes in the Wood" by the Steve Miller Band, 1977
- "Lady Blue" by George Benson, 1978
- "Tell Me What You Want" by Daryl Hall & John Oates, 1981

Chapter 28

CHILDREN'S SONGS
ADAPTED TO POP SONGS

Many nursery rhymes and story songs were adapted to pop music lyrics, producing huge hits with familiar ditties.

"Mockingbird" was recorded by Charlie & Inez Foxx in 1962. It was based upon "Hush Little Baby." It was recorded by James Taylor & Carly Simon in 1974. Country singer Toby Keith recorded the song with his daughter Krystal in 2004.

"London Bridge is Falling Down" was adapted by Brenda Lee for her 1962 hit "My Whole World is Falling Down."

"He's a Good Guy (Yes He Is)" by The Marvelettes, written in 1964 by Smokey Robinson, was a soulful twist on "Did You Ever See a Lassie?" Its tune was taken from the Viennese song "Oh du Lieber," written in 1679 by Marx Augustin. It was re-recorded by Raffi in 1975 as "The More We Get Together," a song written in 1926.

"Ashes to Ashes" by David Bowie in 1969 was inspired by "Inchworm," which was recorded by Danny Kaye in 1952.

Sly & the Family Stone's 1969 hit "Everyday People" includes tunes from the Mother Goose song "Rub-a-dub Three Men in a Tub."

Crispian St. Peter had a smash hit with "The Pied Piper" in 1966. It was a tribute to "The Pied Piper of Hamelin," where he rids the town of rats by playing his flute and driving them off the cliff. The song is about the path to love.

Taylor Swift recorded "White Horse" in 2008, a song about fairy-tale princesses and love. The Rolling Stones' 1967 hit "Dandelion" was based upon nursery rhymes.

Sam the Sham & the Pharaohs had a mega-hit in 1965 with "Little Red Riding Hood," a rock updating of the classic children's story. They had a follow-up song "The Hair on My Chinny Chin Chin." Amanda Seyfried re-recorded it in 2011.

Duran Duran scored a hit in 1982 with "Hungry Like the Wolf." It referenced Little Red Riding Hood and the Big Bad Wolf.

Ray Parker & Raydio had a top 1978 hit song: "Jack and Jill." It was based upon "Jack and Jill went up the hill to fetch a pail of water." The hit R&B song also referred to Little Red Riding Hood.

Tommy Roe had a 1969 song hit called "Jack and Jill." It was part of a string of happy perky songs that also included "Dizzy," "Jam Up and Jelly Tight," "Heather Honey" and "Sheila."

Kenny Loggins wrote "The House at Pooh Corner," about the adventures of Winnie the Pooh. This 1971 song was a hit for the Nitty Gritty Dirt Band. It launched a long career for Kenny Loggins, with hits like "Footloose," "I'm Alright" and "Whenever I Call You Friend."

The Dave Matthews Band recorded "Rapunzel," based upon the fairytale about the German girl who was locked in a castle. The 1998 song had lyrics added to an instrumental called "Punk in 5."

The Elegants had a 1958 hit "Little Star." It was based upon the nursery rhyme "Twinkle, Twinkle, Little Star," written as a poem in 1806. It is sung to the tune of the French melody "Ah Vous Diral-je Maman," published in 1761 and arranged by Mozart.

The Mystics, a doo wop group, had a 1959 hit "Hushabye." It was inspired by Brahms' Lullaby, with the lyrics "lullaby and goodnight." The group also scored a hit with the World War II motivational song "White Cliffs of Dover."

Paul McCartney recorded "Queenie Eye" in 2014. It was based on a children's game, where one person would throw a ball over his head, and the kids would ask "who's got the ball."

"Lazy Elsie Molly" was a 1964 hit for Chubby Checker. Songwriters Tommy Boyce and Bobby Hart thumbed through a book of Mother Goose stories. They found a story about Lazy Elsie Marley, a girl who loved to sleep late.

Country singer RaeLynn wrote a song called "Kissin' Frogs" in 2005. It stemmed from a conversation with her mother, who said, "Honey, you don't need a boyfriend. You're just having fun kissing frogs."

Madonna's 1983 hit "Lucky Star" was based on the children's nursery rhyme "Star light. Star bright. First star I see tonight." In 1986, Run-D.M.C. recorded "Peter Piper," a rap song based upon the fables "Humpty Dumpty," "Little Bo Peep," "Rip Van Winkle" and "Peter Piper."

Johnny Preston's 1960 hit "Cradle of Love" had lyrics referencing four children's songs, "Rockabye Baby," "Jack Be Nimble, Jack Be Quick," "Jack and Jill" and "Hey Diddle Diddle, The Cat and the Fiddle."

Rihanna recorded "Raining Men" in 2010. She said, "If things don't work out with one guy, there are always many more guys out there." The chorus plays on the children's counting song "Eeny, Meeny, Miny, Moe," which dates from the 1850s.

Chapter 29
THEY STARTED AS CHILD SINGERS

C hristina Aguilera began singing at age 8, becoming one of the pop superstars as a singer and songwriter. She has been ambassador for the United Nations' World Food Program and holds a star on the Hollywood Walk of Fame. She has been a coach on NBC-TV's "The Voice."

Julie Andrews became a singing star at age twelve in England. In her twenties, she headlined Broadway in "My Fair Lady" and "Camelot." She reigned in the movies for three decades, including "Mary Poppins," "Thoroughly Modern Millie" and "Victor/Victoria."

Jimmy Boyd burst on the music scene at age nine, signing "I Saw Mommy Kissing Santa Claus." He sang other kid record hits. As a teenager, he appeared on the TV sitcom "Bachelor Father."

Celine Dion began her singing career at age five, composing her first song at age twelve. She became the first Canadian to receive a gold record in France, when she was fifteen. She began the ascent to pop superstar status at age eighteen. After three decades, she is a major headliner.

Annette Funicello began her career at age twelve as one of the Mouseketeers on ABC-TV's popular Disney series "Mickey Mouse Club." She was discovered by Walt

Disney at a dance recital in Burbank, CA. She appeared in the "Spin and Marty" serials and Disney's "Zorro" series. She recorded many records for the Disneyland label, with 1959's "Tall Paul" putting her on "American Bandstand." Then came Disney movies "The Shaggy Dog," "Babes in Toyland," "The Misadventures of Merlin Jones" and "The Monkey's Uncle."

In her twenties, Annette starred in the "Beach Party" movies with Frankie Avalon. She was the TV spokesperson for Skippy Peanut Butter. She evolved into the role model for other teenage idols. At age fifty, Annette was diagnosed with multiple sclerosis and was still a positive role model for the way that she valiantly lived with the disease over the next twenty years.

Judy Garland began singing at age two. As a teenager, she became one of MGM's top stars, notably in "Easter Parade," "Meet Me in St. Louis" and "The Wizard of Oz." As an adult, she became a major concert attraction, one of the greatest singers of the twentieth century.

Debbie Gibson became a major recording artist at age fifteen, with pop classics including "Only in My Dreams," "Out of the Blue," "Foolish Beat," "Shake Your Love" and "Staying Together."

Barry Gordon was a child singer and actor in the 1950s, appearing with such greats as Jack Benny. He had a successful teen acting career in the 1960s and evolved into film production and management. From 1988–1995, he served as President of the Screen Actors Guild.

Lesley Gore was sixteen when she burst on the music scene with the #1 hit "It's My Party." She continued a string of hits, dubbed the essential Girl Group Singer. For five decades, she kept the tradition of teen pop ballads alive, including "You Don't Own Me," "Maybe I Know," "Judy's Turn to Cry," "That's the Way Boys Are," "She's a Fool" and "Sunshine, Lollipops and Roses."

Michael Jackson grew up in a musical family. His father put together a group of his sons, The Jackson Five. They were discovered by Diana Ross when Michael was eleven and signed to the prestigious Motown label. His stylized records and music videos of the 1980's became the benchmarks around which the industry grew. His sister Janet started singing at age seven, also evolving into one of the music industry's top stars.

Frankie Lymon was thirteen when he sang the chart-topping hit record, "Why Do Fools Fall in Love." Lymon was a role model for Michael Jackson.

Brenda Lee started singing professionally at age eleven. She was known as Little Miss Dynamite and belted out so many teen anthems: "I'm Sorry," "Rocking Around the Christmas Tree," "As Usual," "All Alone Am I," "Johnny One Time," "Sweet Nothings," "Break It To Me Gently," "Fool #1," "My Whole World Is Falling Down," "Thanks A Lot," "I Want To Be Wanted" and "Too Many Rivers."

Donny Osmond started singing at age four. With his talented brothers, they were performing at Disneyland when they were discovered by singer Andy Williams. They appeared on the Williams TV show and then became top recording artists in the 1970's.

Marie Osmond debuted as part of her brothers' act on the Andy Williams Show when she was four. Her first hit record, "Paper Roses," came when she was fourteen. She began hosting the Donny & Marie Show on ABC-TV at age seventeen. She appeared in the Broadway musicals "The King and I" and "The Sound of Music." She has hosted TV shows, appeared in concerts and as the TV spokesperson for Nutrisystem.

LeAnn Rimes began performing at age five, performing in musical theatre in Dallas. By age nine, she was an experienced singer and had a major record deal at age fourteen. She became a country music superstar with pop cross-over appeal and international stature.

Taylor Swift began performing at age eleven, becoming one of the world's current superstars. Justin Timberlake began performing at age twelve. Britney Spears began performing at age twelve.

Stevie Wonder started performing at age eleven as a child singer. He was one of the Motown hit makers. Because of his writing talents, Wonder became one of the respected musical performers of the last five decades.

Chapter 30
MUSICAL DIRECTORS, ARRANGERS, BANDS AND MUSICIANS

Music Industry Kingpins

Mitch Miller was one of the geniuses of the recording industry. He had the instinct for commerciality and pioneered many of the components of a robust recording industry. He was classically trained, playing the oboe and English horn. As part of the CBS Symphony, he performed in Orson Welles' "War of the Worlds" broadcast. He was head of Artists and Repertoire for Mercury Records, discovering Frankie Laine and Vic Damone. When he moved over as head of Artists and Repertoire for Columbia Records, he brought both artists.

Mitch Miller discovered and signed Rosemary Clooney, Champ Butler, Johnnie Ray, Guy Mitchell, Jimmy Boyd, Johnny Mathis and Aretha Franklin. Miller insisted that his artists perform pop covers of country and soul hits, thus widening the commercial market for great songs. Rosemary Clooney hated a song called "Come On-A My House," but Miller insisted that she do it, the results being a stratospheric career changer.

227

Mitch Miller knew the public's tastes for pop music and catered to it. He fought and resisted rock n' roll for as long as he could, being the beacon for "good music." Miller had many hits under his own band's name, including "Yellow Rose of Texas" and "The Children's Marching Song." What he is most identified with is what he did next, as host of a TV series and record album series, "Sing Along with Mitch." He influenced so many careers and entertainment genres.

George Martin was often called the "fifth Beatle," in his role as their producer, musical director and keyboard player on their records. He was classically trained, playing piano and oboe. For EMI, he produced classical, jazz and comedy records, capped off with his work with The Beatles.

Hugo Peretti was a dominant musical director and musical producer in several genres. His partner was Luigi Creatore. They started producing children's records in the 1950s for Mercury, evolving into producing pop stars such as Georgia Gibbs. They roved over to Roulette Records, then in the 1960s to RCA Victor, where they produced Elvis Presley, Perry Como, Sam Cooke, Ray Petersen and The Tokens ("The Lion Sleeps Tonight"). In the 1970s, they operated Avco and H&L Records, recording The Stylistics and Van McCoy ("The Hustle").

Music Directors, Arrangers and Conductors

Stan Applebaum was the first to add full string orchestra to rock and roll songs. Stan conducted hits also for The Drifters, Neil Sedaka, Connie Francis (notably "Where the Boys Are"), Bobby Vinton, Joanie Sommers, Sam Cooke, Paul Anka, etc. Applebaum wrote music for 1,500 commercials. Applebaum arranged and conducted some of the most important records of all-time: "Stand By Me" by Ben E. King, "Where the Boys Are" by Connie Francis, "Calendar Girl" by Neil Sedaka, "Johnny Get Angry" by Joanie Sommers and hits by The Drifters: "Save the Last Dance For Me," "This Magic Moment," "I Count the Tears" and "There Goes My Baby."

Perry Botkin was a guitar player and bandleader who worked with Bing Crosby and other greats of the 1930s, '40s and '50s. Botkin played the guitar cues for the "Beverly Hillbillies" TV show in the 1960s.

Perry Botkin Jr. was a masterful arranger and orchestral conductor. He provided lush arrangements for easy listening singers such as Ed Ames, Carly Simon, Friends of Distinction, Shelby Flint, Sammy Davis Jr., Vikki Carr and The Lettermen. He conducted the Capitol house orchestra, the Hollyridge Strings. One of the most popular Christmas records is "Feliz Navidad" by Jose Feliciano, and that's Botkin's arrangement.

Charles Calello was a member of Frankie Valli's group The Four Lovers in the 1950s. When they became The Four Seasons, Calello became the group's music director. He arranged and conducted their hit recordings, often known as the "fifth Season." My personal favorites were Calello's arrangements for Tracey Dey, the seminal recordings being "Gonna Get Along Without You Now," "Teenage Cleopatra" and "I Won't Tell." Calello then served as musical director with Frank Sinatra, Neil Diamond, Ray Charles, Bruce Springsteen and Bobby Vinton. He became arranger and conductor with the Florida Sunshine Pops Orchestra.

Salvatore "Tutti" Camarata was trained at the Julliard School, of Music and worked with the big bands of Jimmy Dorsey, Benny Goodman, Glen Gray, Louis Armstrong and Duke Ellington. He had hit records in the 1940s and 1950s, including "Tutti's Trumpets." Walt Disney hired Camarata to be musical directoɪ of his Disneyland record company. He built a studio, Sunset Sound Recorders in what was formerly a Los Angeles auto repair shop. Among the artists who recorded there included Janis Joplin, The Lovin' Spoonful, Whitney Houston, Van Halen, Ricky Nelson, James Taylor, Sam Cooke, Andy Williams, Barbra Streisand, Barry Manilow, Led Zeppelin, Bob Dylan and Perry Como.

Gordon Jenkins was an executive with Decca Records, recording such stars as Louis Armstrong, Ella Fitzgerald, Billie Holiday and The Weavers. His band had many hit records. He conducted on many of Frank Sinatra's TV specials, the 1957 Sinatra Christmas album and other Sinatra records.

Billy May was a staff conductor with Capitol Records, directing swing albums for Frank Sinatra, Nat King Cole, Vic Damone, Mel Blanc and Nancy Wilson, plus a series of popular children's records, such as "Rusty in Orchestraville" and "Tubby the Tuba." He arranged for the big bands of Glenn Miller and Les Brown. He directed albums for Ella Fitzgerald, Bobby Darin, Stan Freberg, Matt Monro, Mel Torme, Jack Jones and Sammy Davis Jr. May had hit records of his own and music for such TV series as "Naked City," "The Green Hornet," "Mod Squad" and "Emergency."

Hal Mooney was an arranger for Bing Crosby, Judy Garland, Frank Sinatra, Peggy Lee and Billy Eckstine. He became Director of Artists and Repertoire for

Mercury Records, steering recordings of Sarah Vaughan, Dinah Washington and Nina Simone. In the 1970s, he was musical director for Universal Studios, guiding themes and cues for TV series.

Walter Murphy composed, arranged and conducted music cues for the Major-Valentino library, whose pieces were used for soundtracks and radio commercials. One of his tracks was released commercially in 1976. It was "A Fifth of Beethoven," a disco instrumental based upon "Beethoven's Fifth Symphony." The record became a hit for Walter Murphy and the Big Apple Band, spawning a series of records.

Jack Nitzsche was musical director for Phil Spector's Wall of Sound orchestra, backing The Ronettes, Crystals, Bob B. Soxx & the Bluejeans, The Righteous Brothers and others. The Wall of Sound included such studio musicians as Glen Campbell, Leon Russell and Hal Blaine. He played keyboards on recordings with The Rolling Stones, Neil Young and others.

Henri Rene was a staff conductor with RCA Victor, backing such stars as Eartha Kitt, Dinah Shore, Harry Belafonte and Tony Martin. He recorded many instrumental sides. Rene's most memorable hit was "Roller Coaster," which became the theme song for the long-running TV game show "What's My Line." Rene made jazz albums, including "Compulsion to Swing" and "Riot in Rhythm."

Nelson Riddle led the orchestra behind Nat King Cole and Frank Sinatra on many Capitol recordings. He wrote, arranged and conducted theme songs and music cues for hit TV series, including "The Untouchables," "Route 66" and "The Rogues." Riddle was the musical director on such variety shows as "The Rosemary Clooney Show," "The Nat King Cole Show," "The Judy Garland Show" and "The Smothers Brothers Comedy Hour." Riddle had hit records with his own band, including 1956's "Lisbon Antigua" (#1 on the charts). In 1976, I emceed a music symposium with Riddle as the guest. I produced a documentary of his music. While it was playing for the audience, I noticed Riddle's hand behind the skirted table, conducting my documentary in time to the music.

House Bands on TV Shows

Nick Perito conducted on albums and TV shows for Perry Como. He was musical director for ABC-TV's "The Hollywood Palace," "The American Film Institute Awards," "The Don Knotts Variety Show" and "Kennedy Center Honors."

Paul Weston was the musical director on CBS-TV variety shows, including "The Danny Kaye Show" and the "Jim Nabors Hour."

David Rose was the musical director on Red Skelton's TV shows and the Fred Astaire TV specials. He wrote, arranged and conducted theme songs and music cues for NBC-TV shows "Bonanza" and "Little House on the Prairie." He wrote theme songs for other TV series, including "Highway Patrol" and "Lock Up."

Jack Rael was the musical director on Patti Page's various TV shows and her 1940s and 1950s recordings. He discovered her singing on the radio in Oklahoma.

Paul Mirkovich is the musical director and leads the house band on NBC-TV's "The Voice." He has been responsible for more than 2,000 arrangements of songs performed on the show. Mirkovich was formerly musical director for Cher, Janet Jackson, Hilary Duff, Christina Aguilera and the TV series "Rock Star."

Archie Bleyer was the musical director on Arthur Godfrey's radio shows and TV shows on CBS. Bleyer founded his own record label, Cadence, whose stars included The Everly Brothers, Andy Williams, The Chordettes and Bill Hayes. He and his band recorded records under their own name, the biggest hits being "Hernando's Hideaway" and "Naughty Lady of Shady Lane."

Ray Bloch led the orchestra on CBS-TV's "Ed Sullivan Show" for twenty-three years. He also led the orchestra on CBS-TV's "Jackie Gleason Show" for several years in the 1950s.

Herschel Burke Gilbert was musical director for Four Star Productions, composing themes and cues for such shows as "The Rifleman," "Dick Powell Show," "Target: The Corrupters," "Zane Grey Theatre," "Black Saddle" and "Wanted Dead or Alive."

Joe Harnell had several hit records, the biggest being "Fly Me to the Moon." He was musical director on the "Mike Douglas Show" from 1967–1973.

The conductor for seventeen years on Bing Crosby's radio shows was John Scott Trotter. On TV, he led the house band on "The George Gobel Show." He also worked with Vince Guaraldi, scoring Peanuts TV specials from 1966–1973.

Nashville composer, arranger, conductor and producer Bill Walker played on recording sessions with Eddy Arnold and Chet Atkins. He served as musical director on ABC-TV's "Johnny Cash Show."

Harry Zimmerman and Harry Sosnick were the conductors on NBC-TV's "Dinah Shore Chevy Show."

Peter Matz conducted for Barbra Streisand and Marlene Dietrich. He was musical director on "Hullabaloo" from 1965–1966, "Kraft Music Hall" from 1967–1971 and "The Carol Burnett Show" from 1971–1978.

Bobby Rosengarten was a studio musician, playing on recordings with Duke Ellington, Billie Holiday, Harry Belafonte, Barbra Streisand, Miles Davis, Benny Goodman, Peter Nero and Tony Bennett. He played in bands at NBC-TV, including on "The Ernie Kovacs Show" and "Sing Along with Mitch." He was the bandleader on ABC-TV's "Dick Cavett Show' from 1969–1974.

Late Night TV Show Bands

Skitch Henderson was musical director on "The Tonight Show Starring Steve Allen" from 1954–1957. He then was musical director on NBC-TV's "Steve Allen Variety Show." He was also musical director on "The Tonight Show Starring Johnny Carson" from 1962–1965.

Jose Melis was musical director on "The Tonight Show Starring Jack Paar" from 1957–1962. He previously led the music on Paar's CBS-TV daytime show. Melis recorded albums on the Seeco label.

Milton Delugg was the musical director for various NBC-TV shows, including "Dagmar's Canteen" and from 1965–1967 on "The Tonight Show Starring Johnny Carson."

Carl "Doc" Severinsen played trumpet in big bands led by Benny Goodman, Tommy Dorsey and Charlie Barnet. He became a studio musician at NBC-TV in 1949, where he accompanied Eddie Fisher, Kate Smith and Dinah Shore. He was a founding member of the band on "The Tonight Show Starring Steve Allen," taking over as the band's leader in 1967 during Johnny Carson's tenure as host. Severinsen sometimes subbed for Ed McMahon as Carson's second banana, and he proved popular in that role too.

Branson Marsalis is a dynamic jazz performer. He was musical director on "The Tonight Show Starring Jay Leno" from 1992–1995. He was succeeded on the show by Kevin Eubanks as musical director. Rickey Minor led the "Tonight" band from 2010–2014 and then moved over to "American Idol."

The Roots were founded in Philadelphia 1987 by Tariq Trotter ("Black Thought") and Ahmir Thompson ("Questlove"). They became a major hip-hop group. In 2009, The Roots became the official house band on "Late Night with

Jimmy Fallon." When Fallon moved to host "The Tonight Show" in 2014, The Roots became the house band.

Paul Shaffer was musical director on NBC-TV's "Late Night with David Letterman" from 1982–1993 and on CBS-TV's "The Late Show with David Letterman" from 1993–2015. He was previously musical director on "Saturday Night Live" from 1975–1980. "Late Night with Stephen Colbert" features music by Jon Batiste and the group Stay Human. Cleto Escobedo leads the band on ABC-TV's Jimmy Kimmel Show."

Mort Lindsey conducted the band on "The Merv Griffin Show," which aired on Metromedia and CBS-TV. Johnny Mann was vocal director on CBS-TV's "Danny Kaye Show" and musical director on ABC-TV's "Joey Bishop Show. Robin DiMaggio directed the music on "The Arsenio Hall Show" on Fox. Mark Hudson was bandleader on "The Joan Rivers Show." Jimmy Vivino and the Basic Cable Band directed music for "The Conan O'Brien Show" on TBS.

Chapter 31
MUSIC HELPED IN TIMES
OF NEED, PAIN AND CRISIS

Music reflects the times. It sets the tone for lives. It is an important part of the fabric of good times, trying times and painful transition periods.

Motivation and Social Consciousness

The US Revolutionary War was fought from 1775–1783. Songs popularized during the era included "Yankee Doodle," "The Battle of Bunker Hill," "The Liberty Song," "Paul Jones," "Free America," "Johnny's Gone for a Soldier," "The Ballad of Major Andre," "How Happy the Soldier," "Young Ladies in Town," "The World Turned Upside Down" and "The Battle of Saratoga."

From the War of 1812 came "The Star-Spangled Banner," which became the US national anthem. The lyrics came from a poem, "The Defense of Fort McHenry" by Francis Scott Key. It was set to a tune by James Stafford Smith. "The Star-Spangled Banner" was chosen for use by the US Navy in 1889 and by President Woodrow Wilson in 1916. Congressional resolution made it the national anthem in 1931.

Other War of 1812 songs included "The 8th of January," "Sweet Pull of Plymouth" and "The Sailor's Complaint."

The Civil War in America was fought from 1861–1965. Songs from the era include "Battle Hymn of the Republic," "Lincoln and Liberty," "John Brown's Body," "The Vacant Chair," "Dixie's Land," "Just Before the Battle Mother," "When Johnny Comes Marching Home," "Tenting Tonight on the Old Campground," "Battle Cry of Freedom," "Bonnie Blue Flag," "Better Times Are Coming," "Amazing Grace," "Goober Peas" and "The Yellow Rose of Texas."

"Guantanamera" was a poem of Cuban freedom fighters in the Spanish-American War of 1898. The US intervened in the war for Cuban independence. Music was added to the poem in the 1930s. It became a song about national pride. Folksinger Pete Seeger added the song to his concert repertoire in 1963. The biggest hit recording was by The Sandpipers in 1966. It is often played at football games.

World War I was fought from 1914–1918. Songs from that era included "Over There," "Pack Up Your Troubles," "K-K-K-Katy," "It's a Long Way to Tipperary," "Au Revoir But Not Goodbye Soldier," "Keep the Home Fires Burning," "Slavic Woman's Farewell," "The Planets" and "The Last Post."

The Great Depression of 1929–1933 brought songs to life people's minds about their hardships. They included "We're in the Money," "Life is Just a Bowl of Cherries," "Brother Can You Spare a Dime," "On the Sunny Side of the Street," "The United States Needs a Prayer Everywhere," "I'm Going Down This Road Feeling Bad," "When the Morning Glories Wake Up in the Morning," "Tight Like That," "Turpentine Blues," "The Great Dust Storm," "Top Hat White Tie and Tails," "President Roosevelt is Everybody's Friend," "Heading For Better Times," "The Poor Forgotten Man," "Old Age Pension Check," "NRA Blues," "No Depression in Heaven," "Keep Moving," "Yes We Have No Bananas" and "Serves Them Fine."

World War II was fought from 1940–1945. WWII spirit songs included "We'll Meet Again" by Vera Lynn, "Boogie Woogie Bugle Boy" and "Don't Sit Under the Apple Tree" by The Andrews Sisters, "Praise the Lord and Pass the Ammunition" by Kay Kyser, "Sentimental Journey" by Les Brown and Doris Day, "Coming In On a Wing and a Prayer" by The Song Spinners, "There's a Star Spangled Banner Waving Somewhere" by Elton Britt, ""G.I. Jive" by Johnny Mercer, "Der Fuehrer's Face" by Spike Jones and "A Soldier's Last Letter" by Redd Stewart and Ernest Tubb.

Other spirit songs included "Bell Bottom Trousers," "It's a Lovely Day Tomorrow," "On the Swing Shift," "Hot Time in the Town of Berlin," "Lili Marleen," "There'll Always Be an England," "Remember Pearl Harbor," "D-Day Dodgers" and "Fight for Freedom."

Irving Berlin wrote "Any Bonds Today?" and turned his royalties over to the government's war bond campaign. Irving Berlin wrote the song "God Bless America." It was considered an anthem of national unity during World War II and still is performed today. The signature recording was by Kate Smith in 1939. Berlin donated the royalties of that song in perpetuity to the Boy Scouts of America.

British singer Vera Lynn recorded "We'll Meet Again" in 1939. It was an inspirational song in the early days of World War II in Europe, offering hope for better times ahead. The song is traditionally played at the end of Every Liberation Day concert in The Netherlands. It is a global legend, establishing Vera Lynn as a major voice from the WWII era.

"When the Lights Go on Again" was inspired heavily by the 1940 London blackouts, to give people a sense of hope, calm and resolve. It was recorded in 1943 by Vaughn Monroe and Vera Lynn. Lyrics: "When the lights go on again all over the world. And the boys are home again. And rain or snow is all that may fall from the skies above. A kiss won't mean goodbye but hello to love. And the ships will sail again. Then we'll have time for things like wedding rings and free hearts will sing. When the lights go on again all over the world."

World War II era lyrics said it all:

- "I'll be seeing you in all the old familiar places."
- "He's 1-A in the Army and A-1 in my heart."
- "I'll be home for Christmas, if only in my dreams."
- "Long the skies were overcast, but now the clouds have past. All I longed for long ago was you."
- "Though they'll be rain, I'll not complain. I'll get by as long as I have you."
- "Till then, let's dream of what there will be. We'll call on each memory when I hold you again. Please wait till then."

"In the Summer of His Years" was a tribute to President John F. Kennedy. It followed JFK's assassination on Nov. 22, 1963. The song was by Connie Francis, recorded Nov. 24, 1963, with Claus Ogerman and his orchestra. Proceeds of record sales went to the family of a slain Dallas policeman. Other versions of the song were recorded by Kate Smith, Mahalia Jackson, Millicent Martin, Toni Arden, the Chad Mitchell Trio and Bobby Rydell. "In the Summer of His Years" paved the way for other social consciousness records, including Band Aid, USA For Africa, Concert for Bangladesh and Voices that Care.

Other JFK tribute songs included "Abraham, Martin and John" by Dion, "He Was a Friend of Mine" by The Byrds, "Warmth of the Sun" by The Beach Boys, "The Day John Kennedy Died" by Lou Reed, "Born in the 50's" by The Police, "Chimes of Freedom" by Bob Dylan, "God" by John Lennon, "Sympathy For the Devil" by The Rolling Stones, "We Didn't Start the Fire" by Billy Joel, "The Sound of Silence" by Simon & Garfunkel, "Sleeping In" by The Postal Service, "Crucifixion" by Phil Ochs, "Seconds" by The Human League and "Jackie's Strength" by Tori Amos.

Vietnam era songs included "The Battle of the Green Berets," "Waist Deep in the Big Muddy," "Bring the Boys Home," "Saigon Bride" and "For What It's Worth."

On Sept. 11, 2001, terrorists attacked America, putting planes into the World Trade Center in New York City, the Pentagon in Washington, D.C. and in Shanksville, PA. The attacks resulted in 2,977 fatalities, plus injury to the cities and way of life. The music industry responded by staging benefit concerts, motivational songs and making donations to victims.

The songs of 9/11 included "On That Day" by Leonard Cohen, "Undivided" by Jon Bon Jovi, "Hole in the World" by The Eagles, "Courtesy of the Red, White & Blue" by Toby Keith, "What More Can I Give" by Michael Jackson, "Empty Sky" by Bruce Springsteen, "Anniversary" by Suzanne Vega, "An Open Letter to NYC" by The Beastie Boys, "I Don't Know Why" by Amy Grant, "Didn't They" by Taylor Swift, "Let's Roll" by Neil Young, "Tuesday Morning" by Melissa Etheridge, "When New York Had Her Heart Broke" by John Hiatt, "Safe and Sound" by Sheryl Crow, "Snowed in at Wheeler Street" by Kate Bush and Elton John, "Sacrifice For Me" by The Oak Ridge Boys, "The Bravest" by Tom Paxton, "World on Fire" by Sarah McLachlan, "Tell Me Why" by Will Smith and Mary J. Blige, "Song for the Lonely" by Cher, "The Last Fallen Hero" by The Charlie Daniels Band and "I Was Here" by Beyoncé.

The COVID-19 Pandemic crossed the world in 2020–2022, affecting every country. In addition to the health effects, the COVID virus negatively impacted the economy, spurring a recession. The pandemic caused great dislocation in society. Musical tributes of the period included "Joining Hands," "Healthcare Workers Rock," "Spirit of Chicago," "Count Your Blessings," "Don't Stop Believing," "Isolation Song," "Do What You Can," "Quarantine Clean," "I Believe That We Will Win," "Better Days," "Stay Away," "Back to the Basics," "We Are the Warriors," "You Are the Champions," "My House" and "Put Your Mask On."

Zoom and other platforms had been used for teleconferencing and training for several years. As COVID forced most business to become distanced, the Zoom era was widely utilized. Conferences, meetings, professional education and customer service began utilizing cubes of people to contribute to the business.

TV shows went virtual, with guests on talk shows appearing via Zoom. Musical stars staged performances from their homes. World-renowned opera singer Andrea Bocelli took the stage in a deserted Duomo di Milano on Easter Sunday 2020 to perform a concert dubbed "Music for Hope," live-streamed to 3.4 million viewers.

Zoom technology allowed special songs to be transmitted via unique locations. Artists missed the live audiences, but the Zoom performances brought great comfort and encouragement to TV and social media audiences.

Rock star Dave Matthews wrote a song of compassionate understanding after the invasion of Ukraine in 2022. It was titled "Something to Tell My Baby."

Music Industry Giveback

Bob Geldof was leader of the group The Boomtown Rats. He was the driving force behind "Band Aid" in 1984. It was a record featuring the talents of most major British rock stars, to raise funds to assist famine relief in Ethiopia. The song was titled "Do They Know It's Christmas?" Geldof was one of the organizers of the 16-hour Live Aid concert, raising money and awareness for Africa. He became involved in the work of non-governmental organizations and was the leading spokesperson on Third World debt and relief.

Inspired by the work of Geldof and Band Aid, a group of American recording artists organized by Michael Jackson, Kenny Rogers and Lionel Richie supported USA for Africa. A total of 47 top stars recorded the song "We Are the World." That hit record raised funds for relief of famine and disease in Africa.

"Hands Across America," a chain of national events and benefit concert followed. On May 25, 1986, 6.5 million people held hands for fifteen minutes along a path from New York City to Long Beach, CA, across the US The record and concert raised more than $100 million for the humanitarian programs of USA for Africa.

Farm Aid was organized by Willie Nelson, John Mellencamp and Neil Young. Farm Aid concerts have continued every year since 1985.

Live Aid was a benefit concert held July 13, 1985, at both Wembley Stadium in London (attended by 72,000) and John F. Kennedy Stadium in Philadelphia (attended by 100,000). It was organized by Bob Geldof and Midge Ure to raise funds for the Ethiopian famine.

"Music Freedom Day" takes place on March 3 each year. It celebrates freedom of expression, recognizing forces that might suppress musicians. The 2016 event honored the victims of terrorist attacks in Paris, France, in November 2015.

These charity concerts and campaigns were in the tradition of others: John Lennon's 1969 "Give Peace a Chance," George Harrison's 1972 "Concert for Bangladesh," the 1979 "No Nukes Concert" and "Voices that Care."

Entertainers have appeared regularly on telethons. One of the earliest was the "Jim Moran Cancer Fund Benefit," 1950 on WENR-TV, the ABC affiliate in Chicago, IL, featuring Don McNeill, Johnny Desmond, Sam Cowling and Patsy Lee.

One of the earliest national fundraising spectaculars was the "Easter Seals Teleparade of Stars," 1955. It starred Jack Benny, Shirley MacLaine, Van Johnson, Ruth Hussey, Liberace, Robert Sterling, Anne Jeffries, Bob Crosby, The Modernaires, Dick Contino, Kitty Kallen, Don Wilson, Paul Baron orchestra. It was a benefit for Easter Seals, the association collecting donations to aide medical research into diseases crippling children.

The longest running has been the annual Muscular Dystrophy Association Labor Day Telethon. It was hosted for many years by Jerry Lewis, who invited the biggest stars to appear.

After terrorist attacks in the US on Sept. 11, 2001, a telethon benefiting families of victims of New York City terrorist attacks was simulcast on most networks. "America: A Tribute to Heroes," aired Sept. 21, 2001, and starred Muhammad Ali, Bruce Springsteen, Jack Nicholson, Al Pacino, Goldie Hawn, Kurt Russell, George Clooney, Stevie Wonder, Robin Williams, Clint Eastwood, Julia Roberts, Tom Cruise, Paul Simon, Tom Hanks, Willie Nelson, Kelsey Grammer, The Dixie

Chicks, Cameron Diaz, Dennis Franz, Sela Ward, Tom Petty, Bon Jovi, Faith Hill, Jim Carrey, Robert DeNiro, Billy Joel, Ray Romano, Neil Young, Amy Brenneman, Conan O'Brien and Sheryl Crow.

Following Hurricane Katrina, "The Concert for Hurricane Relief" was telecast on Sept. 2, 2005. Viewers were encouraged to donate to the Red Cross Disaster Relief Fund. It was hosted by Matt Lauer and featured such entertainers as Harry Connick Jr., Leonardo DiCaprio, Richard Gere, Tim McGraw, Faith Hill and Aaron Neville.

Hurricane Sandy hit New Jersey in October 2012. "Hurricane Sandy: Coming Together" was a telethon for disaster relief, broadcast on Nov. 2, 2012. Performers included Bruce Springsteen, Billy Joel, Aerosmith, Jon Bon Jovi, Christine Aguilera, Sting, Jon Stewart, Jimmy Fallon and Kevin Bacon.

Top stars performed on records raising money for worthwhile causes

Chapter 32

COVER SONGS

G ood songs are meant to be recorded by multiple artists. The mark of quality cover songs is in the artists adding their own takes on the music. Most music released each year is comprised of re-recorded songs from vast catalogs, cumulative distribution. Thirty-two percent of all songs and artists have been covered.

In the early twentieth century, music publishers would sell their songs to multiple artists. The term Songbook evolved, where writings by well-known composers got recorded many times.

In the Big Band Era of the 1930s and 1940s, bands wrote their own material. Other bands and singers covered songs created by others. As record albums grew in the 1940s, it was common to have covers on the set, along with original material.

By the 1950s, artists went back to songs of the 1920s and 1930s, covering them in updated styles. Connie Francis launched her recording career by recording a 1920s song "Who's Sorry Now" with modern beat, and it set the tone for her future recordings. Groups in the 1950s took the standards and added their flair. Prime examples of that era included all the hits by The Platters, notably "Smoke Gets in Your Eyes," "My Prayer," "I'll Never Smile Again" and "Red Sails in the Sunset."

By the 1960s, LP albums by easy listening artists were common. These were filled with covers of songs originated by rock, soul and country artists. The Beatles were so popular in the 1960s that several of their songs appeared re-recorded by every kind of artist imaginable. Artists releasing albums containing covers of the era included Tony Bennett, Sammy Davis Jr., Marilyn Maye, Jerry Vale, Cleo Laine, Vic Damone, Vic Dana, Kate Smith, Rosemary Clooney, Dean Martin, Mel Torme, The Lettermen, The Four Freshmen, Diahann Carroll, Ed Ames, Matt Monro, Peggy Lee and Julius LaRosa.

Some of the most covered songs of the last 100 years include "Bridge Over Troubled Water" (Paul Simon), "Unchained Melody" (Alex North), "Ain't No Sunshine" (Bill Withers), "Love Me Tender" (Elvis Presley), "Over the Rainbow" (Wizard of Oz), "My Way" (Paul Anka), "St. Louis Blues," "(I Can't Get No) Satisfaction" (The Rolling Stones), "Green Grass of Home," "House of the Rising Sun," "Cry Me a River" (Julie London), "How Deep is the Ocean" and "Hallelujah" (Leonard Cohen).

John Lennon and Paul McCartney had written many of their Beatles songs with cover version adaptability in mind. The most covered Beatles songs are "Eleanor Rigby," "And I Love Her," "Michelle," "Blackbird," "Here, There and Everywhere," "Imagine," "Norwegian Wood," "Let It Be," "Hey Jude," "Here Comes the Sun," "All My Loving," "While My Guitar Gently Weeps," "A Hard Day's Night," "Fool on the Hill," "In My Life," "With a Little Help from My Friends," "Come Together," "Something," "Can't Buy Me Love" and "The Long and Winding Road."

The Beatles themselves did several cover songs on their early albums. Their unique takes on other hits included "Anna" (Arthur Alexander), "A Taste of Honey" (Lenny Welch), "Till There Was You" (Shirley Jones), "Twist & Shout" (The Isley Brothers), "Baby It's You" and "Boys" (The Shirelles), "Chains" (The Cookies), "Act Naturally" (Buck Owens), "Money" (Barret Strong), "Please Mr. Postman" (The Marvelettes), "Mister Moonlight" (Dr. Feelgood), "Devil in Her Heart" (The Donays), "Ain't She Sweet," "You Really Got a Hold on Me" (Smokey Robinson & the Miracles and "Words of Love" (Buddy Holly).

The Beatles covered two Chuck Berry songs, "Roll Over Beethoven" and "Rock & Roll Music." They covered two Little Richard songs, ""Long Tall Sally" and "Kansas City." They covered three Larry Williams songs, "Slow Down," "Dizzy Miss Lizzy" and "Bad Boy." They covered four Carl Perkins songs, "Matchbox,"

"Honey Don't," "Sure to Fall in Love with You" and "Everybody's Trying to Be My Baby."

The Rolling Stones did cover songs, including "Under the Boardwalk" (Drifters), "It's All Over Now" (Valentinos), "Harlem Shuffle" (Bob & Earl), "Ain't Too Proud to Beg" (Temptations), "Around and Around" (Chuck Berry), "Can I Get a Witness" (Marvin Gaye), "Going to a-Go-Go" (Smokey Robinson & the Miracles), "I Wanna Be Your Man" (The Beatles), "If You Need Me" (Solomon Burke) and "I'm a King Bee" (Slim Harpo).

The Dave Clark Five did cover songs, including "Do You Love Me" (The Contours), "Reeling & Rocking" (Chuck Berry), "You Must Have Been a Beautiful Baby," "Over and Over" (Bobby Day), "You Got What It Takes" (Marv Johnson) and "A Little Bit Now" (The Majors).

The most covered George Gershwin songs are "Summertime," "Oh Lady Be Good," "Someone to Watch Over Me," "They Can't Take that Away from Me," "But Not for Me," "Rhapsody in Blue," "Love Walked In," "Nice Work if You Can Get It," "Love is Here to Stay" and "Strike Up the Band."

Public domain songs are covered often, including folk songs and gospel songs. Those include "Amazing Grace," "Take Me Out to the Ballgame," "Star-Spangled Banner," "Happy Birthday to You," "It Had to Be You," "Camp Town Races," "Ave Maria," "McNamara's Band," "It's a Long Way to Tipperary," "Give My Regards to Broadway," "Toyland," "Casey Jones," "The Charleston," "Parade of the Wooden Soldiers," "When the Saints Go Marching In," "Old Rugged Cross," "Beale Street Blues," "Pomp and Circumstance," "Come Though Fount of Every Blessing," "Jeanie with the Light Brown Hair," "Down in the Valley," "National Emblem March," "The Prisoner's Song"" and "Look for the Silver Lining."

Christmas songs are constantly covered because artists want to add their takes on the chestnuts. Christmas music is known in the music industry as an Annuity because it keeps on giving each year. The most covered Christmas songs are "Oh, Holy Night," "The Christmas Song," "White Christmas," "Silent Night," "Last Christmas," "Joy to the World," "Jingle Bells," "Winter Wonderland," "Have Yourself a Merry Little Christmas," "Little Drummer Boy," "Oh Little Town of Bethlehem," "Santa Claus is Coming to Town," "Baby It's Cold Outside," "Oh Holy Night," "Rudolph the Red Nosed Reindeer," "Silver Bells" and "We Wish You a Merry Christmas."

Special Cover Songs

According to the *Guinness Book of Records*, the most covered song is The Beatles' "Yesterday," more than 1,600 recorded versions.

"At Last" was written in 1941 by Mack Gordon and Harry Warren. It was performed by the Glenn Miller Band in the movie "Sun Valley Serenade" and became a hit record. In 1960, R&B singer Etta James recorded an album of mellow standards, with "At Last" being the biggest hit. That became a signature song for the rest of her career. Celine Dion and Beyoncé also had successes with the song.

In 1973, Dolly Parton wrote "I Will Always Love You" as a farewell to her performing partner Porter Wagoner. In 1982, Dolly sang a new version of the song in the movie "Best Little Whorehouse in Texas," in which she starred. In 1992, Whitney Houston sang the song in the movie "The Bodyguard." Whitney's hit single of the song remains her best-known record.

In his 1967 album "John Wesley Harding," Bob Dylan sang his composition "All Along the Watch Tower." Covered by several artists, it is the Jimi Hendrix version from 1968 that remains the biggest hit.

Rock star Janis Joplin recorded several cover songs, "Me & Bobby McGee" (Roger Miller), "Piece of My Heart" (Erma Franklin), "Cry Baby" (Garnett Mimms) and "Little Girl Blue" (Richard Rodgers & Lorenz Hart).

Throughout the 1970s, Linda Ronstadt recorded many cover songs in her unique style. These included "You're No Good" (Betty Everett, "When Will I Be Loved" (The Everly Brothers), "Blue Bayou" (Roy Orbison), "Heat Wave" (Martha & the Vandellas), "That'll Be the Day" and "It's So Easy" (Buddy Holly & the Crickets), "Poor Pitiful Me" (Warren Zevon), "Tumbling Dice" (The Rolling Stones), "Tracks of My Tears" and "Ooh Baby Baby" (Smokey Robinson & the Miracles), "Back in the USA." (Chuck Berry), "Hurt So Bad" (Little Anthony & the Imperials) and "Just One Look" (Doris Troy).

On the country charts, Narvel Felts recorded a string of cover songs from the pop charts, including "Drift Away" (Dobie Gray), "Lonely Teardrops" (Jackie Wilson), "Raindrops" (Dee Clark), "My Prayer" and "Smoke Gets in Your Eyes" (The Platters), "Funny How Time Slips Away" (Jimmy Elledge), "Roll Over Beethoven" (Chuck Berry), "Runaway" (Del Shannon), "Reconsider Me" (Johnny Adams), "Everlasting Love" (Robert Knight), "To Love Somebody" (The Bee Gees) and "Tower of Strength" (Gene McDaniels).

Some artists re-recorded their own songs, including "Breaking Up is Hard to Do" (Neil Sedaka), "Venus" (Frankie Avalon), "I'll Be Seeing You" and "Saturday Night is the Loneliest Night of the Week" (Frank Sinatra), "Candle in the Wind" (Elton John), "Sway" (Bobby Rydell), "Fearless" (Taylor Swift), "Smile" (Brian Wilson), "Do You Love Me" (The Contours), "Still Hungry" (Twisted Sister), "Phaedra" (Tangerine Dream), "Summer Place" (Percy Faith), "Jagged Little Pill Acoustic" (Alanis Morissette) and "Tubular Bells" (Mike Oldfield).

Other top covers included:

- "Proud Mary" by Ike & Tina Turner, remake of Creedence Clearwater Revival's hit.
- "Respect" by Aretha Franklin, originally written and recorded by Otis Redding.
- "Killing Me Softly with His Song" by Roberta Flack, originally recorded by a group, The Fugees.
- Cyndi Lauper's "Girls Just Want to Have Fun" was first recorded by Robert Hazard.
- Al Green's 1974 hit "Take Me to the River" was covered four years later by The Talking Heads, rock group.
- "Tainted Love" was a non-hit for Detroit soul singer Gloria Jones. The British duo Soft Cell had the hit with it in 1982.
- "I Shot the Sheriff," Eric Clapton's 1974 hit was a cover of Bob Marley.

Hank Moore's Picks of the Top Cover Songs

These are some of my favorite covers, some more obscure, included:

- "How Deep is the Ocean" by The Isley Brothers
- "Along the Navajo Trail" and "Frankie & Johnny" by Sam Cooke
- "Clementine" and "I'll Remember April" by Bobby Darin
- "Danny Boy" by Conway Twitty
- "Straighten Up and Fly Right" by The DeJohn Sisters
- "Anything You Can Do, I Can Do Better" by The Majors
- "Slaughter on Tenth Avenue" and "Perfidia" by The Ventures
- "Prisoner of Love" by James Brown

- "Such a Night," "Crying in the Chapel" and "Witchcraft" by Elvis Presley
- "I Got Plenty of Nothing" by Rosemary Clooney and Perez Prado
- "Fools Rush In" and "For You" by Rick Nelson
- "From Me to You" by Del Shannon
- "Friendly Persuasion" by Aretha Franklin
- "Gonna Get Along Without You Now" by Tracey Dey
- "Love is Strange" and "When You Say Love" by Sonny & Cher
- "Graduation Day" and "Tell Me Why" by The Beach Boys
- "I've Got You Under My Skin" by The Four Seasons
- "Alfie" by Stevie Wonder
- "See You in September," "I Got Rhythm" and "My Mammy" by The Happenings
- "Somewhere" and "You Can Have Him" by Dionne Warwick
- "Light My Fire" and "Hi-Heel Sneakers" by Jose Feliciano
- "Chattanooga Choo Choo" by Harpers Bizarre
- "The Happening" and "Unchain My Heart" by Trini Lopez
- "Dedicated to the One I Love" and "Glad to Be Unhappy" by Mamas & the Papas
- "Dream a Little Dream of Me" by Mama Cass Elliot
- "Don't It Make You Want to Go Home" and "Fools Rush In" by Brook Benton
- "Try a Little Tenderness" by Three Dog Night
- "It's All in the Game" by The Four Tops
- "Love is Strange" and "Mary Had a Little Lamb" by Paul McCartney & Wings
- "You'll Never Walk Alone" by Blue Haze
- "Brazil" and "In a Persian Market" by The Ritchie Family
- "I Saw Her Standing There" by Elton John and John Lennon
- "She's Not There" by Santana
- "Only Sixteen" by Dr. Hook
- "Stay" by Jackson Browne
- "Up on the Roof" and "Mockingbird" by James Taylor
- "I Don't Want to Walk Without You" by Barry Manilow
- "War," "Pink Cadillac" and "Fire" by Bruce Springsteen

Chapter 33
BEST ADVICE FROM POP MUSIC LEGENDS

Inspiring Words from Meeting the Legends

Dick Clark said: "Rock had a huge impact. Anything that the older generation hates is usually loved by kids. Nothing changes, and that continues today. Humor is always based on a modicum of truth. Have you ever heard a joke about a father-in-law?"

Diahann Carroll became a Broadway performer in the 1950s and appeared as a singer on all the great TV variety shows. I knew her during the run of "Julia," her 1968–1971 NBC sitcom, the first TV series starring a black female. Her talent extended to recurring roles on other TV series: "Dynasty," "The Colbys" and "White Collar." Diahann Carroll was a founding member of the Celebrity Action Council, the Los Angeles Mission, working with women in rehabilitation. Her film debut was in 1954's "Carmen Jones." She received a Golden Globe award for "Julia" and the Oscar for Best Actress in the 1974 film "Claudine." Diahann Carroll said: "If you're not invited to the party, throw your own. You must keep your sanity as well as know how to distance yourself from it while still holding onto the reins tightly."

I met Kenny Rogers in 1960, when he was performing with the Bobby Doyle Trio. I introduced him in concert in 1976 and 1986. Photos from a 1985 public service shoot for the Houston Police Dept., with Dolly Parton, promoting seatbelt safety. During his 6-decade career, Kenny Rogers released sixty-five albums and sold more than 165 million records, one of the most successful recording artists of all time. He won three Grammy Awards, thirteen American Music Awards, six Country Music Assn. Awards, CMA Lifetime Achievement Award, CMT Artist of a Lifetime Award. Kenny Rogers said: "I have this theory about performers who last for a long time, and that is, if you break it down, music is not as big a part of it as personality and who you are. I think that we are all three people. I am who I think I am, I am who you think I am, and I am who I really am. The closer those three people are together, the longer your career will last. People don't like to be fooled. Don't be afraid to give up the good for the great."

The Beatles appeared in Houston, TX. It was Aug. 19, 1965. I was backstage with The Beatles, one of the radio DJs who introduced them in concert. From John Lennon, I learned that we shared the same birthday (Oct. 9). From Paul McCartney, I learned that his and John's first composition, "Love Me Do," was written in 1957, inspired by The Everly Brothers' "Wake Up Little Susie." Twenty-one Beatles singles reached #1 on Billboard charts, most of any band. "Hey, Jude" enjoyed longest run on the charts: twenty-three weeks. Twenty-five Beatles albums reached #1 in the US. Worldwide album sales topped $600 million.

Chuck Berry was the premiere guitar hero of rock n' roll, bursting on the scene in the 1950s with hits like "Sweet Little Sixteen," "Roll Over Beethoven," "Johnny B. Goode," "Reeling and Rocking," "Maybelline," "Memphis," "Rock and Roll Music," "Back in the USA.," "Nadine" and "You Never Can Tell." He inspired countless musicians since. I met him at the taping of "American Bandstand" in 1972 in Hollywood. I emceed a concert with Chuck Berry on Aug. 12, 1980, held at Hofheinz Pavilion in Houston. His influence on rock, R&B, country and pop music was strong.

Said Chuck Berry: "It's amazing how much you can learn if your intentions are truly earnest. Don't let the same dog bite you twice. Of the five most important things in life, health is first, education or knowledge is second, and wealth is third. I forget the other two."

I met Beyoncé in 2011 at a Dick Clark tribute event in Hollywood, CA. She said: "I get nervous when I don't get nervous. If I'm nervous I know I'm going to have a good show."

From Bill Moyers, I learned these lessons:

- You cannot go through life as a carbon copy of someone else.
- You must establish your own identity, which is a long, exacting process.
- As you establish a unique identity, others will criticize. Being different, you become a moving target.
- If you cannot take the dirtiest job in any company and do it yourself, then you will never become "management."

From Bob Gooding and Neal Spelce, I learned: "Think like a world-class visionary. Grow into the role and not just remain a radio DJ."

One never forgets being in the presence of greatness and their shared wisdom.

Chapter 34
INVENTIONS, EQUIPMENT AND TECHNOLOGY

Music Technology

In 1877, Thomas Edison introduced the cylinder, developed originally for business office use. It was the earliest Dictaphone, whereby messages would be recorded by a needle on a rolling tube. In 1888, Emile Berliner invented the phonograph record, for the purpose of transporting music to consumers. Columbia Records (now Sony) was founded in 1898, followed by RCA Victor Records in 1901. Edison missed his chance to influence the recording industry by sticking with the cylinder medium, not converting to phonograph records until 1912 and finally getting out of the recording business in 1929.

The radio industry began as a multi-city network that piped recorded music into department stores. In 1920, the first radio sets sold by Westinghouse to promote its first station, 8XK in Pittsburgh, PA. In 1926, NBC Radio signed on the air, followed by CBS the next year. In addition to news and other entertainment shows, a large portion of radio programming was attributable to music, and a long growth relationship with the record industry was sustained. Stars came on variety shows to promote their releases, and the era of radio disc jockeys was firmly secured in the public culture.

The media of music distribution was the 78RPM record. It was bulky, breakable and limiting the amount of music on each side. Record companies put multiple discs into sleeves and began calling them "albums," the terminology still existing today. Those albums started as collections of "sides" but became thematic. Further packaging enabled various-artist albums and collections of "greatest hits" (those two categories currently accounting for half of all CD sales, a big chunk of business to be wiped out by going all-digital).

The two major labels went into research and development on non-breakable records that would play at slower speeds, with thinner grooves and more music on each side, producing a cleaner sound (without pops and scratches). The results were Columbia (owned by CBS) introducing the 33-1/3RPM long playing vinyl record in 1948 and RCA Victor (owned by NBC) introducing the 45RPM vinyl record in 1949. Why those speeds? They were combined derivatives of 78RPM, known by engineers as "the mother speed." Today's CDs play at 78RPM, a technological updating of Emile Berliner's 1888 invention of the phonograph record.

The 1930s and 1940s were massive-growth periods for the recording and broadcast industries. Along came other record labels: Brunswick, Decca, Capitol, Coral and jazz imprints. Movie studios got into the record business. Entrepreneurs brought Atlantic, King and other labels to showcase black artists and country music (two major growth industries attributable to the interrelationship of radio and records). Then came the international recording industry, which is the major user of CD technology.

The 1950s saw exponential growth of the recording industry. There were more retail outlets for the music than ever before or ever since. One could buy music at every grocery store, department store and many unexpected locations. There was an industry of sound-alike records, sold at reduced prices. The result was that all families had phonographs, and music was going into cars via radio, thus stimulating record sales and thus encouraging other technologies to bring music into cars in our mobile society.

Due to broad radio playlists, there was ample airplay for every musical taste, and the record industry continued to grow. Independent record labels proliferated, as did recordings by local artists around the country.

With the British Invasion of the 1960s came the reality of the international nature of entertainment. To package and market emerging modern music, media were implemented to make the best possible sounds and reflect the plastic portability of youth traffic. Along came music available on cassette tapes, then eight-track tapes. The music industry experimented with Quadraphonic Sound, and that experiment fell flat after one year.

At every juncture, there were transition periods in the adoption and acceptance of new media. For the first eleven years of 45RPM records and LPs being manufactured, there were still 78RPM discs on the market. Throughout the tape formats, there were still records. With the advent of Compact Discs, there were still records and cassette tapes on the market.

Entertainment Media

Radio: In 1920, the first radio sets were sold by Westinghouse to promote its first station, 8XK in Pittsburgh, PA. In 1926, NBC Radio signed on the air. In 1927, CBS Radio signed on the air. In 1939, NBC covered the opening of the World's Fair and the first football game, baseball game and prize fight were broadcast. The year 1940 saw the first basketball game and hockey match and the first coverage of political conventions broadcast.

Television: In 1898, the first suggestions were made that pictures with sound could be carried across large distances. Movies were introduced in European arcades in 1895. Within three years, research was begun to carry the moving pictures to distant locations. This preceded the development of radio. In 1927, the first test television pictures were sent.

The year 1928 saw the first American home got a TV set. the first regularly scheduled TV programs and the first trans-oceanic TV signal sent from London to New York. The first public demonstration of a color TV model was in 1929. The first closed-circuit TV projected on a big screen in a theatre was in 1930. In 1941, the first licensed commercial television station (WNBT-TV) went on the air. The first commercial cost sponsor Bulova Watches nine dollars.

The year 1945 saw the first public demonstration of a TV set in a department store, 25,000 watching. 1947 saw the first mass production of television receivers, the first broadcast of a joint session of Congress and the first broadcast of a World Series baseball championship. In 1951, RCA unveiled the first community TV antenna system (forerunner of cable TV). In 1952, coaxial cable was laid, facilitating national broadcast transmissions.

1953 saw the first worldwide event coverage: the coronation of Queen Elizabeth (film flown from England) and RCA testing the first compatible TV sets. In 1956, video tape was first used on television production. Originally, tape was used for commercials and portions of programs. By 1958, entire programs were taped and edited for later broadcast. This ultimately spelled the beginning of the end of live television (except for news shows).

Records: In 1931, research into record speeds other than 78RPM ensued. In 1948, Columbia Records first issued long-playing record albums on the market. In 1949, RCA Victor Records first issued 45-RPM singles on the market.

At every juncture, there were transition periods in the adoption and acceptance of new media. For the first eleven years of 45RPM records and LPs being manufactured, there were still 78RPM discs on the market. Throughout the tape formats, there were still records. With the advent of Compact Discs, there were still records and cassette tapes on the market.

45RPM Adapters: These are plastic or metal inserts that go in the middle of 45RPM records, so they can be played on the LP spindle of a turntable. The first adapters were introduced by the Webster-Chicago Corporation. They were made of solid zinc, difficult to insert into a record and almost impossible to remove without breaking the disc. A differently shaped, but similarly difficult-to-use metal adapter was made by Fidelitone. Capitol Records produced what they called "Optional Center" or "O.C. 45" records. These had a triangular cardboard insert with an LP-size spindle hole; the cardboard center could be punched out for playing on 45RPM spindles but could not be replaced.

Tapes: 1946 saw the importing of reel-to-reel recording from Germany to the US 1965 saw the advent of audio cassette tapes.1968 saw the advent of eight-track tapes.

Video cassette tapes: In 1980, the concept of videotape rentals was first introduced. The retail cost of VCRs went below $1,000 for the first time. By 1984, the retail cost of VCRs went below $500 for the first time. In 1985, the cost of blank videotapes dropped below $10.00 for the first time.

Critical Decision, Keeping CDs on the Market

Certain forces in the recording industry have announced intentions to cease production of compact discs and convert their music marketing to digital downloads.

The CD issue (including those who advocate obliterating the medium) is symptomatic of the bigger watersheds that have crippled and ruined large chunks of the music industry:

- Not understanding the business basics.
- Taking decisions away from the creative people.
- Focusing only on the technology, not on the creative output.
- Not understanding the totality of the music industry, with recording as a prime stakeholder, not as the stake driver that it tries to be.
- Failure to learn from the past.
- The trends toward over-formatting of radio.
- Failure to understand and nurture the relationship with radio.
- Failure to understand and nurture the relationship with television.
- Deregulation of broadcasting.
- Failure to collaborate, bundle products or combine efforts to create and sustain advantage.
- Failure to understand and nurture relationships with the retailing industry.
- Failure to plan for the present.
- Trends toward homogenization of culture that resulted in drastic cuts in the quantity and quality of original music programming available.
- Trends away from utilizing and showcasing music.
- Trends away from spoken word and educational usage of recordings.
- The music industry responding to changes and uncertainty by scapegoating the wrong people.

- The international marketplace responding as entrepreneurs by taking up the slack and addressing the "missed opportunities" by the American music industry.
- Making knee-jerk decisions based upon partial information and wrong hunches.

78RPMs were phased out because better technology was developed. Quadraphonic was technology glitz but did not make good business sense. Eight-track tapes were only meant to be an interim medium, until CDs were developed. CDs are the dominant medium and are economical to produce.

Killing CDs is a bean counter move and is contrary to the heart of the music business. CDs enable local bands to have records. Computer downloads are convenience items and impulse purchases. People's listening frequency and intensity is different and reduced through computer downloads.

Nothing still says "record" like a CD in a plastic case, where the album is as much in the packaging as the content material on the disc. Lose the "record album," and the music industry will never be the same.

This is the juncture where the music industry must step back, analyze their decline over the last thirty years and understand the reasons why they must create new opportunities and move forward.

I would steer the music industry toward:

- Stimulating a culture where excellence in music would be encourages, thus improving the quantity and quality of music being recorded.
- Creating a music industry where the products would be more worth buying. There are still higher profits in album sales, rather than Internet song downloads (the modern equivalent to the 45RPM single).
- Thinking of music distribution in directions other than just the Internet.
- Stimulating the global record industry.
- Encouraging TV shows to again feature theme songs.
- Encouraging movies to get back to real musical soundtracks (not just the current drum crashing noise effects). This would re-boot the soundtrack album industry.

- Recognizing that nearly half of all record sales and downloads involves repackaging older music product for new audiences.
- Finding ways to promote local acts around the world.
- Working with radio programmers to get playlists expanded. Music must have the interactive exposure via radio. Nurture programmers of internet radio shows as the best new opportunity for expanding music exposure.
- Understanding better the after-market of music resellers and stimulate that series of opportunities for expanding the reach of musical products around the world.
- Recognizing downloads as "low hanging fruit." Do not put all your industry's distribution in one area, because that one area will always change.

Technology has influenced so many devices and niche industries, including aircraft navigation, alarm systems, analyzers, automated attendants, automobiles, broadband communications, cable fiber optics, call systems, cellular mobile station equipment, clocks, cloud storage, computers, converters, data management systems, digital test equipment, distributors, earth stations, educational and training systems, fiber-optics, lighting systems, message systems, modems, monitoring systems, paging systems, power supplies, radio telephone equipment, railroad systems, receivers, revenue and billing systems, routers, security systems, semiconductors, signaling systems, storage systems, surge protectors, switches, telecommunications devices, teleconferencing, test equipment, towers, transformers, trucks, video games, video systems, wave guides, wireless equipment, work stations, dust busters, cochlear implants and much more.

Areas and industries benefiting from tech innovations include architecture, assistive technologies, banking and finance, construction, energy, healthcare, information technology, manufacturing, medicine, military, nursing, retail, risk management, science, speech and hearing, technology transfer, water treatment, weather forecasting and others.

Chapter 35
MUSIC IN AUTOMOBILES

The first music in cars came from songs people could sing along to, glancing at sheet music. Hit tunes about vehicles in the 1905–1925 era included: "In My Merry Oldsmobile," "I'm Going to Park Myself in Your Arms," "Take Me Out in Your Buick," "The Long Way Home" and "I'm Wild About Horns."

The first car radio was introduced in 1904. By 1920, the vacuum tube was perfected to the point that radio receivers could be viably placed in automobiles. The first car radios were expensive (up to $500). By the late 1930s, push button radios were a standard feature. By the late 1940s, there were millions of AM car radios in use, allowing drivers to hear music, news, sports and dramatic radio programming along their commutes.

The first FM radio receiver was introduced to automobiles in 1953. Chrysler Corporation sought to discontinue car radios as being too expensive and in 1956 introduced an alternative, a 45RPM record player that was housed in the glove compartment. In 1957, lower-cost radios were installed, with power being a hybrid of transistors and low-voltage vacuum tubes. In 1963, a tubeless solid-state radio was introduced. Stereo speakers were introduced for cars in 1960.

Philips introduced the audio cassette in 1964, and a dashboard player with radio and cassette player was introduced in 1968. In 1966, Ford and Motorola jointly introduced the 8-track tape, affording better-quality sound and noise reduction.

In 1984, Pioneer introduced the first compact disc, which compressed music onto thin discs, with incredible sound. CDs began appearing in cars in 1987, and multi-disc changers for home use revolutionized the consumption of music. As CDs appeared in cars, so too did DVDs, where movies and cartoons could be shown to family members in the back of vans and SUVs.

From 2010 forward, musical media adapted for automobile use included satellite radio, Bluetooth, internet radio, USB, iPods, and entertainment centers in vehicles.

The recording industry adapted its products to reflect improving technology and nodding to the importance of automobiles as growing consumption of music. By the late 1950s, heavier base lines and stronger instrumentation gave the records a fuller sound on car radios. Berry Gordy's Motown sound was optimized when heard on car radios. So was Phil Spector's Wall of Sound, and he referred to his thunderous production as "little symphonies for the kids." Same for 1970s rock, which sounded ideal via 8-track tapes and boom boxes.

Cars represent individual freedom, mobility and independence. Pursuing quality of life is more pleasurable, and we see lots of sights, locales and people. Automobiles are inspirational forces.

The twentieth century was typified by the automobile and its support industries (notably energy, highways, retail and parts) as the most significant factors in commerce growth and development. In 1921, President Warren G. Harding proclaimed in that "the motor car has become an instrument in our political, social and industrial life."

Henry Ford introduced assembly-line production and techniques in 1913, using standardized, interchangeable parts. He trained employees in only one or two steps so that each person could work as quickly and efficiently as possible. This large-scale manufacturing is a production model that's been adopted in countless other industries, allowing for mass production that cuts cost. In 1959, Berry Gordy Jr., a Ford employee, designed a record company which would mass-produce hits. It was the Motown sound.

Automaking has changed the economy. Today, 4.25 million people work directly within the automotive industry. Not only has car manufacturing become one of the largest industries in the world, it's also been the driving force behind the growth in the oil and gas industry.

Cars gave people a way to get around quickly. They could travel for work and visit more places. Up until the early 1900s, few people lived more than a few miles from where they grew up. Before cars were invented, moving just a short distance away meant hours of buggy travel on rough roads. Suddenly, people had a new mode of transportation that could get them more places, which meant leisure travel became something folks could afford.

There were population shifts, typified by moves from farms to cities. Demographic changes led to the influx of women in the workforce. Cities experienced economic supremacy. With rapidly increasing affluence, wages were up, and consumer choices were up. These factors inspired business innovations and successes.

Chapter 36

NOSTALGIA WAVES AND
LESSONS FROM MUSIC HISTORY

The biggest sphere of influence on nostalgia is music. Not only do those who grew up when the golden oldies were current, but younger generations like and appreciate classic music.

Songs of certain eras paralleled moral standards. When Frank Sinatra sang "love and marriage go together like a horse and carriage," it typified romantic ballads of the day. In 1956, school PTA groups raised up in arms over Elvis Presley's gyrations on television and over Fats Domino when he proclaimed, "I found my thrill on Blueberry Hill."

A song considered risqué in 1955, "Work with Me Annie" by Hank Ballard and the Midnighters, was banned from radio stations. Singer Georgia Gibbs had a hit with "Dance with Me Henry," the cleaned-up version. The term "Sock It to Me Baby" was given social acceptance when it was used as a comedy line on TV's "Rowan & Martin's Laugh-In."

Nostalgia waves come from repurposing of the music, the fashions, the excitement and how it affects us. The first known use of the term "repurposing" was in 1984. Its definitions and meanings include:

- To find new uses for an idea, product or process.
- Giving a new purpose or use to.
- Finding ways to change, adapt and take to a new dimension.
- To make more suited for a different purpose.
- To re-use for different or expanded purpose beyond which it was originally intended.
- To re-use on a long-term basis without alterations.

Repurposing involves compilations, reissues and highlights, including:

- New content juxtaposed with old content.
- Reissuing on different platforms.
- Combining with platforms that did not exist with the original issues.
- Turning one product into a series.
- Writing about how the original product transformed into more utilization.

There have been waves of nostalgia over the last century:

- For the Victorian era in the 1930s.
- For the 1920s in the 1950s.
- Remembering the 1940s in the 1960s.
- Celebrating the 1950s in the 1970s.
- Revisiting the 1960s in the 1980s.
- Revitalizing 1970s in music of the 1990s.
- Remembering the 1980s in the 2000s.

Platforms for nostalgia music include:

- Oldies re-packaging.
- Nostalgia concert tours.

- Artists appearing at fairs, casinos and festivals.
- Internet websites: Ebay, Amazon, Discogs, MusicStack, etc.
- Comic festivals, record shows and nostalgia fairs.
- Oldies radio shows.
- Internet music history sites.

Defining Nostalgia and its Dynamics

People get nostalgic when they are longing for the past. Restorative nostalgia makes one feel sad and then glad. It is the romanticism of pleasant memories and better than current times.

Nostalgia means reviewing things that you were doing, enjoyable memories of past times. We recall persons and places that you knew at certain times, along with people with whom you shared the good old days. It includes understanding what made times good, applying today's perspectives to past reflections.

Retro-memories deserves attention. It raises our spirit and vitality, with independent and positive emotion. Nostalgia improves mood and social connectivity and enhances positive self-regard.

Nostalgia Bands and Shows

With the dawning of the 1970s, oldies tribute bands burst on the national scene. They included Ten Years After, Flash Cadillac, Commander Cody and Sha Na Na.

Johnny Dee & the Rocket 88s was one of the premier 1950s–1960s party bands. In 1971, I advised Keith Landers, a young musician in Austin, TX. Rather than being just another hard rock group, I suggested that he catch the early wave of 1950s nostalgia and create a band that would faithfully perform the golden oldies. The Keith Landers group became Johnny Dee & the Rocket 88s. In 1978, I emceed the Prince's Hamburgers fiftieth anniversary party, with Johnny Dee & the Rocket 88s performing. Keith led the party band for thirty-three years, and he died in 2011.

A popular nostalgic cover band is Midlife Crisis & the Hot Flashes. Led by David Wadler and Rob Mosbacher, they performed at four Presidential inaugurals. The Big Band Era was kept alive at dances led by the bands of Ronnie Renfrow and Ed Gerlach. Cover bands span much material over its chosen eras.

Tribute bands are plentiful, doing great justice to the artists whose songs they perform. R.J. Diamond performs the songs of Neil Diamond. Brooke Alyson leads the Nightbird Fleetwood Mac and Stevie Nicks Tribute Band. There are hundreds of Elvis Presley tribute artists. The Motor City Revue and others keep the soulful 1960s–1970s hits of Motown alive.

Broadway shows that sparked nostalgia waves included: "Gypsy," "Hello, Dolly," "Cabaret," "Follies," "George M," "Grease," "Beatlemania, "Mamma Mia" (ABBA), Jersey Boys" (Frankie Valli & the Four Seasons), "Smokey Joe's Café," "Hamilton," "Moulin Rouge," "Beautiful: The Carole King Musical," "Tina, the Tina Turner Story," "Summer: The Donna Summer Musical" and "Ain't Too Proud" (The Temptations).

Movies that sparked nostalgia waves included "The Roaring Twenties," "Holiday Inn," "Night and Day," "Al Jolson Story," "Singing in the Rain," "Glenn Miller Story," "Benny Goodman Story," "White Christmas," "Oklahoma," "South Pacific," "My Fair Lady," "Hard Day's Night," "Help," "Yellow Submarine," "Monterey Pop," "Woodstock," "The Last Picture Show," "The Way We Were," "The Great Gatsby," "American Graffiti," "Buddy Holly Story," "Saturday Night Fever," "Thank God It's Friday," "Skatetown, USA.," "Xanadu," "Fame," "Urban Cowboy," "The Cotton Club," "Flashdance," "Footloose," "Stand By Me," "La Bamba, the Ritchie Valens Story," "Dirty Dancing," "The Doors," "Hairspray," "All That Jazz," "Selena, the Selena Quintanilla-Pérez Story," "Walk the Line, the Johnny Cash Story," "Forrest Gump," "When Harry Met Sally," "Sleepless in Seattle," "Across the Universe," "La-La Land," "Bohemian Rhapsody, the Queen Story," "Rocket Man, the Elton John Story" and "Respect, the Aretha Franklin Story."

TV shows that sparked nostalgia waves included "Happy Days," "Laverne & Shirley," "Goodtime Girls," "MASH," "The Waltons," "American Bandstand" anniversary specials, "Dick Clark's New Year's Rockin' Eve," "The Wonder Years," "Mad Men," "That 70s Show," "Downton Abbey," "Deadwood," "When Calls the Heart," "The Crown" and "The Marvelous Mrs. Maisel."

Songs About Nostalgic Memories

- "I'm Getting Sentimental Over You" by Tommy Dorsey
- "Auld Lang Syne" by Guy Lombardo
- "Yesterday," "In My Life" and "Penny Lane" by The Beatles

- "Memories Are Made of This" by Dean Martin
- "When We Were Young" by Adele
- "I Remember You" by Frank Ifield
- "Summer of '69" by Bryan Adams
- "Brown Eyed Girl" by Van Morrison
- "A Case of You" by Joni Mitchell
- "Remember" by Irving Berlin
- "Remember Then" by The Earls
- "Remember When" by The Platters
- "Remember, Walking in the Sand" by The Shangri-Las
- "Remember the Time" by Michael Jackson
- "Good Old Days" by Roger Miller
- "Turn Back the Hands of Time" by Eddie Fisher
- "If I Could Turn Back Time" by Cher
- "Turn, Turn, Turn" by The Byrds
- "In Times Like These" by Mahalia Jackson
- "Living in the Past" by Jethro Tull
- "Days of Future Past" by The Moody Blues
- "Old Days" by Chicago
- "Photograph" by Ringo Starr
- "Remember Christmas" by Harry Nilsson
- "Looking Back" by Nat King Cole
- "Reflections" by The Supremes
- "Do You Remember These" by The Statler Brothers
- "Memories" by Elvis Presley
- "Old Time Rock and Roll" by Bob Seger
- "Garden Party" by Rick Nelson
- "The Boys of Summer" by Don Henley
- "Video Killed the Radio Star" by The Bugles
- "Hey Nineteen" by Steely Dan
- "The Way We Were" Barbra Streisand
- "Wasted on the Way" by Crosby, Stills & Nash
- "Reminiscing" by The Little River Band
- "Yesterday Once More" by The Carpenters

- "Crocodile Rock, Elton John
- "It Was a Very Good Year" by Frank Sinatra
- "It's Hard to Say Goodbye to Yesterday" by Boyz II Men
- "Glory Days" by Bruce Springsteen
- "Jack and Diane" John Mellencamp
- "Heroes" by David Bowie
- "Yesterday's Gone" by Chad & Jeremy
- "Done Too Soon" by Neil Diamond
- "American Pie" by Don McLean
- "All Those Years Ago" by George Harrison
- "Life is a Rock but the Radio Rolled Me" by Reunion
- "The Beat Goes On" by Sonny & Cher
- "Memory," from the musical "Cats"
- "Dreams of Long Ago" by Enrico Caruso
- "When We Were Young" by Eric Burdon & the Animals
- "Abraham, Martin & John" by Dion
- "Kodachrome" and "Me & Julio Down by the School Yard" by Paul Simon
- "The Night They Drove Old Dixie Down" by The Band

Songs that Trigger the Old Days
- "Sing, Sing, Sing" by Benny Goodman
- "In the Mood" and "Moonlight Serenade" by Glenn Miller
- "Boogie Woogie Bugle Boy" by The Andrews Sisters and Bette Midler
- "St. Louis Blues" and "Hello, Dolly" by Louis Armstrong
- "How Much is that Doggie in the Window" by Patti Page
- "Your Cheating Heart" and "Cold, Cold Heart" by Hank Williams
- "Hey There" by Rosemary Clooney
- "Secret Love" and "Whatever Will Be, Will Be" by Doris Day
- "Rock Around the Clock" by Bill Haley & his Comets
- "Hound Dog," "Jailhouse Rock" and "Burning Love" by Elvis Presley
- "Little Darling" and "The Stroll" by The Diamonds
- "At the Hop" and "Rock and Roll is Here to Stay" by Danny & the Juniors
- "You Send Me," "Wonderful World" and "Chain Gang" by Sam Cooke
- "Wake Up Little Susie" and Bird Dog" by The Everly Brothers

- "Rockin' Robin" by Bobby Day
- "Peggy Sue" and "That'll Be the Day" by Buddy Holly & the Crickets
- "Peter Gunn Theme" by Ray Anthony and Henry Mancini
- "Mack the Knife" and "Splish Splash" by Bobby Darin
- "Shout" and "Twist & Shout" by The Isley Brothers
- "Those Oldies but Goodies Remind Me of You" by Little Caesar & the Romans
- "Where the Boys Are" and "Lipstick on Your Collar" by Connie Francis
- "Walk, Don't Run" and "Hawaii Five-O" by The Ventures
- "I Left My Heart in San Francisco" by Tony Bennett
- "Bandstand Boogie" by Les Elgart and Barry Manilow
- "Do You Love Me" by The Contours
- "Breaking Up is Hard to Do" and "Calendar Girl" by Neil Sedaka
- "It's My Party" and "You Don't Own Me" by Lesley Gore
- "Go Away Little Girl" by Steve Lawrence
- "I Get Around," "Surfer Girl" and "Good Vibrations" by The Beach Boys
- "Heat Wave" and "Dancing in the Street" by Martha & the Vandellas
- "She Loves You," "Hard Day's Night" and "I Want to Hold Your Hand" by The Beatles
- "Walk on By" by Dionne Warwick
- "Baby Love," "Come See About Me" and "Someday We'll be Together" by The Supremes
- "In the Midnight Hour" by Wilson Pickett
- "I Can't Help Myself" by The Four Tops
- "My Girl," "Get Ready" and "Ain't Too Proud to Peg" by The Temptations
- "Satisfaction" and "Brown Sugar" by The Rolling Stones
- "Last Train to Clarksville," "I'm a Believer" and "Daydream Believer" by The Monkees
- "When a Man Loves a Woman" by Percy Sledge
- "Respect," "A Natural Woman" and "Think" by Aretha Franklin
- "Light My Fire" by The Doors
- "Brown Eyed Girl" by Van Morrison
- "Dance to the Music" and Everyday People" by Sly & the Family Stone
- "The Dock of the Bay" by Otis Redding

- "Raindrops Keep Falling on My Head" by B.J. Thomas
- "Sweet Caroline," "Cherry, Cherry" and "Heartlight" by Neil Diamond
- "He Ain't Heavy, He's My Brother" by The Hollies
- "ABC" and "Never Can Say Goodbye" by The Jackson Five
- "Signed, Sealed, Delivered, I'm Yours" by Stevie Wonder
- "It's Too Late" and "One Fine Day" by Carole King
- "Joy to the World," "Black & White" and "Never Been to Spain" by Three Dog Night
- "I Am Woman" by Helen Reddy
- "Best of My Love" and "Hotel California" by The Eagles
- "Mandy" and "Copacabana" by Barry Manilow
- "Fame" and "Flashdance, What a Feeling" by Irene Cara
- "Bad Girls," "Hot Stuff" and "Last Dance" by Donna Summer
- "Macho Man," "Y.M.C.A." and "In the Navy" by The Village People
- "My Sharona" by The Knack
- "Old Time Rock and Roll" by Bob Seger
- "Bette Davis Eyes" by Kim Carnes
- "Jessie's Girl" by Rick Springfield
- "Beat It," "Billie Jean" and "Thriller" by Michael Jackson
- "Footloose" by Kenny Loggins
- "We Are the World" by USA for Africa
- "Mickey" by Toni Basil
- "Hurt So Good" by John Cougar Mellencamp
- "The Rose" and "Wind Beneath My Wings" by Bette Midler
- "Material Girl" and "Like a Virgin" by Madonna
- "Dancing in the Dark" by Bruce Springsteen

Quotes About Nostalgia

"I listen to both oldies and contemporary radio stations. I enjoy listening to current stuff because there's an energy to it that's inspiring." (Carole King)

"Kids don't see me as an oldies person when I go onstage. They see me as an energy force." (Dick Dale)

"I'd trade all my tomorrows for one single yesterday." (Kris Kristofferson)

"I don't like nostalgia unless it's mine." Lou Reed

- "Those were the days my friend. We thought they'd never end. We'd sing and dance forever and a day." (Mary Hopkin)

Hank Moore emceeing concerts with the nostalgia showband, Johnny Dee & the Rocket 88s

Chapter 37
PREVIEW OF NEXT BOOK

Pop Music Legends, Book 2, "The Songs and the Stars"

Music for the Ages. Music for the Times
Stories Behind How Songs were Written
The 2000s, Modern Music. The Electronic Music Era. The Download Era
You Must Remember This
Stars for All Time. Forgotten Music Stars
Vocal groups
Sports Music
Tribute songs
Local Music Industries
The influencers. Producers, Music industry executives. The business of music.
Music Merchandising and Memorabilia
Repackaging, Reissues and Compilations of Music
Broadway music
Music from Movies: Soundtracks and Film Tie-In Music
TV Theme Songs and soundtracks

Library Music & Industrial Music. Production libraries, music cues.

International music. Foreign Language Songs. Phonetic cover versions.

Country music

R&B, Soul

Comebacks, Second Acts, Reunions and Reboots

Artwork: Album Covers, Picture Sleeves, Inner Sleeves, Gatefolds, Song-sheets, Booklets

How They Got Their Names

Business of the Music Industry

Timeline, Great Dates in Music History

Concerts and Festivals

Radio: DJs, Record Surveys and Jingles

Instrumentals, Orchestral Legends and Mood Music

Classical recordings

Actors Who Sang, Singers Who Acted. Recording stars from other areas: actors, golden throats, Disney stars, TV personalities, Brady Bunch, California Raisins, cartoon characters, comedians, spoken word

When the Greats Got Together: Teamings, Guest Appearances, Jams, Duets

One-Name Singers

Pop Ballads and Singers. The Superstar system

The Payola scandal era, 1959–1963

Pop Music Compendium

Media that purveyed music. Books & Magazines. Music Websites

Dance Crazes

Custom Pressing Industry

Novelty records: Comedy, Spoken Word, Celebrity Narrations

Hank Moore's interviews with top stars

Why Organizations Click

Music Quiz and Trivia

ABOUT THE AUTHOR

Hank Moore is an internationally known business advisor, speaker and author. He is a Big Picture strategist, with original, cutting-edge ideas for creating, implementing and sustaining corporate growth throughout every sector of the organization.

He is a Futurist and Corporate Strategist™, with four trademarked concepts of business, heralded for ways to remediate corporate damage, enhance productivity and facilitate better business.

Hank Moore is the highest level of business overview expert and is in that rarified circle of experts such as Peter Drucker, Tom Peters, Steven Covey, Peter Senge and W. Edwards Deming.

Hank Moore has presented Think Tanks for five US Presidents. He has spoken at seven Economic Summits. As a Corporate Strategist™, he speaks and advises companies about growth strategies, visioning, planning, executive-leadership development, futurism and the Big Picture issues affecting the business climate. He conducts independent performance reviews and Executive Think Tanks nationally, with the result being the companies' destinies being charted.

The Business Tree™ is his trademarked approach to growing and evolving business, while mastering change. Business visionary Peter Drucker termed Hank Moore's Business Tree™ as the most original business model of the past sixty years.

Mr. Moore has provided senior level advising services for more than 5,000 client organizations (including 100 of the Fortune 500), companies in transition (startup, re-engineering, mergers, going public), public sector entities, professional associations and non-profit organizations. He has worked with all major industries over a fifty-year career. He advises at the Executive Committee and board levels, providing Big Picture ideas.

He has overseen 400 strategic plans and corporate visioning processes. He has conducted 500+ performance reviews of organizations. He is a mentor to senior management. This scope of wisdom is utilized by CEOs and board members.

Types of speaking engagements which Hank Moore presents include:

- Conference opening Futurism keynote.
- Corporate planning retreats.
- Ethics and Corporate Responsibility speeches.
- University—college Commencement addresses.
- Business Think Tanks.
- International business conferences.
- Non-profit and public sector planning retreats.

In his speeches and in consulting, Hank Moore addresses aspects of business that only one who has overseen them for a living can address:

- Trends, challenges and opportunities for the future of business.
- Big Picture viewpoint.
- Creative idea generation.
- Ethics and corporate responsibility.
- Changing and refining corporate cultures.

- Strategic Planning.
- Marketplace repositioning.
- Community stewardship.
- Visioning.
- Crisis management and preparedness.
- Growth Strategies programs.
- Board of Directors development.
- Stakeholder accountability.
- Executive Think Tanks.
- Performance reviews.
- Non-profit consultation.
- Business trends that will affect the organization.
- Encouraging pockets of support and progress thus far.
- Inspiring attendees as to the importance of their public trust roles.
- Making pertinent recommendations on strategy development.

Hank Moore has authored a series of internationally published books:

- *The Big Picture of Business,* four-book series
- *Pop Icons and Business Legends*
- *Non-Profit Legends*
- *The Classic Television Reference*
- *The Business Tree*™ (with international editions)
- *The High Cost of Doing Nothing*
- *Houston Legends*
- *Power Stars to Light the Flame*
- *The $50,000 Business Makeover*
- Monograph series for the Library of Congress Business Section, Harvard School of Business, Strategy Driven, publications and websites.

Follow Hank Moore on:
Facebook: www.facebook.com/hank.moore.10
Linkedin: www.linkedin.com/profile/view?id=43004647&trk=tab_pro
Instagram: www.instagram.com/hank.moore/
Twitter: twitter.com/hankmoore4218
YouTube: www.youtube.com/watch?v=jFax7XZvz0U

Pin Interest: www.pinterest.com/hankmoore10/
Atlantic Speakers Bureau: atlanticspeakersbureau.com/hank-moore/
Business Speakers Network: directory.espeakers.com/buss/viewspeaker16988
Silver Fox Advisors: silverfox.org/content.php?page=Hank_Moore
Facebook book page: www.facebook.com/hankmoore.author/?fref=ts

Additional materials may be found on Hank Moore's website: www.hankmoore.com

A free ebook edition is available with the purchase of this book.

To claim your free ebook edition:

Visit MorganJamesBOGO.com
Sign your name CLEARLY in the space
Complete the form and submit a photo of
the entire copyright page
You or your friend can download the ebook
to your preferred device

Print & Digital Together Forever.

Snap a photo   Free ebook   Read anywhere